The Wonder an

By Jane Bradshaw

"We come unbidden into this life, and if we are lucky, we find a purpose beyond starvation, misery, and early death, which, lest we forget, is the common lot."

Abraham Verghese, *Cutting for Stone*

The Wonder and Chaos of Being by Jane Bradshaw

Copyright © 2016 by Jane Bradshaw. All rights reserved.

No part of this book may be reproduced in any written, electronic, recording, or photocopying without written permission of the publisher or author. The exception would be in the case of brief quotations embodied in the critical articles or reviews and pages where permission is specifically granted by the publisher or author.

Although every precaution has been taken to verify the accuracy of the information contained herein, the author and publisher assume no responsibility for any errors or omissions. No liability is assumed for damages that may result from the use of information contained within.

Printed in the United States of America

First printing, 2016

janebradshaw@yahoo.com

10 9 8 7 6 5 4 3 2 1

Contents

Preface 6
Prologue 8
Part 1 9
   Chapter 1 10
   Chapter 2 13
   Chapter 3 24
   Chapter 4 28
   Chapter 5 33
   Chapter 6 40
   Chapter 7 51
   Chapter 8 58
   Chapter 9 70
   Chapter 10 77
   Chapter 11 86
Part 2 99
   Chapter 13 100
   Chapter 14 105
   Chapter 15 112
   Chapter 16 121
   Chapter 17 133
   Chapter 18 143
   Chapter 19 152
   Chapter 20 164
   Chapter 21 172
Part 3 180
   Chapter 22 181

Chapter 23 191
Chapter 24 204
Chapter 25 214
Chapter 26 228
Chapter 27 238
Chapter 28 248
Chapter 29 259
Chapter 30 266
Conclusion 274

Authors Note

All names of persons included in this memoir have been changed.

Acknowledgements

That I am alive today is due to the love, mercy, patience, and strength of my husband Jake, my children Sarah, Adam, and Lydia, and my best friend Jo. With all of my heart, thank you for loving, supporting, and accepting me, and for staying by my side during the worst days, months, and years of my life. I love you all and will remain ever grateful for all you have said and done and sacrificed to help me survive the horrible death of our Puffmeister.

Preface

The Wonder and Chaos of Being is not a feel good story. It does not have a "happy ending," and there is no "dawning of a new day," when "everything makes sense," "falls into place," or "works out for the best." This story is the true account of a world with a dark and bleary landscape, where nothing is clear or easy to understand—a world in which a mother finds herself after death has snatched away one her children. It is the world I have inhabited since October 24, 2010. A place, should *you* ever find yourself, where you have no knowledge or wisdom. You know nothing. You understand nothing. And nothing feels right anymore. Attempting to make even the most insignificant decision produces panic. Leaving the house becomes a dreaded prospect because the anxiety is so much worse outside of the safety and reliability of home. The most heinous part of this landscape is the debilitating sorrow and mental anguish that flood your mind, body, and every corner of your being. The hurt you experience over the death of one of your children is agonizing. The pain is so brutal it can feel daunting to continue living. You wake up and find yourself on a tortuous, desolate road, upon which you have been thrust without your consent, and it has no foreseeable end.

In this story, no one rises from the dead. No one is visited by the ghost of a deceased loved one who professes peace and joy with his or her new situation and tells everyone to go on happily living. No one immediately affected by the tragedy can see the cup as half-full, find a silver lining, or employ psychological tricks or religious gymnastics to see this tragedy as a blessing in disguise; the aforementioned axioms being the empty comfort of well-meaning friends. All who are within my immediate family, primarily affected by the events in this story, are struck dumb and hopeless. Grief is not pretty, nor is it easy, but it is a part of this life. This story presents the guts of my raw grief.

Some will not want to read this account because child mortality is something no one wants to contemplate. It is depressing. There is also an unspoken fear that in reading a book about a child's death, you might be tempting fate. If you worry about that kind of voodoo, then by all means, don't read this. If one day your child dies, read it then. At least read some grieving mother's story. It might help. A little.

I used to think, as most probably have, I couldn't live if one of my children died. Then, my 13-year-old son died. What I have been doing would probably not be considered living, but surviving. That would be an accurate description. Surviving has been complete hell. Having a loving, supportive spouse, three sensitive and emotionally aware children, and a generous, encouraging best friend has made a difference. Prior to this tragedy, my "tomorrow is a new day" attitude and "where there's a will there's a way" perspective always kept me moving through life's trials. My dad even used to occasionally refer to me as a "Pollyanna." However, no positive attitude or new perspective could bring my son back to life. There was no comfort; there was only death. The one thing that gave me a shred of hope I could make it was seeing other moms who were surviving and who were farther down this same horrible road. I dedicate this story—of death, sorrow, and perpetual heartache—to my Sammyboy, and to every mother so unfortunate as to have experienced and be surviving the death of one of her children.

Prologue

Fluffy, white, snowflakes appeared, floating down from the endless dark sky, drifting toward my face, and settling on my cheeks and nose. After sitting alone on our porch swing for several hours, drinking vodka and chain smoking, I stood to go inside, lost my balance, and collapsed. I lay on my back in the nearly two feet of snow blanketing our front yard and had not yet found the resolve to get up. Everything in the world seemed hushed and still. Watching the falling snow was soothing. The Smirnoff that warmed my blood or Sammy's rabbit fur, Russian-style hat that insulated my head, or both, prevented me from feeling the frosty air, the icy wind, and the wetness of the snow. Maybe it was the heavy cloak of grief that covered my heart, my mind, my whole self, that numbed me to the frigid weather. Regardless, I wasn't cold and all seemed quiet and untroubled. *This wouldn't be such a bad way to go,* I thought to myself. *If I lie here long enough, maybe I will just fall asleep and freeze to death. Dying like this probably wouldn't hurt. I would just fall into a deep slumber: only I would never wake up. I wouldn't have to open my eyes from the dark nothingness to remember Sammy is dead, and I will never see him again. Good god, what a sweet relief.* The faces of my beloved husband and remaining children came to mind as I imagined them finding my lifeless body. Their anguish from our recent, heinous loss would be multiplied by my death; I couldn't do that to them. I attempted to force open my eyes and sit up, but the vodka haze and snowy bed had anesthetized me, and I was relatively pain-free for the moment. *If I could just stay right here, in this place, feeling this way...* I dreaded the passing of that transient reprieve and the brutal heartache I knew would return. I didn't want to live with that burning, consuming agony that filled my chest and head and body, every moment of every day. *I might doze off before I make a conscious choice. Then, I could be free from this soul crushing misery without having to feel guilt for the additional sorrow my death would bring my people.*

Part 1

Life is sorrow

-Buddha

Chapter 1

"Life is a long preparation for something that never happens."

-W.B. Yeats

A bright and clear sunrise can foster the illusion that everything is as good and lovely as the brand new day. Although the sunshine casts beautiful shades of pink and orange that spread and color the horizon, the sun also reveals the dark deeds of the night. At the same time a mom is stepping outside into the warmth of the morning sun and breathing in dewy, fresh air, police cars are at an emergency department interviewing a young woman assaulted on a college campus overnight, at a playground from which a child disappeared the previous dusk, even at a residence in a cheerful neighborhood where a 13-year-old boy hanged to death sometime before daybreak.

Life often mimics that same illusion as the beauty of a sunrise. Just as you celebrate the arrival of your own personal, glorious dawn—when you have finally reached a place of peaceful, happy homeostasis—mayhem strikes (or is revealed). Life's easy, trouble-free days are the exception, not the rule. Marion Stone in the novel *Cutting for Stone* eventually understands this reality of life, which is that "The uneventful day [is] a precious gift."

That is the nature of life—one finds a place of peace only to have it interrupted repeatedly by calamity. It is the reason for the first tenet of Buddhism, "life is suffering." Despite this grim truth, it remains a miracle that *we exist*. Evolution has worked in such an incredible way that we *have come into being* and experience life. If—throughout our various tribulations—we can hold onto the *wonder of being*, or at least cling to the belief that *someday we will once again be amazed by the miracle of being*, that just might pull us through the *chaos* and the *horrors* of being.

March 2015

Among the myriad emotions I experienced in the first days and weeks following my son's death, I felt surprised and perplexed that the particular child of mine who had died was Sammy. Of my five children, I had worried the least about Sammyboy ever getting seriously hurt (and fear of him dying, of course, hadn't even been on my radar). Throughout his short life, Sammy had continuously displayed impressive athleticism, and because of his physical strengths, he had rarely even ever been injured. I used to joke that Samuel had received every bit of the physical ability that God (or as I would now say Mother Nature or evolution) had portioned to be distributed among my offspring.

The first time I took note of Sammy's physical capabilities was a day when the children were all very young, and I was having homeschool with them. For the first time, Sammy, age 3, was joining his brother Peter, age 6, and his sister Sarah, age 5, for P.E. I told them all to sit on the floor in a straddle position. Peter and Sarah spread their legs in their usual barely-greater-than-90-degree angle, but when I glanced at Sammy, I was taken aback to see his legs stretched out in a 160-degree angle. After I told the kids to lean forward and stretch, Peter and Sarah moved a few inches toward their toes and stopped, but Sammy leaned forward until his face was only a few inches off the floor. Peter, Sarah, and I stared open-mouthed at our little Sammy. After that, I began to regularly observe things that evidenced Sammy's abilities. When he would jump off small ledges, although the other kids stumbled or fell forward upon landing, Sammy didn't. He landed and stuck hard to his position. By the time he was 4-years-old, Sammy was able to maintain a perfect L position while holding onto a horizontal bar above his head. So, when our horrible family tragedy occurred, it didn't make sense to me that Sammy was the one who had died; and yet, he was.

When he was quite young, Sammy naturally assumed the role of protector for his siblings. Once, when our family was returning home after visiting another family, Adam (then 3 years old) tearfully told us how one of the host's children had pushed him. Sammy (then 5 years old) immediately scowled and piped up, "Adam, the next time we are at somebody's house and one of their kids pushes you, you tell me and I'll punch 'em!" And when he said, "punch 'em" his voice got low and growly the way it sometimes did when he was angry. Another time, several years later when I had taken the kids roller-skating, a few boys bullied Adam in the restroom. My little dreamer had gone in by himself, forgetting my family rule of no one going alone into a public bathroom. The bullies didn't physically harm Adam; but, they were several years older than he was, and they (one, in particular) were harsh in their verbal teasing and mean in their behavior, looking over and under the bathroom stall Adam occupied. Visibly rattled and upset, Adam skated to where I stood talking to Lydia, Sammy, and Sarah and told us about the incident. With pride I confess, I watched the following events unfold. After asking Adam to point out the offensive meanies, Sammy quickly skated to catch up with them. In one smooth motion, while flying past the mean boys, Sammy slid his right foot out in front of the worst offender, causing the surprised bully to tumble to the ground. Sarah skated up to the fallen boy while he was getting to his feet and coolly informed him he better not do anything else to anyone in our family. He looked innocently at the pretty brunette lecturing him, until she pointed out her little brother Adam, and realization came into the bully's eyes. Sammy skated closely by Sarah just then, and the bully, noticing him, stared cautiously as he passed.

 Sarah then finished her speech. "That boy you are watching? The one who tripped you? He is another one of my brothers." The bullies gave my children a wide berth for the rest of the evening. Generally, Sammy respected authority and was a rule follower, but if someone messed with one of his siblings, caution and adherence to a strict rule of law were thrown aside as Sammy the Body emerged.

 Sadly, no one protected Sammy the night he died. I hadn't even realized he needed protecting; and had he needed protection from himself or from someone else?

Chapter 2

"What hurts so bad about youth isn't the actual butt whippings the world delivers. It's the stupid hopes playacting like certainties."

-Mary Karr, *Lit*

Wednesday, October 20, 2010
Four Days Before Sammy Died

It was a sunny, crisp October morning, and I wasn't scheduled to work. I loved my job as a registered nurse, and I loved the friendly hospital where I was employed (and had been born and given birth to two of my five babies). Having recently picked up several extra shifts, I was thrilled to have a day off. As a bonus, it was a weekday so all of my children would be at school. Once I taxied everyone to their respective locations, I would drop into Starbucks and treat myself to a lovely Pumpkin Spice Latte and a blueberry scone.

My second child and oldest daughter, Sarah, had already left the house for the day. A sophomore in high school, Sarah turned 16-years-old right before the school year started. Every day the previous summer, she practiced driving so she would pass her driver license test the first time she took it and be able to drive herself to school. She would have practiced every day even if she hadn't been allowed to drive herself, because that is Sarah.

Sarah does not fail any kind of test. Ever. She is my most driven, disciplined, and responsible child. I sometimes tease her she was born a miniature adult. At age 2, she was the youngest of my children to be potty-trained and at age 4, the youngest to learn to read. On her own initiative when she was 5-years-old, Sarah would inform me she had packed the swim bag with towels and goggles for everyone and placed it by the front door—an hour before we had to leave. Like me, Sarah loves planning, organizing, and list making. When she was 7-years-old, she would even sit next to me as I wrote out our two-week meal plan and grocery list, carefully transcribing them into her own notebook. Sarah is kind, thoughtful, and gentle, a pleasant soul to those whose company she keeps.

I often refer to my two daughters as "my sugar and my spice." Sarah, my quiet, sweet, older girl, is my sugar. My talkative, sassy, younger girl and youngest child, Lydia, is my spice. Both of my two daughters' unique personalities equally delight me

When Lydia was only a toddler, my mother would regularly tell me, "This one is full of spit and vinegar!" Spit and vinegar, indeed. Lydia is the kind of girl people often call "a pistol." She is direct, free with her opinion, and frequently thinks aloud. Because she lives in the present moment and is very observant of her surroundings and details, Lydia makes an excellent family detective. She can always find her dad's misplaced wallet or recall the color of skirt worn by the sales lady—20 minutes after we leave a store. She is creative, can take forever picking something out (too many exciting choices to narrow down the decision) and she is tough.

That morning in 2010, I took a deep breath as I entered Lydia's room. I never knew what to expect from my spicy girl. At age 11, she was in fifth grade, and her school started an hour later than did the boys'. Every weekday, I roused Lydia to wake up and get dressed, before I left the house for five minutes to drive the boys to school and return home. "Time to rise and shine, Schmoo," I whispered, bending over her where she slept sprawled across her bed.

Before I could straighten, Lydia had thrown her arms around me, locked her hands behind my neck, and exclaimed, "Cuddle with me!" That is my little firecracker! Sometimes, I find this type of behavior from Lydia amusing and delightful; other times, it greatly irritates me. I'm not certain if that is because she demands what she wants rather than asks, or because I find her timing inconvenient—probably both. Aside from my preference for sweet requests rather than blunt commands, I am more task oriented and (at that time) followed a school-day morning agenda: 1) Wake Lydia. 2) Take boys to school. *Not*- 1) Wake Lydia. 2) Cuddle with Lydia for ten minutes. 3) Take boys to school. For one week earlier that school year, I actually scheduled an allotted time for a morning cuddle session with Lydia. Alas, it was too hard for me to stop and vege during the morning rush, so I dropped it from our schedule. That day, I had about five minutes before I needed to leave to take the boys to school, so I climbed into bed next to Lydia and tried not to worry about whether Adam, my forgetful son, had combed his hair or brushed his teeth.

Not only my daughters, all of my children are quite different from each other. In October 2010, I was mother to five: Peter, 17, Sarah, 16, Samuel, 13, Adam, 12, and Lydia, 11. Back when I had only two or three children, in order to better understand each of their blossoming personality and behavioral differences, I began researching and reading vast amounts of information about personality types. I stumbled across the Myers-Briggs Type Indicator information (MBTI) and with eagerness plunged into that theory (I am aware the professionals prefer The Big Five, but as a layperson in psychology, MBTI worked great for my purposes). Learning about each child's specific type was instrumental in my understanding and accepting of his or her inherent nature and in helping me to parent and nurture accordingly. At age 20—when I knew everything about everything—I assumed the most critical components in shaping my future children, in addition to regular, firm parenting, would be an abundance of love and understanding. When my babies were born already partially programmed, I experienced a bit of a rude awakening. In my carefully laid parenting plan, I had over-looked one factor that is equally important to the nurture element: each child's specific *nature*. Although all of my children were nurtured in the same home, with the same love, training, and very similar early life experiences, all five evidenced substantial differences from one another almost from the moment they emerged from my womb. In time, I discovered each child's distinct personality type. The knowledge of their inherent dispositions enabled me to recognize what could appear as disobedience might simply be absent-mindedness, or what could appear as a mean-spirited remark might just be a candid observation. One would think in having five children, two of them might have come out with the same type; no two of mine had. To this day, the personality type knowledge I gleaned during those years of research and reading (in combination with many years of loving and growing my children) continues to be helpful, not only in my parenting endeavors but with all of my relationships.

Over the years, in order to ascertain my children's specific personality types, I tested each child multiple times with the MBTI information. When I tested Sarah, her result was ISFJ: I-Introvert, S-Sensor/takes in information through her senses, F-Feeler/privileges peoples' feelings above facts, and J-Judger/prefers decisions made rather than keeping options open. The SJ types are often called, "The Traditionalists," a perfect description of dependable, well-behaved Sarah. Lydia—my spitfire and saucy girl—is part of the larger group type called, "The Experiencers." She is an ESTP: E-Extrovert, S-Sensor/takes in information through her senses, T-Thinker/privileges facts over feelings, and P-Perceiver/prefers to keep her options open. Lydia likes to see, smell, touch and try everything for herself, so "The Experiencers" is a fitting group for her.

After my five-minute cuddle with Lydia that October morning, I jumped up before she could wrap a leg around me and yell, "Noo, don't leave yet!" Rushing out of her room, I called the boys. "Sammy! Adam! Time to go!" They came to the front door with their backpacks, and I quickly inspected their hair and teeth. Sammy and Adam, my two middle children, were as opposite as a short, blonde-haired, hazel-eyed, quiet, athlete could be from a tall, brown-haired, brown-eyed, talkative, brainiac.

As I suspected, my fourth child and youngest son, Adam, a sixth grader, had yet to brush his teeth, a typical oversight for my absent-minded boy. While I was cuddling with Lydia, he probably had been daydreaming about his favorite TV show, *Dragonball*, as he slowly ate his breakfast. Sammy and I went out to the van, and Adam ran to brush up.

An abstract thinker, Adam is always thinking of out-of-the-box ideas. He is clever, quirky and bright. He is considered—and is proud to be—a nerd. Adam loves chess and other games of strategy. He is gifted at debate and public speaking. In Myers-Briggs, he is an ENXP: E-Extrovert, N-Intuitor/takes in information through abstract thought, X-right in the middle of thinker/feeler/sometimes privileges facts over feeling, but sometimes feelings over facts, and P-Perceiver/prefers to keep his options open. Adam is aptly classified as part of the group type called, "The Dreamers."

My third child and middle son, Samuel, a seventh grader, had likely been ready to leave for school for five minutes. His hair was combed and teeth were brushed (albeit, haphazardly). Very much a "typical" boy, Sammy was categorized in the same general MBTI group as Sarah, "The Traditionalists." Sammy was task oriented; when given a job, he quickly completed it without fuss. He rarely got into trouble, dutifully completed his homework (although his handwriting was atrocious), and quietly did what was expected of him. He was easy-going, pleasant, and funny, and he was an exceptional athlete. His body was like a machine, the only weaknesses being his allergies and exercise-induced asthma. Sammy was a naturally cool kid with a good heart. His MBTI type was ISTJ: I-Introvert, S-Sensor/took in information through his senses, T-Thinker/privileged facts over feelings, though not nearly as strong of a T as Lydia, and J-Judger/preferred decisions made rather than keeping his options open.

Since my divorce in 2005, my firstborn child and son, Peter, lived solely with my ex-husband Lucas. In 2010, Peter was a junior in high school and, sadly, I rarely saw him. On the Meyers-Briggs, Peter tests (at least he did when he was under 12-years-old) as an ENTJ: E-Extrovert, N-Intuitor/takes in information through abstract thought, T-Thinker/privileges facts over feelings, and J-Judger/prefers decisions made rather than keeping options open. His group type is called, "The Conceptualists." Independent, logical, and skeptical, Peter likes talking about ideas and theories. Although he is quite intelligent, from a very young age Peter struggled to remain focused when reading, writing, or completing tasks. He was easily distracted and couldn't pay attention, and he had occasional aggression, anger, and irritability problems. I suspected he might have ADHD. When I began home educating Peter, I quickly realized these problems were a liability to his learning. Through reading books about teaching, particularly children who were left-brained or those who suffered ADHD, and by trial and error, I discovered one way to side step his learning troubles (without medication). I completed most of his schooling orally with him.

When I first filed for divorce and separated from Lucas after 12 years of marriage, Peter (then 11-years-old) was shocked and quite disgruntled and became very upset with me. Change had always been hard for Peter, and a marital break-up was a massive adjustment that was just too much for him. He and I had always been close, and I thought that would be enough to help him get through the transition without many problems. I was wrong.

The divorce wasn't easy. It took a full year and became fairly ugly. Lucas was a minister, and my decision to divorce angered him. He fought hard and dirty. Frankly, I was shocked and devastated by his ugliness throughout our divorce, which, in my mind, confirmed my suspicion about his (lack of) love for me.

During the year it took to go through the divorce, Peter—strongly against his will—lived with me and the other kids (I had temporary custody). He seethed with anger and kept insisting on living with his father. His response and reaction completely blew me away. He didn't just say he preferred to live with his dad. He was raging mad. He went from regularly telling me he loved me and I was his best friend, to telling me he hated me and didn't give a crap if he ever saw me again in his entire life. I took Peter to a child psychologist for a while to help him work through his fury, but to no avail. Before we went to court for the final hearing, after much deliberation, several discussions with my own father, and many sleepless nights, I gave Peter his choice of residence. To my utter frustration and sadness, he chose to live with Lucas.

Following the divorce, most of the time he still didn't want to come to my house to visit, and I didn't force it. He was very determined, acted quite ugly, and was often full of anger. When I insisted he come, he made life extremely challenging for me and the other kids. Eventually, I told him he didn't have to come if he hated it so much. I thought and hoped with time, his anger would resolve and he would want to start visiting again, especially if I wasn't forcing it; he didn't.

Although going through the divorce was brutal and very sad, my oldest child essentially cutting me out of his life was excruciating. I never dreamed Peter would react the way he had. Over the years, I suffered great heartache and shed an abundance of tears over him. I missed him, and it tore me up that I wasn't involved with the entire last third of his childhood. There were a few occasions when he indicated he was ready to have a relationship again, and that he was okay with having regular, scheduled visits. He would even say he loved me, had always loved me, and hadn't meant the things he had said in the past when he was 11, 12, and 13-years-old: "I hate you", "You are my ex-mom", "I don't care if I never see you again in my life," "I know you love me, you've told me a million times, and I don't care." With his help and preferences, I would set up a bedroom for him at my house and be full of hope, but every time nothing would come of it. He would just not return for four months, six months, or ten months. When I would finally see him again, it was as if he had never said or implied anything about resuming visits or reconnecting with me.

As of October 2010, the last time I had seen Peter had been in June. We went to lunch together (one of a very few times), and while I attempted to converse with him, letting him direct the flow of conversation, I came to a realization that I shared with Peter. I told him I thought I had become cauterized to him. The things he said and did no longer cut me too deeply; they no longer caused my heart to bleed. My intent was not to be hurtful, but I had no fear of that. Peter didn't seem to get hurt feelings. To him, everything was just information, just data. I'm not sure why I even shared my thought with him. I think that upon realizing it, as I had been listening to Peter talk, I simply was thinking aloud and being open with Peter about it. Maybe I hoped it would move our relationship away from a trend where it seemed Peter's goal included wounding or hurting me.

Despite the difficult divorce and the subsequent painful behavior and choices of my oldest child, my life had finally reached a beautiful place. In 2007, I married Jake, a man with whom I had been friends in high school and dated briefly in college. Life with Jake was what I always hoped marriage would be—a happy, peaceful existence with your best friend, lover, and favorite person. The children had quickly taken to Jake and even started calling him "Dad;" they didn't do it to replace their biological father, but because they felt Jake deserved to be called Dad and they looked to him as a dad (in addition to their dad Lucas). Jake had never been married nor had any children when we reconnected (both of us then age 33). For many reasons, we decided we would not add more children to our life together. So, Jake would never biologically father any children, a fact of which the children were aware and that played a part in their decision to call him "Dad." Jake jumped into our family with both feet, assuming responsibility for a wife and four children. He also would have accepted Peter, had Peter not opted out of our lives. We all (excluding Peter) settled into a routine, and began enjoying our individual lives as well as our happy family life.

As we started that beautiful fall day in 2010, and Sammy and I waited in the van for Adam to brush his teeth, none of us had any warning our days of easy joyfulness would soon be abruptly ending. We thought we had been through our family's karmic allotment of hard times, that life had settled down, and that it was just a regular week.

Sammy and I were listening to the radio when Adam came running out, and we drove to school singing to one of their favorite songs, "Numa Numa." I hadn't taken the kids to get their Halloween costumes yet, and as we were driving, Sammy asked, "Mom, can you take us to the party store soon so we can pick out our costumes before all the good ones are taken?"

"Ohh, good thinking, Puff," (one of my nicknames for Sammy). "How about we go today after I pick you guys up from school?"

"Yes!" shouted Adam.

"Awesomesauce!" yelled Sammy.

They loved Halloween, especially Adam who always relished the opportunity to dress up as the misunderstood villain. In history class, Sammy had been studying ancient Greece, and Jake and I had recently watched the film *300* with him after he practically begged us. He loved it so much he wanted a Halloween costume that resembled the characters in the film. True to his type, Sammy always selected costumes that were more traditional; he loved to be the manly protector of women, children, or any who might be needful of protection. For several years in a row when he was younger, Sammy had dressed up as Buzz Lightyear (one of his childhood favorites), and the last three years he had gone as a medieval knight. Lydia was thinking she would wear the genie costume she had worn for her Arabian Nights-themed birthday party the previous month, but she hadn't decided for sure.

After enjoying my latte' and scone that day and running a few errands, I picked up the kids from school, and we drove to the party store. We found a Hercules costume that was perfect for Sammy. Adam was still undecided (what a surprise-*not*. Adam is a P—according to the MBTI—and he likes to keep his option open), so I would have to take him back again after he gave it more thought. We drove home and the kids helped me with a few chores.

We began the task of straightening up our family room by sorting through the massive collection of books cluttering our bookshelves. We placed in piles for removal, textbooks from when I was in nursing school, curriculum guides and books from my years of homeschooling, and some religious books that no one was reading.

It delighted me to see my quickly growing boys carrying the stacks of heavy books out to the garage. Because Sammy had been making the change from boy to young man over the previous few months, I took particular joy watching him. His back had broadened, his forearms had become sinewy, and his neck had grown thicker. He was handsome with his sweet, squinty eyes, his dirty-blonde hair, his puffy lips, and his muscular body; I figured he was going to be a heartbreaker.

 That night, we attended Sarah's Concert Choir performance at her high school. She took great satisfaction singing with the choir, and her pleasure gave me pleasure. I was also able to check out a certain boy in whom she told me she was interested who also sang in the choir. In fact, when Jake picked Sarah up from school one day the previous week, he had noticed the blonde-haired boy standing with her, engrossed in her conversation. When Jake asked about it on the way home, Sarah nonchalantly said the boy was just a friend. When Jake told me about it later, he informed me that although Sarah might feel that way about the boy, the boy was definitely interested in Sarah. Since then, I had noticed several flirty comments on Sarah's Facebook wall from the boy and had been teasing her a little about it. I made efforts to stay aware of the goings-on in my children's lives and to engage with them about those things.

 One of my parenting goals was to try to really know, understand, and be in tune with my children. I wanted to be aware of who they were and what was going on in their hearts and minds. I felt that made the difference between being a good mother and being a great mother. Further, I encouraged the kids to be aware of each other and to observe, watch over, and look out for one another. I wanted my children to feel like our family was a team, pulling all together through life. I believed that connectivity helped to develop a sturdier foundation for each family member and made us all stronger. That increased stability founded a sense of well-being and emotional connection for us and made our home and family life pleasant and loving.

 Having an emotionally warm and happy home had been a goal of mine since childhood. I wanted to be a supportive, encouraging wife and an attentive, loving mom, and I hoped to make my home a warm and happy oasis. With enough planning, care, and work, I thought all of that was possible. I never would have believed that after 12 years of marriage, I would feel exhausted, defeated by my efforts, done. My sincere commitment to God had not been enough to save my first marriage or help me to live with it any longer—so much for faith. I never would have believed after years of pouring myself (my love, energy, and attention) into my precious babies, one of them would come to despise me and no longer want to sustain a relationship—so much for love. I certainly never considered one of my beloved children would come to a premature, tragic end—so much for hope. "Now abide faith, hope, and love; but the greatest of these is love," a bible verse and motto of my youth, would eventually be thrown into the garbage heap with most of my other young dreams. However, at that time in the fall of October 2010, all was not yet lost; faith and love had been trampled upon, but not entirely, because I still had hope.

Chapter 3

"Blessed is he who expects nothing, for he shall never be disappointed."

-Alexander Pope, *Letter to Gay, October 6, 1727*

October 21-23, 2010

The Last Days Before Sammy Died

Thursday, October 21, Jake and I took the kids to a performance of the musical, *Fiddler on the Roof*. Occasionally, we tried to do things all together in our efforts to build family solidarity. In addition, I wanted to stretch the children's thinking by exposing them to great art, music, literature, and theater, which I felt were an important part of shaping and sculpting their young minds. Prior to the show, Sammy and Adam grumbled that we were making them go to a play, and even worse, a musical! Alas, Sammy hated musicals. Apparently, I had failed as a mother, or perhaps it was one of those instances where nature was trumping nurture. Surprisingly, after the show both boys said they thought it was good, and—miracle of miracles—they liked it! They didn't even mind that all the way home, the girls and I kept loudly singing "Tradition!"

I worked the next day, Friday, October 22, and Jake took the children to school. I knew I wouldn't be finished at the hospital until 4:30 pm, so I arranged with Sarah to pick up the little ones. Lucas usually came to my house at 6:00 pm every other Friday to collect the kids for his weekend visitation with him (and Peter). However, Sarah wanted her car over at his place that weekend, so Lucas told her to bring the kids with her to his house at 6:00 pm rather than him coming to get them. Sarah had only been a licensed driver for two months, so I hadn't yet allowed her to do much driving with all three of the little ones in her van. Although she had picked them up from school several times when I was still at work, our house was only two minutes away from their schools (which were right next to each other). Additionally, it was the weekend of the University Homecoming football game, so I knew traffic Friday evening would be heavy with football fans coming from out of town. Sarah making the ten-minute drive on the interstate during rush hour with the little ones in the car concerned me. Instead, I told her to go directly to her father's house after she picked the kids up from school, which meant I wouldn't make it home from work in time to see them before they left for the weekend. I hated to make that sacrifice, but I was worried about their safety and thought it wiser for them to drive earlier right after school. I would later regret that decision.

Saturday, October 23, I worked, and it was a relatively uneventful day at the hospital. During my lunch break, Sammy called to ask me a question. He was getting a new black hoodie and didn't know what size he needed. Sammy liked his sweatshirts, hoodies, and t-shirts to be a little baggy, and, uncertain of his current size due to his recent growth, I suggested he call Dad to double-check what I had told him. Jake is very detail oriented and always aware of tiny facts regarding the children.

That evening, Jake and I ordered Domino's pizza for dinner, cuddled on the couch, and watched a movie. The house was quiet with the kids gone. Before bed, I caught up a little on Facebook. There was an article in the newspaper about a man who was shot dead, essentially, for being in the wrong place at the wrong time. While stopping for gas at around 2:00 am at a filling station, he lost his life in a random gun shooting. Reading the article reminded me of something my dad used to say to my siblings and me.

Jane's Facebook Wall

My dad always used to tell us, "Nothin' good happens after midnight."

Missouri Daily Newspaper

Man shot dead in Break Time parking lot

A 22-year-old man was shot to death early Saturday morning at a convenience store.

Becky S- "My dad used to say that to me when I was a teenager and wanting a later curfew!!!"

Jane B: "Lol:) I am glad to say that about 5 years before my dad died, I finally realized that he was almost NEVER wrong!! And I told him that regularly :) (Not to imply that the victim was at fault, but the general principal of nothing good after midnight is true!)"

Another old friend from high school, with whom I had just reconnected on Facebook, posted on my wall,

Paula B- "Hey, it's good to find you here. How are you doing? You look sooo happy. I'm so happy for you!"

Jane B- "Good to see you too! I am very happy:) I have a wonderful husband, my children are a constant source of love, joy, and excitement, and I get paid to do what I love, which is be a nurse!"

I changed my profile picture, and Sarah commented from over at Lucas's house. That was one of the things I loved about Facebook! When Sarah was at her father's every other weekend, we could stay in touch.

Sarah B L- "Me gusta your profile pic:) It's really cute!"

Jane B - Muchas gracias! Me gusta your soul :)"

A little while later, Jo (my best friend since college) posted an article about long lasting friendships, and she commented:

Jo M-"You're my longest female friendship—19 years and counting! Love you, Jane!"

Jane B- "Awwww thanks, MFJ," (one of our little code names, which meant, My Friend Jo). "Our current schedules (me working every day and you going to class in the evening) are seriously causing me to lose brain cells by lack of cranium usage from not getting to talk to you! I miss you! Oh and Happy Anniversary btw!" (We casually acknowledged the anniversary of our friendship each fall.) "I love you too!"

"Nothin' good happens after midnight," had been just one of the *hundreds* of aphorisms and axioms my dad used to say. I loved all of his pithy bits of wisdom, and I missed them; I missed *him*. It had been a long, sad year and a half since Dad's sudden and unexpected death. Losing him had been particularly difficult because he was the parent with whom I had been much closer; I think that was because we were much more alike than my mom and I, who had always seemed to misunderstand each other. Over the previous few months, I had *finally* shaken off the heaviest part of the grief and had been able to start appreciating and enjoying life again.

At the beginning of October, Jake received great news concerning a serious cardiac condition he had been fighting throughout the previous year—he was completely healed—and for that we were ecstatic! After losing my Dad, I had been terrified at the thought of losing Jake too. Fortunately, with the help of our great physician and some fantastic meds, we had managed to jump that health hurdle. The chaos of life had crashed in on us, as it is want to do, but thankfully, it appeared we were back in blue skies again.

11: 44 pm- After I finished up on Facebook for the night, Jake and I turned out the lights and went to bed. Life was good, and we only expected it would get better. We were clueless that while we slept that night, across town in a different house, very bad things would be happening after midnight.

Chapter 4

> "Life changes fast. Life changes in the instant. You sit down to dinner and life as you know it ends."
>
> -Joan Didion, *The Year of Magical Thinking*

Sunday, October 24, 2010

I was scheduled to work that morning but had been called off due to low hospital census. After I received the 5:00 am call letting me know I wasn't needed for the first four hours of the shift, I happily fell back asleep snuggled up next to Jake. At 9:40 am, my cell phone rang again. Hoping I wasn't being called in to work, I rolled over and grabbed it. I didn't recognize the phone number. When I answered, a high pitched shrieking voice screeched through the receiver and blasted my ear drum. For about two seconds, I was confused by the screams, and then I recognized the distraught caller's voice. I sat straight up in bed, startled. The screaming caller was Sarah.

"Sarah? Sweetie? What's wrong?" I asked, completely alarmed. I strained to decipher her words through the broken, anguished cries, but she was nearly unintelligible. "What did you say, Sweetie? You need us to come over there? To Lucas's house? Right now?" I asked, trying to keep my voice calm and reassuring.

"Yes!" she wailed loudly.

"Okay, Sweetheart. We're coming over right now. I love you."

Jake, who had been in a deep sleep, awoke when he heard Sarah's screams through my phone. We scrambled out of bed, making little eye contact, and threw on our clothes. I was extremely concerned and was trying not to panic. I knew my daughter well. I had never heard her so discomposed. I could think of nothing that would excite such hysterics in her or cause her tell us to come over to my ex-husband's house right then, both of which were firsts.

We rushed out of the house to the van and started racing across town. "Maybe Sammy and Lucas got in a fight and Sammy wants to leave or something?" I said. The previous year or two, Sammy had been having increased irritation and frustration in his relationship with Lucas.

Jake shook his head, "I don't think so."

My cell phone rang, and I looked at the caller I.D. When I saw it was Lucas, my stomach tightened and the panic surged. Lucas and I rarely had any contact; it was unusual for him to call me.

"Did Sarah call you?" he asked when I answered.

"Yes," I replied, and then silence; I didn't know what else to say.

"Are you on your way?"

"Yes. We are about four minutes away." There was only silence again. Then, I asked, "Is everything okay?"

"No, it's not," he replied gruffly.

"Okay. Well, we'll be right there." After I hung up, I looked over at Jake. "It must be really bad if he is calling me."

"Yeah," Jake quietly agreed as he briefly glanced at me. Both of his hands were tightly gripping the steering wheel, and he was intent on driving. As we flew down the highway, it crossed my mind that if one of the kids were hurt we should be going to the hospital and not to Lucas's house. *But that's what it has to be*, I thought. *One of the kids must be hurt...*

As we turned onto Lucas's street, I saw emergency vehicles everywhere. My heart faltered for a moment and then started beating fast and hard. Fire trucks, an ambulance, a crime squad van, and police cars all crowded the road between our location and my ex-husband's house. Jake slowed, trying to maneuver around the vehicles in order to reach the driveway. By then, I was frantic. I removed my seatbelt, scooted to the edge of the seat, and put my hand on the door handle ready to bolt. Something very bad had happened, and I had to make sure all of my babies were safe. There were too many vehicles on the street to get through, and we were going too slow. So, I yelled, "Just pull over! Pull over to the side of the road!" Every molecule in my body was screaming, straining to get to that house and see the happy, healthy faces of my children. Jake pulled over, but before he had completely stopped, I threw open my door, jumped out, and started sprinting down the street to Lucas's house. I couldn't help it; I was near hysteria. Approaching his lawn, I saw Lucas, grim-faced, standing in the grass near his front door. I barely took note of him before I scanned the yard for my little ones; I saw none of them. When I reached him, Lucas shook his head back and forth. His arms were folded across his chest, one of his hands under his chin.

He didn't look at me as he spoke.

"Well, he's gone. Sammy's dead," he said. I just stared at him, my brow furrowed and my eyes squinted into tiny slits. I tried to think, to understand. His words had absolutely no meaning to me. What the hell was he saying?

"What?!?" I screeched, completely confused. *Wait: Did he just say, 'Sammy's gone? Where?! Where has Sammy gone?* I thought.

"Sammy's gone. He hung himself," he stated.

"He...hung...?" I faltered, still failing to comprehend what he was telling me. He turned and walked away, and I was left standing in the grass, open-mouthed, staring dumbfounded at his receding back.

His words made no sense. I didn't know what in the world he meant by saying, "Sammy's gone." But the words, "He hung himself," were burning through the turmoil in my mind; and then, "Sammy's dead," detonated like an atomic bomb inside my brain. My mouth, my mind, and my heart made one enormous scream. All of the truth, knowledge, and wisdom I had ever known exploded in a bright flash. All my sense of self dispersed. My knees shook. My bladder released, and a warm stream soaked my jeans. A white-hot scream rose within the fragmentation inside my skull and rushed out of my mouth. A tortured howl pierced the air. A loud ringing filled my ears, and I felt as if some invisible essence—which was me, or my spirit, or my sanity—began wafting away from my body and into the great unknown.

Jake was in front of me then, grabbing me by my shoulders and trying to catch my gaze with his. "Sweetheart, what happened? What's wrong?" An intense tug from deep inside my gut snapped my horror-stricken, fleeing spirit back to my body. It didn't want to be there. I didn't want to be there. I wanted to be free from my physical form to search through the universe for my beautiful boy. I needed to be free—to exist apart from the constraints of my flesh—to leave the wretched dimension in which I was stuck. *Where is Sammy's spirit? Where is he now? He must still be right around here?!* But, my beloved, my best friend, my lover, my husband was holding me, staring with alarm intently into my eyes, keeping my spirit tethered to my body. His face, his presence, his love, grounded me enough that I was able to speak.

I shrieked, "Sammy's dead! He…hung himself?!" He looked at me as if I had just spoken in another language; his mind could not register my words. I was unable to say more. An animal wailing emitted from deep within my bowels. I wanted to run like crazy. I wanted to pull out my hair. I wanted to fall and roll around on the ground thrashing and foaming. I was lost in agony. My spirit raged to be released, to fly, to seek, to search, but it was safeguarded for the time by Jake, who possibly had saved my spirit/soul/sanity/mind from ripping itself apart in its frantic attempt to break from reality to go find the spirit of my child.

How long I remained in that state—moaning, screaming, teetering on the brink of mentally breaking away—I cannot say. Police officers, firefighters, and other uniformed people silently stood around, unable to say or do anything to relieve my misery. They had no answers. They could offer no reassuring words. Over and over I wailed, "My boy! My sweet boy!" I screamed. I cried. I shook my head. I rocked my body.

Gradually, awareness crept over me of Jake quietly weeping by my side—his face a mask of shock, pain, and befuddlement. He looked as if someone had struck him hard across the head with a two by four, leaving him stunned, confused, and hurt. I moved closer to hold him, and to be held by him, but—for the first time since we had reunited many years before—I found no comfort in his embrace. We were both critically wounded. Our hearts and minds were shattered. Our lives forever changed. The final flicker of hope I still carried inside of me, which had survived all of life's previous blows, was extinguished, completely snuffed out. All hope for life, for happiness, or for the future was gone. My child, my son, my Sammy Soft Skin was dead.

Chapter 5

> "Like the pain of a bad wound, the effect of a deep shock takes some while to be felt. When a child is told, for the first time in his life, that a person he has known is dead, although he does not disbelieve it, he may well fail to comprehend it and later ask—perhaps more than once—where the dead person is and when he is coming back."
>
> -Richard Peters, *Watership Down*

October 24, 2010, Sunday Morning Cont.

    Jake and I were dumbfounded and aghast. Why had it happened? A terrible thought formed in my mind: *What if Sammy was taken as a consequence of me having an abortion years ago?* The thought sickened me, and I was overcome with madness as an enormous weight of guilt pressed down upon me. *Oh my god,* I wondered. *Am I the cause? Am I to blame? Was our beautiful, sunny boy taken because God really does exist and he is somehow balancing the scales?* I turned wild-eyed to Jake and whispered my thoughts into his ear.

    He immediately shook his head and sliding an arm around me, whispered, "No, no, Sweetheart. This has nothing to do with that." But, really, he didn't know. He was only saying what he thought would soothe me. It was difficult to shake the feeling, and I was briefly filled with rage at a god who would exact payment of Sammy's life for my debt of a blueberry-sized embryo of cells and tissue. If that was the case, I wanted nothing to do with such a god. That wasn't how I parented my children, and I would expect more from a god.

    Sarah and Adam moved slowly, dazed, through the front door of Lucas's house; Peter followed, his hands stuffed in his pockets. Sarah's tearful face looked guarded, deeply pained, and troubled. Adam was pale, and he looked drawn, shocked, and confused. Peter seemed very closed off and pensive, and he didn't walk toward me or Lucas but made his way to the side end of the front porch and stood there alone. Peter's body language was bizarre. He seemed to be deep in thought, and I saw something else... Anger? Scorn? As I looked at him, a huge knot formed in my stomach. I felt a terrible sense of foreboding, and then, horrified, I thought, *Oh dear god, he knows something. He was a part of whatever happened.* It was disquieting. It was disturbing. The very idea caused my knees to feel weak, sent a sharp pain into my already screaming heart, and made me want to claw at my face. *Oh my god... Not anything like that. Please. But surely not. That's ridiculous.* I tried to push it out of my mind and turned to look at the other kids.

Upon seeing Jake and me, Sarah and Adam came over to us, and we embraced them. I had no words of comfort for my children. I didn't know what to say. I no longer had any wisdom. I no longer knew anything. I began to babble. "This makes no sense. It makes no sense. Sammy was happy! He had me take him to get his Halloween costume on Wednesday?! He picked out a Hercules costume!" They had no words. They could offer no answers. They were in shock. They were bewildered. They were in distress. And they were only children.

Awareness crept over me that the officers seemed to be observing us. It felt strange, like we were some freak show, and they couldn't look away even when I stared pointedly at them in irritation at their rudeness. *Good grief, why are they just staring at us?! Wait... They aren't staring at us; they are observing us. They are noting our individual responses.* The gears of my mind started spinning, and I tried to assemble my thoughts to determine and make sense of what happened. I pondered the believability of Sammy taking his own life, but suicide didn't make sense. I knew I couldn't be aware of everything that went on in my children's heads, but for me to have been oblivious to all signs and behaviors indicative of the kind of depression that would have foreshadowed a suicide, seemed doubtful. If it *wasn't* suicide, how the hell did he end up hanging?

Peter continued to stand silently by himself, his hands in his pockets and his face showing a strange countenance. In my mind, a red warning flag went up. Peter seemed particularly standoffish, he wasn't crying, and he didn't look shocked or numb. He seemed to be brooding on his own thoughts.

I needed to go look at the death-scene to see if I could figure anything out about what had happened. I also needed to see Sammy's face. I had to see him. I was his mother. I was supposed to always look out for him and be there for him.

Lucas stood in the driveway (where I think he had been since our arrival) speaking to or being questioned by an officer. I made my way over and said to the officer, "I would like to see where this happened, and I need to see Sammy. Is that okay?"

The officer looked at me silently for a moment. He then said, "The detectives and crime squad members are canvassing the scene and taking pictures right now." I paused, processing what he had said. *Does that mean they suspect foul play? Or is canvassing a scene something they always do when a death has occurred outside a hospital and the deceased was young and healthy?*

"Oh. Okay. Well, when they are finished can I go look?" I asked.

"Yes, when we are finished," the officer told me.

My cell phone chimed, and I looked to see a text message from Jo. "Wakey?" That was our standard morning check in before we phoned each other. Pressing the speed dial, I lifted the phone to my ear. When I heard her voice, my throat was too thick and swollen to speak. The tears began to flow heavy again. The words I tried to say were crowded out by a sob filling my mouth. Our nineteen years of friendship and shared experiences of childbearing, breast-feeding, homeschooling, church going, husband divorcing, adult schooling, adult dating, ex-husbands, and more, had knit a strong cord of love and friendship between us. I handed the phone to Jake.

He cleared his throat and managed to say "Hi, Jo." Pause. Jake faltered and said, "Sammy... hung himself." His words sounded ludicrous. Jo had known Sammy since his birth, and she would be just as flabbergasted as we were that he might have taken his life. Jake said, "Yes, he hung himself." He paused, and then he said, "No, he's gone." Jake hung up and told me, "she's on her way."

An officer who overheard the phone call came over to us. "I told Lucas earlier, but when you call people to notify them, it's better not to explain what happened if they're going to be driving. It can be too upsetting and driving becomes a safety risk. It's best to say there is an emergency and to please come."

I felt panicky and turned to Jake, "We told Jo what happened, and she will be driving!" He assured me Jo was cool in a crisis and would be fine. I called my mom, but she didn't answer. I called my sister Valerie, my sister Laura, and my niece Victoria, but none of them answered. It was Sunday morning. They all were probably at church. I sent a text message to Victoria, who (since she was a college student) might just still be sleeping. I told her there was an emergency, and she should go to the church, notify everyone to come to Lucas's house, and I would explain when they arrived. Victoria texted back and said she would do it.

It was then I realized I hadn't yet seen Lydia. Looking around, I asked Sarah, "Where is Lydia?" She told me Lydia had spent the night with Mary (her best friend from church). I walked over to Lucas, with whom I'd had no conversation since I arrived, and asked him about Lydia. He explained that she spent the night with Mary who brought her to church that morning. When he was notified of an emergency, he left her at church.

I was certain she was freaking out. Knowing her, she had realized the other kids never arrived, saw Lucas rush out, and was trying to figure out what was going on. Lucas asked, "Should I have Amber (his girlfriend) go back to the church and pick her up and bring her here?"

"Yes," I told him. "She will be anxious and worried, wondering what is happening. She will want to be here."

Jake and I sat on the driveway waiting for the detectives to finish their work. *Why is it taking them so long?* I wondered. I looked at the crime squad van parked on the street. *They must be confirming this is an actual suicide and not something else. I spoke to Sammy on the phone yesterday when he called me at work. He seemed totally normal. He didn't sound sad, mopey, angry, or upset. Was he struggling with something of which I was unaware? He has a lot of friends and is well liked at school. I wonder if Kyle* (Sammy's best friend) *knows anything?*

Searching my phone contacts, I found the number for Kyle's mom and pressed dial. Part of me felt ridiculous for calling at such a time; but I had nothing to do except wait, and I wondered if Sammy's best friend might have some information. When Kyle's mom answered, I told her what had happened. I asked if she would share the news with Kyle and see if he was aware of anything that had been bothering Sammy. In less than ten minutes, she called back. Kyle was shocked by the news. She said he was unaware of anything troubling Sammy. They had played Xbox online together Friday night, and everything had been fine. Kyle got on the phone to talk to me. He was baffled. We talked a little, but he had no information to explain why his best friend would have suddenly taken his own life. "Thanks for your help, Kyle." I felt a subtle shift in my mind as to Kyle's position relative to our family, from "He *is* Sammy's best friend," to "He *was* Sammy's best friend."

Lydia arrived and walked apprehensively down the sidewalk in our direction from several houses away. As I rose and started toward her, Lucas (who still stood at the top of his driveway) said, "Just wait until she gets over here." He seemed to be self-conscious about the chaos unfolding in front of his house. He had always shown more concern for appearances than I. Indeed, a few neighbors were standing out on their driveways watching. I hadn't noticed.

I looked at Lydia and saw fear and anxiety on her face as she took in all of the emergency vehicles and personnel. I couldn't get my arms around her soon enough, and (disregarding Lucas's suggestion) I walked quickly toward her. When I reached her, I gently hugged her.

"Sweetheart," I said, "Something's happened. Everything is going to be okay, but… Sammy's dead." She started crying and we hugged some more. Then, she opened a small notebook she was carrying to show me something she had written earlier after Lucas left the church. "Something bad has happened. None of the other kids ever came to church. I hope Peter and Sammy weren't in a car accident."

She closed the notebook and said, "I knew something bad had happened."

"I knew you would know," I answered.

We walked back toward the house and sat on the driveway. Two cars arrived with my mother, my sister Valerie and her husband Vince, their twenty-something daughter, Victoria, and my sister Laura. I stood, feeling ever so slightly pacified to see them, my mother and sisters, my people who had known me from birth. As they walked toward me, I managed to say, "Sammy's dead." They had no reaction and showed no emotion—nothing.

Valerie then said, "We know. Lucas already told us." Irritated, my eyes tightened toward a squint. It wasn't Lucas's place to tell my family, and more importantly, for safety reasons, the officers specifically told us not to disclose the information to anyone who would be driving. They reached where I stood with Jake, Sarah, Adam, and Lydia, and I tried to push aside my irritation. I wanted to be enveloped by familial love.

All of them hugged all of us—with the exception of my mother. In a perfect display of how differently we thought and operated, my mother continued to walk up the driveway toward Lucas, where she embraced him and then stood quietly talking to him. My blood pressure immediately shot up, and my heartbeat pulsed uncomfortably in my temples. *Mother?! I am your child! And my child has just been found hanged to death. Why on earth would you console my ex-husband—with whom it is no secret I have a strained relationship—before me?!* My perspective was skewed red with the blood of my dead son, and I didn't have it in me to feel anything but offended.

"Nice, Mother. You chose to console your asshole ex-son-in-law before your own daughter," I said. It was stupid. It was immature. It would be counter-productive and achieve nothing aside from invoking her quiet, long-lived anger. On most days, I could hold my tongue, but not that day. My child was dead, and I didn't care what anyone thought about anything I said.

I couldn't read the expression on my mother's face as she looked at me, but she stood still for a moment, her mouth set in a tight line. Then, she moved slowly back down the driveway toward me and said condescendingly, "Now, Jane, don't be like that. This is not the time for that." My first instinct was to snap back at her, but I didn't have the emotional energy for a fight or to explain why her actions had stung me. I reached out and hugged her, but the damage was already done. I could read it on her face. *This is gonna come back and bite me*, I thought. *Why can't dad be here?! He never would have done what she just did. He and I were like-minded in so many ways, including our understanding of loyalty. When he was living, I always felt I had a safety net under me. No matter what was going on or how difficult the circumstance in which I found myself, he could and would provide support, reassurance, wisdom, and resources. But, he is dead. Besides, this event is like the one time he was unable to offer me any help: his own sudden death. I am experiencing one of the two things in life that are permanent: death and taxes* (something Dad used to quote). *I don't know why I am thinking this. I guess because I am thinking of Dad, and it is one of the many things he used to say. I get it now. You can change almost anything in this world if you try hard enough, but not death. Sammy is dead, and even Dad couldn't change that if he were here. He would, however, have comforted me first.*

Chapter 6

"Grief turns out to be a place none of us know until we reach it. We anticipate (we know) that someone close to us could die, but we do not look beyond the few days or weeks that immediately follow such an imagined death. We misconstrue the nature of even those few days or weeks. We might expect if the death is sudden to feel shock. We do not expect this shock to be obliterative, dislocating to both body and mind. We might expect that we will be prostrate, inconsolable, crazy with loss. We do not expect to be literally crazy, cool customers who believe their husband is about to return and need his shoes."

-Joan Didion, *The Year of Magical Thinking*

October 24, 2010, Sunday Morning, Cont.

We stood near the end of the driveway quietly talking in shock and disbelief. I mentioned that when the cops were finished I wanted to see where it happened, and I wanted to see Sammy. Valerie's husband, Vince, said he didn't think I should see Sammy in his current condition, because that would remain my last memory of him. My heart throbbed in fitful protest at the thought of seeing Sammy dead and possibly still hanging, but I tried to tune out my feelings to think it through. I still felt the need—the urgency—to see him. I asked Laura her opinion. Though I am an extrovert and she an introvert, we think alike in many ways. She was hesitant to offer an opinion (as is generally the case with Laura), but then she said, "I am afraid if you don't go look him over now, you will regret it. You always like to know all of the information and be given all the facts." I knew she was right as soon as she said it. I had to see him to really believe he was dead, and I needed to see where it happened to understand or make some sense of how it happened.

I hugged and kissed Sarah, Adam, and Lydia and told them to go with the rest of my family members to Aunt Valerie's house, and we would come there in a bit. I told Lucas that Peter also could go with them and he could pick him up later. My family members left and took the kids, including Peter, who rode with my mother. Vince decided to stay and look over things with us.

The detectives came out of the house and informed me I could go inside and look at the scene and view Sammy's body. With trepidation, I took Jake's hand and followed the detectives into the house. It was the first time I had ever been inside my ex-husband's house. Dread filled me as the detectives led us downstairs.

Outside of Sammy's bedroom, I noticed a coat hanger on the floor beside the door. The hook part had been untwisted so it was straight. A detective who was watching informed me, "Peter said Sammy's door was locked, and he got that coat hanger to unlock it." That was weird. Sammy never locked his door.

As I walked into Sammy's bedroom, a detective pointed to one of the open double doors to a closet. "Here...," she trailed off. I stared at the unremarkable door. There was nothing visible to indicate it was the place of Sammy's death. Not a scratch or a scuffmark to show my sweet boy had been hanging there.

"Why are there no scuffmarks on the door?" I asked. "In fact, there are no marks of any kind on the door. Wouldn't he have been kicking and flailing for several minutes before he died?" I tried to recall information I had learned in nursing school. "Yes, he should have had residual oxygen in his lungs that would have kept him alive for a minute or two, during which he would have been kicking and struggling," I said, puzzled.

"Sammy would have left marks and probably a hole in this flimsy door," said Jake, examining the door. "He was strong." The detective just looked at us. She said nothing.

There had to be some sign of what happened. I looked back at the door. There wasn't. I looked for a chair or piece of furniture, anything Sammy could have stood on to hang himself. I didn't see a single thing. "Was there a chair or something that has been removed that he stood on to get up into the noose?" I asked.

Again, the detective just looked at me for a few seconds and then said, "We found no chair or stool or anything." I looked back at the door to try to figure out how in the world Sammy could have gotten up in a noose without something to stand on. I attempted to open the closet door far enough to brace it against the outer wall, but the hinge didn't allow it to open that far. It stopped at about 190 degrees. I held it there to see if it was steady enough to climb on if a person tried to shimmy up the side, but it began swinging back and forth as soon as I put any weight on it. I looked around for something—a bookshelf, a box, a piece of wall trim—he might have used to stand on. There was nothing. I had no idea how he managed to get himself up and into the noose.

"Where is the noose?" I asked.

"It wasn't a noose," the detective said, "it was a nylon strap from a duffle bag, and it was one big loop. The other detectives have removed it."

"What do you mean, 'it wasn't a noose?'" I questioned her.

"It wasn't tied to make a noose. The two ends of a neon duffle bag strap were tied together in a knot, so the strap was just a big loop. It was hooked over the door hinge in the corner, and he was hanging with his back against the door." Again, I tried to imagine how he possibly could have gotten into the strap. Assuming he could have somehow gotten his head up through the loop with nothing to climb on and while the door was moving around, what was his intent? It didn't look like a suicide attempt, not with the strap tied in a big loop like a lasso. Could he have just been messing around with the strap, trying to climb up his door, and… accidentally landed with his head inside the strap?! Maybe he was bored, was messing around with the strap, and decided he would see what it would feel like to hang? Again, how did he get his head into the loop? And he wouldn't have tried that without a chair in place. Sammy had more common sense than all the rest of the kids combined, excluding Sarah. No, that didn't even remotely sound like something Sammy would do. He was brave and fearless, but he wasn't reckless.

"Do we know if it happened last night or early this morning? Was Sammy wearing his clothes from yesterday or something else?" I asked.

"He was wearing the clothes he had on last night," the detective said, "and we aren't sure of the time of death yet, but based on lividity, my guess would be sometime between 11:00 pm and 2:00 am."

Adam and Sammy had told me weeks before (when I asked them why they kept coming home so tired) that all three of the boys had been staying awake downstairs until 3:00, 4:00, or 5:00 am for the past several months on their bi-monthly weekend visits to Lucas's house. So there was a good chance they all still would have been awake between 11:00 pm-2:00 am.

We left Sammy's room and moved into the TV room, where the lead investigator, Detective Higgins, appeared to be waiting to speak to me. "Do you have any ideas about what happened here?" I asked. "I mean, what does it look like to you?" She stared at me for a moment.

"We are exploring several possibilities, one of which is something called The Choking Game. It is a trend among kids, where they use a strap or a necktie or something around their neck long enough to pass out. They get sort of a high from doing it. Sometimes, something goes wrong, like the strap doesn't release, and then it is fatal." That didn't sound like something Sammy would try. Generally, Sammy followed the rules. He hadn't gotten in trouble for anything almost ever in his life. Also, just recently I had talked with the children about how dangerous it was to be choked, even if it didn't last for very long. I explained that it could cause a stroke and then paralysis on one side of the body. The reason I had even discussed the topic with the kids was that for various reasons throughout the previous year, Peter had repeatedly been putting his hands around Sammy's neck!

"Hmm, okay." I said. "Anything else?"

"Well, there is autoerotic asphyxiation, but it doesn't look like that. He was fully clothed, and there weren't any materials that are usually found at those scenes. We will talk to some of Sammy's friends and classmates and teachers to see if we can find out any more information."

"Oh," I said, "to see if maybe he was depressed, and we just didn't know it? Or to see if he and his friends have been playing this choking game or something?"

"Yes," Detective Higgins replied. "Can you give me the names of some of Sammy's good friends?"

"Sure," I told her.

Then, I overheard Lucas talking to a detective, and my ears perked up. He was saying, "Like I said, when I came downstairs this morning to let the dog out, the only unusual thing I noticed was the fan on in the kids' bathroom. I turned it off and let the dog out."

I jumped in, "Why was that unusual?"

Lucas turned to look at me, "Because the boys never turn on the fan." That was true. No matter how bad they might stink up the bathroom, I had never known any of them ever to turn on the fan. Someone had to have intentionally turned it on. All of the kids were aware that at my house I turned on a bathroom fan every night and had since Adam was born. He had been a colicky baby, and I hadn't wanted his crying in the middle of the night to wake the other kids. Through the years, I continued to turn on a fan to create a white noise buffer to help everyone sleep. Lucas didn't do that at his house. My suspicion was that someone turned on the fan to buffer noise. However, Sammy wasn't very calculating. That didn't seem like something he would do.

"We need to speak again with your son," Detective Higgins said to me. I immediately knew she was referring to Peter, but my motherly protectiveness surged a little.

I didn't want her to draw any conclusions by my assumption that she was talking about Peter, so I asked, "Which son?"

"Your oldest," she answered. My stomach turned over. They had noticed his strange behavior too.

"He has gone to my sister Valerie's house with the rest of the family. You are welcome to go there to question him." I said, and then, "You want to question him because you thought his behavior was odd this morning?"

She paused a moment before saying, "We just need to ask him some more questions about some details." She was suspicious of him, and he certainly had acted very strange. He hardly spoke to anyone and pretty much kept off by himself. He seemed to be deep in thought and showed no emotion at all. I had felt an uncomfortable knot in my stomach all morning regarding Peter.

"Just so you are aware," I told her, "Peter has always been a little different; he tends to be socially awkward. However, I did think he was stranger than usual today."

At that, Lucas piped up, "Well, that is not necessarily surprising considering what happened."

Detective Higgins nodded her head, as if in agreement that the circumstances of the morning might explain Peter's peculiar affect. She then said, "I would like to ask you three—Jane, Jake, and Lucas—some questions now. Would that be okay?" We all agreed and followed her into the library.

"How long have you been divorced?" The questions began. "How long have you and Jake been married?" To Lucas, "Have you remarried?" Then, referring to Lucas and me, "Would you say that you two have an amicable relationship?" I looked at Lucas, curious to hear what he would say.

Nodding his head, he glanced briefly at me and said, "Yeah, I would say it's amicable." I was only mildly surprised by his response. "Amicable" was not the correct adjective to describe our relationship. Lucas seemed to despise me since our divorce, and we had been unable to rationally talk through or work through almost anything since the day we separated. I looked back at Detective Higgins, who was watching me.

"I wouldn't classify our relationship as amicable. Basically, we have no relationship. We almost never communicate with each other about anything. There aren't necessarily fights between us anymore, but that's because there's no communication. There hasn't been for several years now." It wasn't how I had hoped or wanted our post-marital relationship to be, but that was how it was.

She made notes, asked some more questions, and eventually asked "Do Peter and Sammy get along? Was there any jealousy between them?"

Again, Lucas spoke up and said, "Yeah, they get along. Just a week ago, Peter took Sammy to see a movie." Lucas's answer was disingenuous. Peter *had* struggled with mild jealousy toward Sammy since they were young.

The detective then turned to me for my answer. "Well, Peter *did* take Sammy to a movie a week ago, for the first time ever, and in the last few weeks they seem to have been getting along better than usual. However, Peter has always struggled with some jealousy toward Sammy for various reasons: Sammy is athletic and good at every sport, Sammy is muscular and limber, Sammy has straight, silky hair—those kinds of things. That being said, I do think Peter loves his brother." I finished. Detective Higgins scribbled in her notebook.

The detective finished her questions, and we walked back into the TV room. Then, we saw Sammy. A black body bag partially unzipped on a gurney, revealed Sammy's head and upper chest. I moved slowly to stand by my poor child's side. He was completely still and pale. He almost looked like he was sleeping. His lips were their usual fullness. His skin had its usual smoothness. I found myself thinking, *If I concentrate hard enough, I can send a message to his spirit, and he will open his eyes and be alive*. I stared at him and thought really hard, *"Sammy, come back! Be alive!"* He remained motionless and without breath. My son, my little "Pookie," who had grown inside my womb and nursed at my breast, who had confused L's and Y's so he'd said, "I Yove you," and called yellow, "lellow," who had grown into a handsome, young teenage boy of 13, was dead. My sweet boy was really gone. The reality was brutal. If there was anything I could have done to bring him back to life, I would have done it. I would have cut off my legs. I would have gouged out my eyes. I would have made a deal with Hades and spent eternity by the river Styx if doing so would have meant Sammy could live.

I looked at Lucas who stood on the opposite side of the gurney, across from Jake and me. If I thought the tragedy of one of our children dying might have allowed him to forget our failed marriage and awful divorce and have a modicum of solidarity through parental mourning, the illusion was quickly dispelled. His eyes did meet mine for about two seconds, and I reached out to him over Sammy's body. We had a brief, small hug (he offered one arm and a partial lean-in), then he dropped his arm and his eyes back to Sammy.

I shifted my gaze back to my lifeless son. I leaned over to look closely at his sweet face. It sickened me to see the vile, purple ligature mark on the front of his neck. My brain shifted into nurse assessment mode. His face looked normal. He didn't have blood coming from his eyes, nose, mouth or ears. He didn't have an engorged tongue. His eye sockets were not bulging. He didn't have any petechiae (broken capillary vessels that look like tiny red dots) on his face. He didn't have a dried trail of saliva coming from his mouth. He didn't have dried tear-stains coming from his eyes. For all of those things, I was grateful. His eyes were closed, and I considered opening them. For clinical reasons, I wanted to see if he had any petechiae in his eyes, but the thought of looking into his lifeless, vacant stare was too disturbing. I would later learn that he had no petechiae in his eyes, per the medical examiner.

My child was dead. Life had become a sickening nightmare from which I would never wake. I looked at my ex-husband again. We shared many sweet memories from Sammy's early childhood. I continued to stare at Lucas, but he wouldn't look at me. I waited for him to raise his eyes, but he didn't. He wouldn't. I was right in front of him. He knew I was attempting to connect, but he was unwilling. I could feel the anger building inside of me. I was disgusted that he could not momentarily rise above his disdain for me for divorcing him, in order to mourn together over our child. Finally, I just said, "How can you still believe in a loving God?" I have no idea why I said that. I didn't believe in God anymore, but Lucas still did. It stung that Lucas would not allow himself to be present with Jake and me to unite in sorrow over Sammy. Was I trying to sting him back by pointing out the ridiculousness of him worshiping a deity who couldn't even protect one of his own shepherd's children? Over the next several days, months, and years, I would learn that it didn't take much cage rattling to draw out the mad-as-hell grieving Momma. Nevertheless, Lucas remained silent in his own private world, and because of my stupid comment, I had probably just provided him fodder for one of his sermons. Wonderful, he would equate me with Job's wife.

I returned my attention to my son. I had seen Sammy. There was nothing more I could do for him, at least not right then or right there. The officers were waiting to take his body to the medical examiner where an autopsy would immediately take place. The detectives wanted to get over to Valerie's house to ask Peter more questions. My living children were waiting for me.

We all went out to the front yard. They wheeled the gurney carrying Sammy's body through the grass. Less than 24 hours before, he had called me at work. Less than 12 hours before, he had been alive watching a movie with his brothers. Somehow, he ended up hanging. Somehow, he ended up dead. Somehow, my beautiful boy was lifeless inside that black body bag. Jake and I wept and held on to each other as Sammy's body was loaded into the van. I had failed my child. I was his mother. It was my job to keep him safe. All of my efforts to protect him from choking hazards, electrical outlets, dangerous objects, strangers, mean dogs, and speeding cars had been for nothing. It was all for nothing. I felt helpless. The invisible veil of parental protection I had always deluded myself into believing was secure around my child, had been ripped apart, and Sammy had been snatched away. I couldn't really protect my children like I always thought I could. The van transporting Sammy's body left to go to the medical examiner's office. There, his body would be cut open, peeled back, probed and tested as they looked for the cause of death. Jake and I walked to our van in silence.

Shortly before I filed for divorce, I started smoking. At first, it was just a few cigarettes each night on the back deck as I sat with Lucas, who smoked a cigar and sipped on a glass of brandy. A few months later, I was a single mom of five going through a divorce, and the stress level in my life skyrocketed, as did my number of daily smokes. I continued the habit throughout the divorce, night school, nursing school, dating Jake, remarriage, my first nursing position, and my dad's death, until August 2010, when I finally quit and started wearing nicotine patches. The day Sammy died I was on Step 3, the last step. I had nearly finished and was close to being nicotine free, but as we left Lucas's house, I turned to Jake and said, "Stop at the first gas station." I slid my hand under my sleeve and ripped off the patch.

I cracked open the window and lit up as Jake drove away from a Break Time. "Okay, did Peter seem really off to you?" I asked.

"Yes," he replied, without hesitation.

I took a deep breath and said, "I have this… horrible feeling that he was involved, somehow."

"So do I," Jake said, darkly.

"I don't think Sammy would have intentionally killed himself," I told him.

Jake turned his eyes from the road to catch mine for a moment, "He wouldn't have."

I called Jo. After we had talked for a few minutes, I said, "It doesn't make sense to me that Sammy would kill himself. I have this terrible feeling in my stomach that there is more to the story."

"Regarding Peter?" she asked.

"Yeah, how did you know?"

"Because I have a bad feeling too," she said. "When I got off the phone with Jake earlier, I just stood there, dazed. Carl (Jo's partner) came over and said, 'What's wrong?' I said, 'I don't think I heard Jake correctly.' 'What did you hear him say?' Carl asked. 'Sammy hung himself,' I told him, 'but that doesn't make any sense. Sammy wouldn't hang himself.' I paused for a moment, and then I said, 'But I know who would hang him: Peter.'"

"You thought that? And said that?" I asked her.

"Yes." She answered. She had known both Sammy and Peter since each of their births. She also knew the history of their interactions with each other, the good as well as the bad. Jo often seemed to have spot on gut instincts about things. I couldn't begin to count how many times over the years she had correctly intuited something with little to no information. I don't know if I felt better or worse that Jo's mind had also turned to Peter in seeking the answer as to what happened—probably both.

"There are so many things about this that don't seem to make sense, like there was no chair or stool or anything for Sammy to have climbed on to get up into the noose," I told her. "Also, the noose wasn't tied like a noose; the ends were just tied together to make a big circle. He was hanging from a neon duffle bag strap that was looped over the door hinge. There's a lot. I will explain it all to you when you get here. Peter was strange all morning. Something was up with him, I'm just not sure what."

"Okay," she said, "I will be at Valerie's in about an hour."

Chapter 7

"The pain and broken heart were blocked off for a little while, leaving me numb with disbelief. Shock is what Dad called it."

-Karen Ann Hopkins, *A Temptation Novel Book 1*

The afternoon of October, 24, 2010

The first hour at Valerie's house was a blur. I talked to people. I sat. I stood. Stepping outside to smoke, Jake accompanied me. "You know," I said, "I don't think this is going to be as bad as it was when Dad died. Maybe going through this once with his death has prepared me." Jake stared at me in silence, concern all over his face. "You think I am wrong? That I am just in shock or something?" I asked.

He looked perplexed and troubled but finally said, "Yeah, Sweetheart. I think you're in shock."

Several months later, when thinking back to that conversation, I would be astounded. I was completely oblivious to the agony I would live with for years. I experienced a brief window of numbness from the awful pain. Since then, I have talked to others who have had the same experience. Perhaps, it is the body's way of trying to protect itself, to give a racked and heated brain a brief respite from a tragic event. Maybe our body shields us when we are overloaded and in danger of losing our mind. I don't know. I do know it was a mercy to have had a small allotment of nearly complete numbness during that long, horrendous day. That numbness would return, off and on, throughout the next several days and months. I learned to accept the numb moments as gifts from my central nervous system.

Back inside the house, I noticed Peter sitting alone at the kitchen bar. His manner still seemed defensive, and his affect, standoffish and cold. I considered whether to tell him or not that the detectives were coming to question him again (as a matter of procedure, when the police were called to the scene at Lucas's that morning, they had already questioned all of the children). If Peter had done something wrong or had somehow played a part in Sammy's death, I didn't want to tell him the detectives were coming. I wanted his response, when questioned, to be unguarded. However, if he was acting so bizarre because he was traumatized by Sammy's horrible and inexplicable death, I wanted to prepare him. I didn't want him to freak out when the detectives arrived. He was my child, my son. I loved him. That Peter had been the most challenging of my children when they were all young, or that he had been extremely difficult and hateful since Lucas and I separated in 2004, in no way diminished my love for him. He would always be my child, I would always love him, and I would always want the best for him. My motherly instinct to protect my oldest son, who had to be traumatized, was just as strong as my instinct to determine and understand what had happened to Sammy. What I knew was that Sammy was dead. Involvement of Peter in Sammy's death was undetermined. Peter's level of disconcertment by the detectives coming there to question him again was something I could control by merely telling him of their impending arrival. Although his behavior was strange, and I had a growing sense of dread in my gut that he was somehow a part of whatever happened, my motherly instinct to protect overcame any other concerns; and I thought, surely, my gut—which kept telling me Peter was guilty of something—was off.

"Peter," I said to him, gently and calmly, "it's no big deal, but the detectives have a few more questions to ask you. They are coming here in a little while." His face paled slightly, and he appeared a little alarmed.

"Why?" he asked. "I already told them everything."

"I think they just want to go over things again. They will probably ask Adam and Sarah some questions also," I said to ease his anxiety (although I didn't know whether the other children would be questioned again or not).

I would come to regret informing Peter. If he was innocent of any wrongdoing and had played no part in Sammy's death, he couldn't have said anything wrong. If he were guilty of something, perhaps he would have been startled by the detectives coming to question him again and may have inadvertently been forthcoming. Had my dad been alive, I would have asked his opinion before warning Peter. As he had many times, Dad probably would have told me to keep my mouth shut.

Jo arrived, and we went outside. Her face was soothing to me. We had known each other since before Sammy was born, before any of my children were born, before I had even married Lucas in 1992. We embraced and wept. I lit up a smoke and started at the beginning. She occasionally took my cigarette for a drag as I told her the details of the day, specifically, Peter's behavior and the oddities of Sammy's death. Jo was not a smoker, but it was a day for smoking. When I had shared everything I knew, she nodded, we hugged again, and we walked back to the house. We knew we would be parsing through the details of Sammy's death for days, months, years, and possibly decades. Really, for the rest of our lives.

Once we were back inside, Lydia came marching over to me and firmly stated that she wanted to know exactly what had happened to Sammy. I hadn't told her anything except that he had died. "Mom, I want to know!" she said firmly. I had been considering if I should tell her or not. If I could have kept the details of his death from her, I would have. I didn't want to chip away at her remaining childhood innocence with the gruesome truth. I thought it would be impossible to keep it from her though, and if she were to find out, I wanted it to be from me. I took her into my sister's bedroom for privacy.

"Okay, Sweetheart, this is bad. Prepare yourself. Peter and Sarah found Sammy hanging from his closet door this morning."

Tears started streaming down her cheeks and after a few moments she said, "Someone must have broken into the house overnight and done that to him. Lucas forgets to lock the basement door all the time."

"Oh, Sweetie," I held her. "I don't think so."

"Well, did the police check for footprints outside the door or fingerprints on the doorknob?" she asked.

"I think they checked for footprints outside Sammy's window, Lydia. Also, they looked to see if dust on the window seal had been disturbed, but they didn't find anything suspicious."

"But Sammy wouldn't do that to himself," she wailed. "I know he wouldn't!"

"I don't think he did it on purpose, Lydia," I reassured her. She kept throwing out possible scenarios, proclaiming Sammy would never take his own life, and that he wouldn't have done it accidentally because he never hurt himself. That persistence exemplified Lydia, and even she, at 11-years-old, knew her brother well enough to recognize suicide was in direct conflict with Sammy's fun-loving, silly confidence. After a while, I told her I loved her and that hopefully the police would get to the bottom of it.

I thought about Lydia's insistence that Sammy wouldn't have accidentally hung himself because he never got hurt. She was right. Sammy was a beast, a fact we had all known since he was toddler when Lucas and I had dubbed him "Sammy The Body". He was like one of those action movie people with the amazing moves who always land on their feet and leave you scratching your head wondering how they did something. His physicality was his greatest gift. I had always thought if we could find a sport that didn't aggravate his allergies and exercise induced asthma, he could become a professional athlete.

After pondering Lydia's astute observation, I found myself sitting on the couch with Jake, talking softly with an old friend. It was then that I noticed my mother, Vince, and Lucas had disappeared. "Has anyone seen my mom?" I asked those around me. No one seemed to know where she had gone. The coincidence of those three missing at the same time seemed odd. I discreetly asked Jake to go see if something was going on.

He came back shortly and whispered in my ear, "Your mother is upstairs in the library talking with Vince and Lucas." *What the hell?* I thought. Apparently, my dad—true-to-form—had purchased life insurance policies on each of his grandchildren when they were born. Mother was discussing Sammy's policy with my ex-husband and my brother-in-law but, for some reason, hadn't included Jake or me; I did *not* understand her thinking. If she wanted to discuss something important related to Sammy's death, she should have talked about it first with us. If she felt that telling me about the policy would have been too distressful for me, or if she thought that insurance was something the men should handle, she should have at least pulled Jake into the conversation. I felt uneasy. Lucas and I had been unable to have any kind of positive relationship since our marital separation (a fact of which my mother was well aware), and, frankly, I didn't trust him. Among a host of ugly things, he had said and done during our divorce, he had revealed some personal and private information I had shared with him over the years (insecurities I'd had early in our marriage and a few unpleasant events from my childhood) in an attempt to secure full custody of our children by proclaiming I must have a personality disorder. His hateful, scorched earth mentality had been surprising and hurtful. If that wasn't enough to dissuade Mother from fraternizing with him, I would have thought she would feel disinclined since at no time following our divorce had Lucas even shown Dad the courtesy of a wave or a handshake. However, Dad was gone, and my mother's faith was very important to her. Not only was Lucas a Christian, he was a minister. In comparison, I was the first member in our family to get a divorce, I left a minister, and I left the faith and became an atheist, which was shameful to my mother. I wasn't loud and proud about my change in beliefs, but Mother knew. To say the least, it didn't sit well with her. Sixteen months before, for example, when Jake had been diagnosed with a serious, life-threatening cardiac issue that had a 75 percent mortality rate within five years of diagnosis, Mother had informed me she would not pray for God to heal Jake. She would pray that God would use the situation—Jake's illness, his failing heart, and potentially his death—to bring me back to the Christian faith. Following that unpleasant conversation, things hadn't smoothed out much with my mother (not that we were ever very close, as I have said, but things between us had definitely been worse since my divorce, Dad's death, and then Mother's heartless comment about not praying for healing for Jake.) Needless to say, I didn't feel comfortable with the meeting taking place in the library.

    I wished I hadn't extended an invitation to Lucas to come over. Every time I tried to do right by him, I felt he always took advantage. My attempts at charitable understanding and accommodation were not reciprocated and usually resulted in me feeling vulnerable and disrespected as the children's mother and his co-parent (although, candidly, Lucas hadn't invited himself into the discussion in the library.)

    "Good grief," I said to Jake, and we went upstairs.

    When we entered the library, the conversation seemed to falter. "What are we discussing?" I asked, not trying to hide the mistrust and irritation in my voice. My mother looked at me and briefly explained the insurance policy, and then they all left the room. I was mystified at Mother's decision to disclose the insurance policy at that time and in that manner with Vince and Lucas. Since my father's death, Mother had taken took over all of Dad's business. Dad had purchased, developed, sold, and rented a great deal of land and property over a 50-year span in our small city and acquired a substantial amount of wealth, all of which Mother was managing. Since she assumed control, Mother had been working closely and on a daily basis with Vince. She relied heavily on him, so I could understand that, but why include Lucas?

    Over the next several days, Mother would state she felt it was time to mend fences with my ex. I'm not sure how she thought her being friendly to and inclusive of Lucas would result in Lucas and I getting along better. I had no delusions regarding my future relationship with my ex-husband. Even if I hadn't had the history of our exchanges to inform me, it became clear when he couldn't openly mourn with me as we stood directly over our dead son. Mother opening up the family and the channels of communication with Lucas in her attempt to help heal the breach would do nothing but allow Lucas unnecessary information and access to our lives and cause me to feel exposed and the need to be more attentive. In addition, I knew that while he would be very pleasant and cordial to my family members, Lucas would never extend that courtesy to me (or Jake) as well as that the affectation of respect and cooperation with my family would be just that: a tool to advance his own agenda, whatever that might be.

The detectives arrived and took Peter to a private room for questioning. As soon as they finished, Lucas left with Peter. The detectives did talk again briefly with Sarah and Adam. When they finished, I wrote down the female detective's phone number. "Is it okay for me to call you later to ask some questions?" I asked.

"Certainly," she answered, and they left.

Our friends who came to support us slowly headed home, and soon after, so did our extended family members. Jake and I were exhausted, and we gathered Sarah, Adam, and Lydia, and headed home where we would all, most likely, have a sleepless night.

As soon as we left Valerie's house, I called Detective Higgins. "Did you find out anything new when you talked with Peter?" I asked.

"No," she told me. "He pretty much said everything just like he did this morning."

"Oh. Okay. Also, can you tell me about the 911 call?"

"Sure," she said. She concisely relayed the details of the 911 call, but it provided no new information, except to show Peter's responses during the phone call were just as strange as they had been that morning. I felt deflated. I'm not sure what I had hoped to learn. I guess I thought something would stand out, point to, or provide a little understanding about what happened to Sammy.

Chapter 8

"You'll get over it…" It's the clichés that cause the trouble. To lose someone you love is to alter your life forever. You don't get over it because 'it' is the person you loved. The pain stops, there are new people, but the gap never closes. How could it? The particularness of someone who mattered enough to grieve over is not made anodyne by death. This hole in my heart is in the shape of you and no-one else can fit it. Why would I want them to?"

-Jeanette Winterson *Written on the Body*

Walking through the front door of our house, I saw a pair of Sammy's shoes on the floor and one of his hoodies hanging on the coat rack. I stopped looking at anything and walked straight through the house to the back deck. Jo quickly followed. After making a few cocktails for Jo and me and grabbing a beer for himself, Jake joined us on the deck. We all sat quietly with our drinks. My brain was sluggish, but I thought back to Dad's funeral (which my siblings and I had managed) to try and remember what I needed to do next. "We have to figure out who can officiate the funeral," I said.

For the first year following the divorce, I took the kids to different churches as I searched for a new fit (obviously, I couldn't continue to attend the church that Lucas pastored). I also started asking a lot of questions and reading a much broader scope of material, including Steven Pinker, Michio Kaku, and Richard Dawkins, which led to many adjustments in my thinking and my beliefs. To the point, I had no current minister. I needed to find someone to preside over the funeral, and it had to be someone that Lucas would accept. I thought the one person on whom we could agree and feel comfortable with was Lucas's brother Bruce. He was a college campus minister; I had always liked him well enough, and I felt he had a good heart. I also liked his wife and children. They were the uncle, aunt, and cousins to my children with whom we had spent a good amount of time. Most importantly, Bruce had known Sammy his entire life. Running the idea by Jake and Jo, they agreed that Bruce would be a good choice.

"Okay," I continued, "I guess I need to call the funeral home and set up an appointment." Jake and Jo stared at me. It felt like we were actors in one of Hitchcock's episodes of *The Twilight Zone* or something. It didn't feel real. Jo googled the telephone number for the mortuary, and I called. "Hi. My name is Jane Bradshaw. I am calling because my 13-year-old son died last night, and I need to plan a funeral." The words seemed foul and ridiculous coming out of my mouth. They felt wrong to say, almost as if they were a lie or I was playing a part in some horror film. No effing way was Sammy dead: except he was. The gentleman was very polite and told me to come in the following morning at 10:00 am.

After I hung up, Jo said, "You might want to call or email the kids' principals to give them a heads up about what happened. There will probably be talk at school and a lot of upset kids."

"You're right," I said. As she had mentioned, there would be a lot of upset kids, which would lead to a lot of talk. There would be rumors. Sammy's best friend, Kyle, knew Sammy had been found hanging. Another friend of Sammy's, who lived next door to Lucas, also knew. The cops had been speaking with the neighbor friend when we left Lucas's house. I didn't think Sammy committed suicide, and I didn't want all of Sammy's friends to think that unless the police discovered evidence that proved it really *was* suicide. It would get around, though, that Sammy had been found hanging and thus assumed a suicide. Jo looked up the email addresses on my laptop, and I sent messages to the principals and a few of the counselors.

Shortly afterward, my phone rang. It was the principal of Sammy and Adam's middle school. Once again, I had to speak repulsive, horror-film words that didn't feel real. We talked for a bit, and she was very kind and sympathetic. I explained we were unsure exactly what had happened to Sammy but that he was found hanging. I told her the detectives didn't think it was suicide and had begun an investigation. Because I knew a few of Sammy's friends were aware he had been hanging and that people usually talk, I should have advised the principal differently than I did. I should have said the counselors could go ahead and tell the students Sammy was found hanging, but the police didn't think it was suicide and were investigating. However, I couldn't bear for so many people to know he was hanging, and I was hopeful—for Sammy's sake—it wouldn't get around. I told the principal it would be best for the counselors simply to say Sammy had suffered a terrible accident. Over the next few weeks, much to my dismay, rumors that he committed suicide by hanging would spread like wildfire.

Throughout my life, I have always tried to prepare myself for bad things by considering worst-case scenarios. I hate being caught off guard. I used to fret when the kids went swimming that one of them would drown. If they rode in a car with someone else, I would be concerned they would be in an accident. Not one time had it ever crossed my mind to worry about any of my children being hanged to death. Nothing in my life had ever shocked me more.

Sarah came out onto the deck. She looked pitiful, distraught and troubled. I tried to pull her on my lap, but she was drawn too far inside herself for that. She looked terribly sad, of course, but she also seemed antsy and bothered. The events of the day had been so utterly devastating and confounding, and I realized we hadn't had the opportunity to really talk. Sometime during that chaotic day, she told me Peter had found Sammy, then she had seen Sammy and called 911, but that was all. She looked like she needed to talk. 'Sweet Pea," I said, "Do you want to tell me what happened now, starting from last night?"

"Okay," she started, sounding uncertain and fearful. "Lucas went to the football game. He left around 5:00 pm because he was going to tailgate before the game. None of us wanted to go, so we all stayed home. Lydia spent the night with Mary. I had just gone to bed when I heard Lucas get home around 11:00 pm. I got up, went into the kitchen, and saw Peter and Adam come up from downstairs. Lucas told us that in the morning, he would leave for church at the usual time, but we could sleep in, skip Sunday school, and Peter could drive us to church for regular service. Then, he said it was time for bed, and he told Adam he could sleep with him. I went back to bed."

"Wait. So Adam slept upstairs with Lucas and not downstairs in his own room?" I asked.

"Yes."

Peter and Sammy were alone downstairs, I thought.

"And last night, did Sammy come upstairs when Peter and Adam did?" I asked.

"No. Only Peter and Adam came up. I didn't see Sammy upstairs last night."

"When was the last time you remember seeing him?" I asked. Sarah thought for a few seconds.

"Earlier in the night, I went downstairs to get a DVD. Sammy, Peter, and Adam were watching a movie on the couch: something called, *Legion*. I leaned over Sammy to grab a DVD, and he said, 'What movie are you getting?' I said, '*Mulan 2*'. He laughed a little bit, and I said, 'I can't help it. I love Disney movies," and he smiled at me." She paused.

"And that was the last time you saw him?" I asked.

She thought for a minute, "Yeah. I didn't see him upstairs last night."

"Okay, go on." I said. "You went back to bed and then what?"

"This morning, I got up and was putting on my make-up in the living room. Peter came into the living room and said, 'Come downstairs; I need to show you something.' I went downstairs with him, and he stood outside Sammy's room. I was like, 'What?' And he said 'In here.' Then, he walked into Sammy's room. He leaned over and picked up some fake hatchet off the floor, and started tossing up and catching it. I followed him into Sammy's room, but I still didn't see anything. So, I said, 'Well, what?' And he lifted his leg and used his foot to push the closet door farther open."

"Sammy was there," she said flatly.

"You mean, Sammy was hanging there?" I asked.

"Yes," she answered. A blank, yet strained, dead-eyed expression crossed her face, and then she said, "My first thought after I glanced at Sammy and looked back at Peter was, 'Oh my god. He's killed Sammy and now he's going to kill me.' But then I thought, 'That's ridiculous.'"

Upon hearing Sarah verbalize her horrible suspicion, everything in the world seemed to screech to a halt. I couldn't think for a moment. I couldn't move. I couldn't breathe. The fact that Sarah thought and feared that Peter had killed Sammy was devastating to me. I knew my daughter well. Sarah was level-headed, responsible, and very fair. She was not disposed to dramatics. That her first instinct was Peter might have killed Sammy was damning.

"You actually thought that, Sarah?" I asked, "I mean, you thought that right then, when you first saw Sammy, and not just later when you thought over it all again?"

"Yes," she said.

"Did you tell this to the detectives?"

"No," she said.

"Why not?" I asked.

"I don't know. I felt bad for thinking it, and I thought it was stupid of me."

"Okay," I said. "Go on."

Her little face was so troubled. "Sammy looked normal, like he just had his eyes closed and was sleeping or faking sleep. And Peter seemed so casual, not like anything was wrong. And he was tossing around that hatchet thing. So, I thought 'they *have* to be playing a joke on me'. I mean, if it was *real*, Peter would be acting different."

"I guess I was staring at Peter because he goes, 'What? I found him like this?' So, I said, 'Very funny', and went back upstairs. I started doing my makeup again, but I had a bad feeling in my stomach. I heard Peter go out into the garage, and I thought I would run and check on Sammy and make sure he was okay before Peter came back in."

"I was hurrying downstairs, but Peter came right back in from the garage and started following me down. He said, 'I poked him with a stick, and he didn't move.' I started running to Sammy's room. I grabbed his arms, and they were cold. He was stiff, and I noticed that his feet were blue. Then, I started screaming and crying and shaking him. I yelled at Peter to call 911, but he said, 'Isn't it a little late for that?' I was like, '*No*, Peter that's what you're supposed to do!' I pulled out my cell phone to call 911, but Peter grabbed it from me. He was like, 'We need to call Dad.' We kept arguing about it. Then, he tried calling Lucas, but there was no answer. I was crying. And we kept arguing because I was saying we had to call 911, and he was saying we needed to go get Lucas. I tried to grab my phone back from him, but he was holding it out and away from me so I couldn't get it. Then, we went back upstairs to the kitchen, and we were still fighting."

Sarah continued, "Adam came into the kitchen then and started to go downstairs. I stopped him and said, 'No, Adam, you can't go down there. Go sit on the couch.' Then, I kind of yelled at Peter and said, 'Well, are you going to tell him what happened?!' Peter looked over at Adam and said, 'Sammy's dead.' Then, he told me I needed to take Adam and get in the car, and we would go to church and get Lucas. And then I got the phone back and called 911, but when they answered, I couldn't say anything. They were saying, '911, what is your emergency?' but I was crying too hard to talk. So, I handed the phone to Peter, and he talked to them." She stopped and took a deep breath. She looked totally miserable and depleted, but slightly relieved that she had told us what she had seen and thought.

"Then what happened?" I asked. She seemed tapped out though and about to shut down.

"Umm, while Peter talked to them, I got Lucas's home phone and called you. Then, the emergency people got there and took over," she finished. I had questions, but it was obvious she had shared what she knew and didn't want to talk about it anymore for a while.

My mind was reeling from everything she had said. The horrible feeling I had regarding Peter, started to feel like a heavy stone in my gut. "Okay, Detective Higgins said during the 911 call, when they asked what the emergency was, Peter said his brother was hanging. They asked if there were any adults home, and he said there weren't. They told Peter to cut the strap that was holding Sammy up. He got a knife and cut the strap. Then, they told Peter to begin mouth-to-mouth resuscitation. Peter told the operator there was 'gross, brown stuff' in Sammy's mouth, and they told him to scoop it out with his finger and begin resuscitation efforts. Then, the EMTs arrived."

When I stopped speaking, I looked at Sarah. Again, I felt the urgency to ask her more questions, but her face was strained. She was visibly anxious, and I needed to let her be. She had seen her brother hanging. It had happened when there was no parent at home, and she had shouldered some unbearable responsibility. Making it worse, she suspected her older brother was somehow responsible for what happened, and she was scared. I ached with pain and sorrow for my poor daughter. "Thank you for being so helpful, Honey," I said to her, searching my brain to find words to soothe her. "Thank you for calling 911. You were right. That's what you were supposed to do. I'm sorry you had to see Sammy like that and go through all that. I love you." I hugged and kissed her, and she slipped back into the house, ready for some solitude.

The more Sarah had talked, the more uneasy I had felt. Why had Peter seemed so casual when he was telling Sarah to go with him to see Sammy? Since he had already discovered him, shouldn't he have been freaking out or at least have displayed a sense of urgency? Why in the world would he be casually tossing around a toy hatchet with Sammy hanging three feet away? Peter must not have realized Sammy was dead yet. After that, when Sarah went up to finish her makeup, Peter said he poked Sammy with the stick, and that is when he must have realized Sammy was dead. Immediately following that, Sarah realized Sammy was probably dead, freaked out, then said they had to call 911. But, Peter said, "Isn't it a little late for that?" So, he obviously knew Sammy was dead then? Yet, he never had a freak out moment. He never cried, seemed surprised or shocked, or screamed: no visible reaction. How could a person see his or her little brother dead and hanging, yet show no response or emotion? Also, regardless of whether Sammy was dead or still alive, wouldn't Peter have known the police had to be called? To be fair, although Peter was smart, he didn't necessarily have much common sense. It was possible he didn't know the police had to be called. However, it wasn't as if he had simply been ignorant or ambivalent about calling the cops. He had grabbed Sarah's phone from her, which made it seem like he was *against* calling the police. Why would he be against calling the cops? What accounted for his aloof behavior during the entire morning? Why had he seemed so removed from it all? Nearly everything he had said seemed odd. For example, when he casually said, "Come here, I need to show you something," Or after Sarah first saw Sammy, when she looked back at Peter and he said, "What? I found him like this." The only thing that made sense of *all* of Peter's strange behavior was if he already knew Sammy was dead, and he was trying to look casual and not guilty.

    After Sarah told us what happened and went back inside, I turned to stare at Jake and Jo. We were all thinking the same thing—Sarah, our responsible, mature, intelligent girl had serious questions about Peter's involvement in Sammy's death. After hearing her more detailed account of the morning, with all of Peter's comments and responses, so did we. Peter's behavior seemed beyond strange. He *had* to have something wrong with him, perhaps Asperger's or an empathy disorder, *or* he was guilty of something; maybe both. Nothing else seemed to make sense.

I called Detective Higgins and told her about a few details I had learned from Sarah. Then, I shared with her what Sarah told us was her first thought when she saw Sammy.

Detective Higgins said, "Well, we really don't put much weight into things she might say now, impressions and what not. We tend to go with what is said by a witness right away. If she is picking up any vibes from others or has overheard conversations, she can be trying to please someone." I could see the reasoning behind her logic, but I knew Sarah. She wouldn't fabricate anything like the detective described; she was too honest and too fair-minded. I didn't even think sub-consciously Sarah could say something just to please, certainly not about something so important. It wasn't in her nature. Sarah was very conscientious and very good. In fact, it was her goodness that had prevented her from sharing her thought to the detectives in the first place. She felt bad for even having that terrible thought. The fact that she told me about it indicated that after considering it all day, she still had that fear or else she wouldn't have told me. She was much too discerning, just, and cautious. Sarah might be a little naïve, but she was no conspiracy theorist. She generally had a hard time believing bad things about people, tending to think the best, not the worst.

I said, "Oh, I see. Well, she told me that was her first thought when she first saw Sammy. I asked her if she had shared this with you, and when she said she hadn't, I asked her why not. She said she felt bad for thinking it and figured it was just some ridiculous fleeting thought."

"Okay," said Detective Higgins, "thanks for telling me."

The detective told me they were going to the Sprint store at 8:00 the following morning to unlock Sammy's cell phone (none of us could remember his password). They wanted to look through his voicemails and texts. If we would like, we could join them. If there was anything on Sammy's phone that could give us any clue as to what happened, I wanted to know right away. I would definitely be there.

I called Lucas and told him about the funeral home appointment time. "Also, I am meeting the detectives at the Sprint store tomorrow morning at 8:00 if you would like to come. The last thing is I am fine with Bruce officiating the funeral if you and he would be comfortable with that." To the third point, he said he would consider it, talk with Bruce, and let me know. The call was finished.

"We ought to go tuck in Adam and Lydia," I said to Jake, and we went inside to find them. Their faces looked tired, but also sad, uncertain, and afraid. My heart ached for them. Their lives had changed and would continue to change in innumerable ways, but there was nothing I could do about it. Sammy's life had changed too. There was nothing I could do about that either. With that thought, a bolt of pain shot through my heart, and my knees felt weak. I said to Jake, "Honey, I think they will do better to sleep in our room tonight and possibly for several nights or weeks." Looking back at them, I saw relief on their faces. "Okay. Brush your teeth, bring your pillows down to our bedroom, and Dad and I will tuck you in." In ten minutes, we all four were lying in our king sized bed. Jake rubbed Adam's back, while I scratched Lydia's.

We lay with them for about 30 minutes to help them relax, but they were not yet asleep. We knew that might take a while, in spite of the fact that I had given them both 50mg of Benadryl.

Upstairs on the couch, Jo was quietly talking to Sarah. We sat with them. We all were quiet. We all felt numb. "I can't believe he is dead," I mumbled. "I just can't understand what happened. It doesn't make sense to me that Sammy committed suicide. He was happy. He wasn't upset about anything that I knew of. Was he depressed, and I missed it?"

"Well, if he was, we all missed it," said Jo, "and I don't think that's the case."

"When I was taking him to school on Monday or Tuesday," said Jake, "he was telling me again about how he wanted my black truck when he turned 16!"

"Sammy was happy," Sarah stated firmly.

"He wouldn't do this to himself," added Jo. "You know I would tell you if I thought that was what happened, Jane. I know you always want the truth. Suicide doesn't make sense."

"Sammy wasn't depressed," stated Jake. "He was a happy boy. No way did he do this to himself on purpose."

"I agree with Dad," said Sarah.

"So, what was up with Peter?" I asked. "His behavior when he found Sammy was bizarre, as if he already knew Sammy was dead so he wasn't shocked. Could he have played a part? I mean, if maybe they were trying 'the choking game' the police mentioned, only it went wrong? And then, Peter freaked out and hung him to cover it up?"

The horror of thinking and verbalizing that my first-born son might have somehow killed my second son was sickening, overwhelming, horrifying. A wave of nausea hit me hard, and I nearly vomited. Sammy was dead. My sweet, sunny boy was gone. I had no idea why, except for a dreadful feeling that Peter was involved. My heart was screaming in open-mouthed horror. The tears started again, and I began to sob loudly, without control. Weeping, Jake put his arms around me. Overcome with sorrow, Sarah lay her head on my shoulder and cried, and Jo stretched her arms around us, unable to restrain her own tears any longer. Bawling, wailing, sobbing, and moaning erupted from me—from us all. The ravaging grief consumed us. My own deep lamentation over the sudden, violent, unexpected death of Sammy was raw and terrible. I cried and cried and raged against the injustice. The knowledge that I would never see him again, that there was no way I could get him back, was agonizing.

Eventually, the tears slowed and stopped. There was nothing left to say. We headed to bed. Jo slept with Sarah. Jake and I moved quietly into our bedroom and lay down together—face to face— next to Lydia and Adam. For some reason, that night and for several months after, I couldn't sustain eye contact with him. Jake and I were close. He was my best friend. He knew every good and bad detail about me and my life. I had always been able to express my deepest thoughts, feelings, and secrets easily with him. We understood each other. We had a nightly practice of lying quietly in bed facing each other. If one of us felt a little anxious, overwhelmed, upset, or disturbed, the other could sense it and feel it and we talked it out. When all was well, we enjoyed our private bubble of love, peace, and tranquility, and words were unnecessary. Staring intently into his eyes that night was impossible. I could sense an enormous black hole that was either my grief, or his grief, or our grief together, and it was too wide and deep to face directly. I felt I would be swallowed into it and would never climb back out. It was too much. I could not be fully present with all of that emotion. I wasn't ready or able to handle that much truth and pain. Avoiding eye contact, I scooted closer to him, and we held each other. I didn't explain my feelings to him. I was too exhausted. The feelings weren't even really something that could be talked out, but he sensed it. He knew. He didn't need an explanation.

My mind refused to rest. I grew anxious. There was no way I would be able to sleep for hours at least, if I would be able to sleep at all. I was plagued with thoughts that would become a nightly mantra. *What was Sammy feeling when he died? Was he scared? Was he mad? Was he sad? Was he confused? Did he feel pain? Was he hanging there, all alone in his room, all night long?* And Sarah. She had to live with that image—of Sammy hanging—for the rest of her life. Lying there with one grim thought after another only increased my anxiety and pain. I got up and went to the computer.

I had to plan a visitation and a funeral to honor my child.

Chapter 9

> "Pain can kill, all on its own: the body goes into shock and shuts down."
>
> -Teri Terry, *Slated, #1*

Monday, October 25

A gut-wrenching wail shot up my throat and had pushed itself forcefully out of my mouth before I even opened my eyes the following morning. I could hardly catch my breath. I rolled toward Jake who was rolling toward me, and we grabbed on to each other. Oh my god, the agony... Sammy was dead. The strange cries that erupted from me sounded like a wounded animal. Only when I felt small hands rubbing my back and my feet did I remember Adam and Lydia had slept with us. My motherly instinct to protect my little ones enabled me to partially subdue my squalling. While I didn't feel I needed to hide all of my grief from my children (it would have been odd and wrong if they didn't see me crying about the death of their brother) I wanted to protect them from the worst of it. That would be hard on them, and everything was going to be hard enough. I wiped my face and hugged them. I told them they might see me crying a lot for a while because I was sad about Sammy, but everything would eventually be okay. I didn't know what else to say to reassure them. I told them to go see if Jo was awake and to get themselves some cereal. After they left, I returned to my safety nook under Jake's arm and resumed crying. I had to make a concerted effort to control and stifle the flow of the crying—not just let it all out—because I didn't want it to spew forcefully from me in screaming and wailing, further distressing the children. Controlling my crying was like opening a shaken two-liter bottle of soda. You have to untwist the cap slowly, incrementally, allowing tiny amounts of gas to escape or else it will just explode and soda will spray everywhere. The sorrow inside of me was just waiting to burst and shoot out of me any time I took off the cap. It wasn't easy trying to stifle the raging geyser of pain, but I did it. That suppression became a regular practice throughout the next several years.

Eventually, we got up and silently dressed. Jo took Adam and Lydia to Kohl's to help them pick out clothes to wear for the visitation and funeral. Sarah was still sleeping. Jake and I drove to the Sprint store. When we walked in, the detectives were already at the counter. Lucas was standing over to the side of the store with Bruce. Detective Higgins reached out, took Sammy's phone back from a store employee, and slipped it into her pocket.

I made my way over and asked the detective a question I had been considering; should the detectives search the kids' computers at both our house and Lucas's for possible clues? Out of the corner of my eye, I noticed Lucas striding quickly over to join us. As I finished speaking, I looked at Lucas's face and read suspicion in his gaze. *What does he think I am saying? What could I say to the detectives that would cause him to look so irritated?* I repeated what I had said so he didn't feel excluded.

"I was asking Detective Higgins if she thought looking through the kids' computers at our houses might give us any ideas about what happened. I mean, if Sammy was looking up anything on the internet about the choking game or something." Lucas appeared displeased with the idea.

"I don't really see how anything on a computer could explain why Sammy did this," he said. *Interesting choice of words, "why Sammy did this,"* I thought. Had he already concluded that Sammy simply committed suicide? Didn't he want as much information as possible to understand why Sammy was dead, even if it was suicide? Why resist having more information?

"Another thing I wanted to clarify," I said, "Sarah says that when you returned home from the game and yelled down that it was time for bed, Peter and Adam came upstairs but Sammy didn't. Adam says the same thing." Lucas's jaw clenched. I wasn't trying to insinuate that he was lying. I figured he was just mistaken about this detail, and I wanted us all to be clear about every detail possible so we could unearth the truth about what happened.

"No, that's not right," he said. "All three boys came upstairs. I saw Sammy." His response was annoying. Adam wasn't usually observant of concrete details and might be mistaken, but not Sarah. She was much better with details than any of us. Sarah was almost never wrong about facts, and Lucas was just as aware of that as I was. Perhaps Sammy came upstairs after Sarah went back to her bed and Adam had gone to Lucas's bed. I had asked Sarah if that was a possibility though, and she hadn't thought so. She was pretty sure everyone had dispersed from the kitchen at the same time. Why was Lucas being defensive? Was he not even going to *consider* if Peter played a part? Didn't he think Peter's behavior had been odd? Maybe, he really hadn't noticed. Lucas was absent-minded, often lost in thought, and could have missed a change in Peter's behavior. Perhaps, he truly had no doubts about Peter. If that was the case, complete transparency would only clear things up, so why the opposition to searching through the kids' computers? The only other scenario I could imagine where Lucas had seen Sammy after returning from the football game, but Sarah hadn't seen Sammy upstairs, was if Lucas had gone *downstairs* and had seen him there. If that was the case, though, he would have said it. Unless Lucas was hiding something...? Was Lucas covering for Peter? Or for himself? Could Sammy already have been dead when Lucas got home from the game? Why did Lucas seem so irritated when I suggested that perhaps Sammy hadn't come upstairs? Possibly, because he is a proud man who rarely admits mistakes. Or was he trying to cover up something and part of his working narrative required him to have seen Sammy upstairs after the game. Knowing Lucas's inattention to detail, it was of note to me that while he said he didn't find Peter's behavior outside of normal, he not only *noticed* the bathroom fan on downstairs, he thought to mention it to the detectives.

"Well, they unlocked the phone for us, so we are set," said Detective Higgins, and we all walked out of the store.

Once outside, I tentatively asked the detective "Could I look at Sammy's texts with you?" I wondered if there would be some texts between Sammy and a friend about the choking game or something to help explain the why of Sammy's death and give me a little peace of mind. I didn't think we would find anything, but I hoped. A small part of me even wondered if we would find a distress message to someone from Sammy. Lucas, who had started walking toward his car, heard my request, turned, and headed back our way. Once again, he appeared suspicious and displeased.

"Of course you can," she answered, pulling out Sammy's phone and handing it to me. Apprehensively, I took it and started searching. The most recent message was from Sammy to his cousin Garrison, but it was from Saturday morning. Lucas had taken all of the kids downtown for the homecoming parade that morning, and Sammy had been trying to connect with his cousin who was also at the parade. There were no more recent texts. I checked the call log to see if he had called anyone or received any calls. The last two calls were made Saturday: one from Sammy to me, and the other from Sammy to Jake. When I saw those, my heart lurched painfully. The call to me was to ask about his sweatshirt size. After talking to me, he had called Jake. That was the last time either of us ever heard his voice. I handed the phone back to the detective. "We will go through his texts and voice mails and see if we find anything," she assured me.

Jake and I debriefed as we drove back home to pick up Sarah. The previous night, she had told us she wanted to go with us to make Sammy's funeral arrangements. Even though it would be emotionally taxing, I felt including Sarah in the funeral plans was the right decision. Her participation in planning the arrangements would allow her to feel some small sense of control. As a J (Myers-Briggs), I knew Sarah felt better when decisions were made and not still undecided and up in the air. She also felt less anxious when she knew what to expect. Sarah had no control over the fact that her brother was gone. Allowing her to participate in the funeral plans would help her feel a little less out of control, and knowing the specifics of the visitation and funeral so she would know what to expect would help her to feel a little less anxious attending them.

We picked Sarah up from the house and made our way to the funeral home. The funeral director seated us in the planning room next to Lucas and Bruce and then left to go gather his paperwork. Lucas turned to me. He appeared to be calculating something in his head, and then he said, "Say, did you observe anything strange about Peter's behavior, yesterday?" His question puzzled me. The previous day, Lucas had been standing quite near when I told the detective I thought Peter's behavior throughout the morning stranger than usual. He had even replied and said he attributed it to the extreme circumstance, so he already knew what I thought. In addition, since our divorce, my impression was that Lucas had stopped trusting my motherly judgment. My opinion on any subject held no value for him, so his question was perplexing; he had to have a specific reason for asking it, and it wasn't because he wanted to know what I thought. I glanced briefly at Lucas's brother and thought it must somehow be for Bruce's benefit. They had likely discussed it, especially with the detectives singling Peter out for questioning. Perhaps Lucas was attempting to give the appearance of keeping an open mind.

Finally, I replied, "Yes, I did."

"Hmm," he quickly responded, "I didn't see anything very different from how he was at your dad's funeral." Ah, there it was. What he really had wanted to say. I started to respond, but the director came back in the room, sat down, and picked up his agenda. I remained silent. I knew my opinion wouldn't sway Lucas's thinking anyway. Peter certainly was different than he had been after my dad's death. I wasn't sure if Peter had cried at Dad's funeral, but he did appear a little sad. He hadn't been aloof or detached following dad's death. He was definitely acting very differently. Was that even a fair question to ask? The deceased was his 13-year-old brother, not his 73-year-old grandfather. At the very least, Peter had been the first person to find Sammy. He had been required to be the acting adult until the paramedics arrived. Peter should be acting differently, and, indeed, he was acting differently. Lucas's question felt like a setup, complete with assigned witnesses, an attempt to eliminate Peter from suspicion by asserting Peter's reactions normal for Peter. As if the hanging death of your brother and the stroke of your grandfather would elicit similar emotional and psychological responses. The problem wasn't that Peter was acting differently than he had at my dad's funeral; the problem was that Peter was acting differently than I had ever seen anyone act after a loved one's death, not to mention a teenager finding his own younger brother hanging. Lucas seemed intent on guiding everyone to believe that Peter was just being Peter, and his behavior was perfectly normal.

The planning session began with Lucas informing us Bruce had agreed to officiate, and we settled days and times of the visitation and funeral. I told them I planned to make a picture video for the visitation, and I would bring some of Sammy's personal things to display on tables in the back of the sanctuary. I wanted rubber bracelets, imprinted with Sammy's name and nickname, for Sammy's friends to wear, so we started discussing which nickname would be best. I suggested, "Sammy the Body?" That didn't feel right since it originated from long ago when Lucas and I were still married. I next said, "What about Puffy?" But I quickly said, "Wait, no. He wouldn't want that on his friends' bracelets."

I recalled a day back in 2005. Sammy had been in first grade, and I was walking him into school. As we neared his classroom, he turned to me and leaned in for a quick hug. As he did, I said, "Bye Puffy, have a good day."

Sammy looked at me, leaned back in, and said quietly, "Um, not to hurt your feelings, Mom, but could you not call me that at school?"

"Oh okay," I whispered, tickled and trying not to smile. "Bye, Sammy," I called out firmly in a 'This-guy-is-mature-and-tough' voice and not in my 'I-love-you-my-little-Puffmeister' voice. When Sammy was a toddler, he had very full cheeks. In fact, his whole body had been round and plump, and so I began calling him, "Puffy" and "Puffmeister" and "Puff the Magic Sammy." I continued calling him Puffy through the years. I think he liked my special names for him, just not in front of his friends.

My thoughts returned to the funeral home where I sat, dejected. The sadness of what we were doing hung in the air, but there was nothing we could do except keep moving forward.

Jake spoke up and said, "How about his gamer tag? Hot Pocket." Sammy was a gamer. On the computer, he played *World of Warcraft* and *Runescape*, on his Xbox, *Modern Warfare*, *Call of Duty*, *Halo*, and *Assassins Creed*. For all of his gaming, he used the game tag, "Hot Pocket." We all agreed that was the perfect nickname, and the one Sammy would have wanted us to use.

We continued to go through funeral details until, with glazed, defeated eyes, we all sat quietly. We were out of steam, and the director took charge. "Okay, why don't we go downstairs and select a casket." No one spoke as we followed him down the hall. I saw Valerie sitting in a chair in the lobby area, and I talked briefly with her. "Sweetheart," I said to Sarah, "why don't you sit here with Aunt Valerie while we go downstairs?" I knew she wanted to participate in the planning, but selecting a coffin for his body would be particularly difficult. Just two days before, she had been joking and laughing with Sammy downtown at the Homecoming parade. Just two days before, Sammy had playfully teased her about her love for Disney movies. That had been their last conversation, the last time she had seen him alive. When she had seen him next, less than 12 hours later, he was hanging from his closet door. She didn't argue with me and took a seat next to Valerie. Clasping hands, Jake and I went downstairs.

Chapter 10

"The only education in grief that any of us ever gets is a crash course. Until Caroline had died I had belonged to that other world, the place of innocence, and linear expectations, where I thought grief was a simple, wrenching realm of sadness and longing that gradually receded. What that definition left out was the body blow that loss inflicts, as well as the temporary madness, and a range of less straightforward emotions shocking in their intensity."

-Gail Caldwell, *Let's Take the Long Way Home: A Memoir of Friendship*

Afternoon of October 25

I reluctantly entered the casket display room. Over the previous 18 months, I already had visited that room twice: April 2009, when my dad had passed away, and July 2009, when Jake and I made our own funeral plans following Jake's cardiac issue. Coffins encircled and filled the entire room. Looking at them, I was filled with dread at the thought of putting Sammy's body in one and burying him underground. In the future, when I thought about where Sammy was, I would see him in a dark, suffocating coffin deep down in the dirt. For 30 seconds, I considered cremating him rather than burying him. Upstairs in the planning room earlier, we had noticed beautiful glass spheres containing different colored glitter and iridescent smears. When I had inquired about them, the director told me families who chose cremation could have a portion of their loved one's cremains swirled into one of those shimmering spheres. Although I loved the idea of keeping a part of Sammy with me via his ashes in a beautiful orb, I quickly dismissed the notion. Thinking about Sammy's body being placed in a furnace or stove and burned until only ash remained, horrified me. I wanted to preserve the physical form that had been my son for as long as possible. Jake gently guided me around the room. The caskets were different colors, styles, types of wood and metal, and casket interiors. Noticing a blue one, Sammy's favorite color, Jake led us over to look at it more closely. The outside was blue metal, the inside, satin. Because Sammy enjoyed the feel of satin, he would like the interior. Obviously, he wouldn't be aware of what the inside of the box felt like, but I would. Each corner of the casket exterior had a place to affix a plaque. From a catalog, we could choose four plaques reflecting some of Sammy's interests. "Okay. This is the one," I said, flatly.

Just the previous March, I had excitedly chosen the theme, the colors, and decorations I knew were Sammy's preferences for his 13th birthday party, a celebration of his life. Seven months later, I was choosing the colors, materials, and other items I thought his preferences for his funeral, a lamentation of his death. One brought pleasure, seeing my beautiful son growing slowly into a man. The other brought horror, seeing his arrested development. The juxtaposition of Sammy's life and death, and the accompanying intense sorrow, squeezed roughly around my heart.

Leaving the funeral home, we headed downtown to a local florist's shop. Mother and Laura were in the back selecting their arrangements when we arrived. Shortly after we were seated, Valerie walked in with Lydia trailing after her looking upset. Lydia hurried to my side and whispered that when they entered the store, Aunt Valerie told the owner her nephew had committed suicide. Angry, Lydia said, "I told them, 'No, he didn't. That's not what happened,' and the man and Aunt Valerie just looked at each other." My gut squeezed tightly. Why would my sister say such a thing? We didn't know why Sammy was hanged, but I didn't think he had intentionally taken his life. It felt wrong on Sammy's behalf to call it suicide if it was an accident and a horrible injustice if the cause of his death was something worse. Sammy could no longer speak for himself, but I could—and would—speak up for him.

I walked over to Valerie. "Don't be telling people your nephew committed suicide," I growled. "The police don't think that Sammy took his own life, and it wrong to tell people he killed himself if that isn't what happened. You don't know anything so don't talk to people like you do." Valerie stuttered trying to find words to defend herself.

Finally, she said, "I'm sorry." Bursting into tears, I threw my arms around her and hugged her. I loved my sister, and our family had taken some hard hits over the previous few years. We were all weary. I knew she meant no harm by what she had said. Of course, people were going to assume Sammy committed suicide since he was found hanging. Unless one was aware of all the peculiarities of his death scene, suicide was the reasonable conclusion.

"In the future, if people ask you what happened tell them he had a terrible accident and leave it at that," I told her. "Now, take me to the person with whom you were speaking so I can rectify this." She led me back to the front of the store where I clumsily tried to explain to the owner that my son had not committed suicide but had suffered a terrible accident. I sounded like a naïve mother in denial, but what else could I do? We finished picking out our flower arrangements and drove back home.

When my dad died, each of us in the immediate family placed something special in his casket to be buried with him. Jake and I wanted to do the same for Sammy. I immediately thought of one item I should bury with him if I could make myself part with it. When Sammy was six months old, I conceived again and started making a baby quilt that I intended for the new baby (Adam). It was sea foam green, white, and pink, with white appliquéd lambs. Sammy saw me work on the blanket every day for several months. When it was all pieced together and only the quilting was left, Sammy—then 13-months-old—started sitting next to me as I stitched, holding the completed part of the blanket on his lap. When I gave him permission, he would take the blanket and carry it all around the house with him. By the time I finished the quilting, the blanket belonged to Sammy. He dragged it everywhere with him during the day and slept with it every night. He loved his "byankie." Although he eventually stopped taking it everywhere, he always kept it at the end of his bed. He never put it away in his closet with other mementos and special things he outgrew. The day he died, it still lay across the end of his bed. I wanted to keep his Blankie. The thought of parting with it poked sharply into my aching heart, but keeping it for myself didn't feel right. Sammy would want it with him, so I planned to cover him with it before we closed the casket.

In addition to Blankie, I wanted to put a shared piece of jewelry on Sammy and myself. I decided a gold heart that could be engraved and then separated into two pieces would be perfect. With each half of the broken heart charm on a chain around our necks, Sammy and I could wear our halves forever. I thought and hoped that would help me to feel a connection to my son as he lay buried beneath the earth. I called Victoria, whose fiancé owned a jewelry store, and asked her to handle it.

Jake knew right away what he would put in the casket. He and I had been dating privately for ten months when I first introduced him to the children; I wanted to make sure he was a keeper before I let the children become attached. Prior to their introduction, when I told the children about Jake, Sammy had been a little concerned and apprehensive. He had asked what I would do if Jake ended up being mean to him and the other kids. I reassured him if Jake ended up being a meanie, we would "boot him to the curb, post haste!" But from the first moments on the evening they met, it was obvious they would be close. Within two weeks of that meeting, while I was tucking Sammy in one night, he said, "Mom, you should hurry up and marry Jake before he marries someone else." After another week had passed, Sammy started feeling badly that Jake had to go home to an empty apartment every night when he left our house. One night as Jake was preparing to leave, Sammy came running out of his bedroom. "Jake!" Sammy yelled, holding out Lambie—one of his favorite stuffed animals—for Jake. "Take Lambie home with you so you won't be all alone and lonely at night!" As hard as it would be to let Lambie go, Jake would be placing him in the casket so Sammy would never have to be alone or lonely at night.

As Sarah and I brainstormed possible options for her, we talked about how she and Sammy had each said they wanted a tattoo when they turned 18 and how cool it would be if we could get them matching tattoos. Unfortunately, we discovered it is illegal to tattoo a deceased person. I tried making the case that the autopsy and embalming processes were performed on a deceased person, that I was Sammy's mother and I gave permission, that he had always wanted a tattoo and would think it was awesome, but there was no wiggle room.

Late in the afternoon, the funeral home called to inform us they had finished embalming Sammy, and we could go see him. As we had not yet delivered the clothes for them to dress him, they told us he was only wearing a hospital gown and was not yet in his casket. I knew what I would be seeing, but my psyche was still jarred when I walked into the big, empty room and saw Sammy lying alone on a metal table in a hospital gown. My mouth was so dry I couldn't swallow as I moved across the room to Sammy's side.

Once again, I found myself wishing I could summon Sammy's spirit and return it to his body. I repressed the impulse to shake him by his shoulders and yell, "Heeey Sammyboy! Wake up!" How had some brilliant scientist not yet discovered how to turn a person back on! I no longer believed a person had a spirit separate from their body. I thought that the spirit-like component of a human being was a function of our higher brainpower (as compared to other animals). A deceased person was similar to a computer with a severed power source. More than ever though, I understood the *powerful* pull of the God/Heaven-when-you-die religious belief, and why even in our highly educated twenty-first century world, many people still believed it. When a loved one died, what could be better than believing death was not the end of the road but only a brief separation? Yes, it is sad that you won't get to see Sammy for a while, but one day when you die, you will get to see him again and spend eternity with him in Heaven! As I have already mentioned, the maddening thing was that until two or three years before Sammy's death I *had* believed in all of that! I had believed in God the Father, God the Son, and God the Holy Ghost, and that every person had an eternal spirit and the opportunity and choice to spend forever in Heaven (or Hell for those who didn't ask Jesus to come into their heart and "save" them.) What comfort and hope I could have had if only I had still believed! What a difference it would have made if I still could have had the *joy of knowing* I would get to see Sammy again in Heaven one day, and the *comfort of believing* that my Heavenly Father was in control of everything; I only needed to trust in Him! The reassurance of believing that nothing happens outside of the will of God so it is all a part of His plan is such alluring bait. I was raised in a Baptist home. I had first married a man who became a minister! For most of my life, I earnestly believed it all! And believing it had been wonderful. But, in my 30's, I started questioning everything, and after much research, reading, critical analyzing, and a desire for truth over comfort, I let those beliefs go, one by one. To my mind, there was as much chance of resurrecting those beliefs, as there was of resurrecting Sammy. I still wished for it, all the same. If, somehow, I *could* have made myself believe in God, Heaven, and eternal life again, I *would* have. Religion was too strong of a narcotic not to crave it during the worst of times; too bad I was already immune to the drug.

Since he couldn't be brought back to life, I thought about how nice it would be at least to take Sammy's body to our house instead of burying him. His body would have to be preserved so as not to decay, but it had been done before, in Russia, for Lenin and Stalin—people who committed crimes against humanity—so why not for my innocent Sammy? I even could have a glass coffin made for him. It was a passing, crazy idea, but what can I say, I was a desperate, crazed mother wanting to hold onto as much of my child as possible.

I began slowly scrutinizing Sammy's body, looking at his arms and legs, skin, neck, nearly every visible place, for anything I might have missed before. I found nothing. The only mark I saw to indicate something had happened was that hateful, purple ligature mark on the front of his neck. The total stillness of his body was disconcerting: no chest rising and falling, no shifting of eyelids, nothing. That absolute stillness was the thing that silently screamed at me that all was not well; life no longer animated him. *Why did this happen? Why did he have to die?* I thought. My brain heated up in agitation at the unsolvable problem of Sammy being dead and me not having a solution. *One minute he was breathing, and the next minute he was gone. Life is just so fucking fragile.*

When we got back home after seeing Sammy, Mother and Laura were in my kitchen, and they were cleaning. It was soothing to have them there. They brought platters of lunch meat sandwiches and coolers with ice and cans of soda inside, which was nice as neither Jake nor I had thought much that day or the day before about feeding either ourselves or the children. Jo and Valerie slipped out to Kohl's and purchased clothes for Jake and me for the visitation and funeral. When they returned, Jo led me to Lydia's room to try on several black outfits. I appreciated what they had done, but honestly, I didn't care what I wore to the funeral. I thought I should wear a sackcloth and cover my face with ashes like the mourners in the Old Testament, because why not? My child was dead!

I kept having flashes of Sammy wearing only a hospital gown and of being all alone on that metal table in the funeral home. I felt bothered that he was not yet in his casket. The thought of him there by himself, with no one that loved him, with none of his special things, in the dark, all night, made my broken heart throb angrily. "Honey," I called out to Jake, "Would you go back to the funeral home and cover up Sammy with his blanket? And take White Tiger to lay next to him?" White Tiger was an enormous stuffed animal we had gotten Sammy a few years before, which he loved and always kept in his bed. On some level, I knew I was being ridiculous. Sammy wasn't there. I knew he had no awareness of his condition or that he was alone. I couldn't help it. I couldn't stand the thought of my sweet boy all alone, displayed on that table with nothing over him. He seemed defenseless, unprotected, helpless. Jake was putting on his shoes when I decided to go with him. I wouldn't be able to see Sammy's body much longer, and I didn't want to miss an opportunity. We left the kids at the house with Jo and went to do for Sammy what he was unable to do for himself: we covered him up with his blanket and set White Tiger next to him to watch over him. It was completely pointless, but doing it made me feel a little better about leaving him. I considered staying all night in the funeral home room with him, but the responsibility to be home and available for my living children prevented me. Jake and I quietly got back in our van and cried for Samuel all the way home.

The sleeping arrangement the previous night had been a little too crowded with Jake, Adam, Lydia, and me all in our bed. After we returned from the funeral home, we made a pallet on the floor of our bedroom for Adam, and Lydia slept in our bed. Jake and I cuddled with each of them, scratched their backs for about 15 minutes, then switched spots, and repeated. They wanted and needed reassuring physical touch and comforting affection from us. Jo slept with Sarah again.

After tucking in Adam and Lydia, I opened my laptop to write Sammy's obituary. I was unable to construct a single sentence. I thought the newspaper should just print, "Sammy is dead!? What the hell?!" Every neuron in my brain felt agitated. My mind was too fevered to form an intelligent thought. The strain of trying to write about Sammy's too brief life left me anxious and nauseated, and, eventually, I asked Jake to write it. He said he would try.

We still had to select some things to arrange on the tables in the church for the visitation service. When Jake finished the obituary, we went into Sammy's room. Sometime over the previous week, my silly boy had placed his paintball goggles on his piggy bank, so the piggy was looking through them. Seeing the goggled piggy started a wave of emotions: fondness and affection for Sammy's silly, random sense of humor, quickly followed by a blast of motherly love and tenderness, then, sharp, searing pain because he was gone, followed by a huge descending grey cloud of sorrow. I looked away from his piggy bank and saw his light saber. Sammy had been a Star Wars fan. In the corner of the room were the jeans and t-shirt he had worn four days before. We started setting things aside: his hockey stick and ice skates, his Xbox controller, a baseball trophy. After a while, it was too much. It hurt too badly, and we had to stop. We lay on Sammy's bed sobbing, heartbroken.

Unable to sleep again that night, I got up to look through my photos of Sammy. I set aside pictures for the video and poster display boards. Every picture I had of Sammy had become priceless: a beautiful toddler with chubby baby cheeks and silky straight hair, at each of his early birthday parties—Toy Story-theme, Superman-theme, Batman-theme, Teenage Mutant Ninja Turtle-theme—at his birthday parties four years in a row at Empire Roller Rink, riding a big-boy bike with training wheels, posing with his siblings, playing, laughing, spoon-feeding his baby brother, Adam, playing dress-up with Peter and Sarah, and hugging his baby sister, Lydia. Every picture was a reminder of happy times he would never have again, happy times which we—I—would never again experience with Sammy. I loved looking at the pictures, but I also hated it. Seeing my beautiful son experiencing life and knowing those moments were all over felt like someone was repeatedly stabbing an icepick into my heart.

Chapter 11

"It's odd, isn't it? People die every day and the world goes on like nothing happened. But when it's a person you love, you think everyone should stop and take notice. That they ought to cry and light candles and tell you that you're not alone."

-Janetina McMorris, *Letters from Home*

Tuesday, Oct 26

Two Days After Sammy Died

I awoke to uncontrollable wails erupting from me again. The pain was wretched. I tried to stifle my loud animal-like cries, to let it out slowly so as not to wake and upset my sleeping children. Fortunately, it was only 4:30 am so they were still deep in exhausted sleep. Jake had awakened and turned to embrace me. My heart felt as if a large chunk had been ripped out leaving only a mangled heap of cardiac muscle, which continued to pump amidst the spewing blood. Jake and I cried and held onto each other in our misery. Eventually, we fell back asleep.

At 10:30 am, tired and puffy-eyed from crying and not sleeping well, Jo, Sarah, and I entered my beauty salon for hair appointments. It felt bizarre and wrong to be going to a salon to have our hair styled. As a matter of fact, everything I was doing seemed absurd compared with Sammy's location and state of existence. I was cuddling with my husband. Sammy was lying dead on a table. I was eating a turkey sandwich. Sammy was lying dead on a table. I was having my hair styled. Sammy was lying dead on a table. I didn't know what else I should be doing though, except maybe lying on the funeral home table holding my dead child?

As we entered the salon, I spotted a woman who worked there whose daughter was a friend of Sammy's, so she knew what had happened. Her eyes were red; she obviously had been crying. The other stylists also seemed to know what had happened, and I was glad. It would have been worse if no one at the salon had known about Sammy's death and acted normal. To me, the world had stopped turning. When people around me moved along like it was a normal day getting gas, buying groceries, or talking about football, I wanted to scream, "Stop! Sammy is dead! My child is dead! Show some respect!" The salon had a sober and somber atmosphere, and for that, I was grateful. We sat quietly through our appointments, and Jo quickly edited the obituary Jake had written the night before. It had to be submitted by 11:00 am in order to be printed in that afternoon's paper.

As my stylist worked on my hair, I thought about the plans for the funeral the next day and what other things I might want to do during the service. When my children were young, I read aloud to them every night. It was one of my favorite things to do with them. I acquired a large library of picture books, but there were a few that were favorites of the children that I read frequently: *Is Your Mama a Llama?*, *Goodnight Moon*, *Jamberry*, *Caps for Sale*, *Curious George*, *Peter Rabbit*, *The Story of Ferdinand*, *The Napping House*, *Tikki Tikki Tembo*, and *Time for Bed*. I read *Time for Bed* aloud to the kids so many times I memorized it. Jake, and before him Lucas, read it to the children many times, as well. For years at bedtime, both before and after the divorce, I would start reciting the lines from the book to the kids: "It's time for bed, little mouse, little mouse, darkness is falling all over the house." I decided I wanted to read *Time for Bed* aloud during the funeral service. I thought if Jake, Lucas, and I alternately read it aloud it would demonstrate the unity of our love for Sammy.

When we returned home from the hair salon, Jo left to go to a bookstore to pick up a new copy of *Time for Bed*. She was then going to meet up with her family who had arrived and checked in at a hotel. Jake and Sarah lay down for naps, Lydia was with Tori, and Adam was quietly playing on the computer. The house was silent. It was nice to have the quiet for about five minutes, and then I started wishing some of my extended family members were with me. The house was too quiet, and I could hear my screaming heart.

In several hours, I had to attend Sammy's visitation. I needed some vodka to settle the panic rising in my gut. When I reached my kitchen, however, the vodka bottle had disappeared from the freezer. It was nowhere to be found. As a matter of fact, I could find no wine, beer or alcohol of any kind in my kitchen. I remembered then that my mother had been at my house cleaning my kitchen the previous night. Mother, a Baptist, was an absolute, committed teetotaler who thought everyone else—particularly her children—should be also. I had no doubt I would find our alcohol if I checked the previous day's trash. I went in search of the trash bag. She had taken that too.

Jake and Sarah woke up and went to the grocery store to pick up a newspaper. We wanted to make sure Sammy's obituary had been included and that it looked half-way respectable. We knew it would not be a perfect piece of writing; we had hardly managed to get it written let alone do much editing. In spite of that, we hoped it would communicate what a wonderful boy Sammy had been.

Samuel Lagunas, 1997-2010

"Samuel Bradshaw Lagunas, 13, died from a tragic accident Sunday, Oct. 24, 2010."

"A memorial service will be held at 2pm, Wednesday, Oct. 27, at Mercy Christian Church with burial at Parkway Cemetery to follow. Visitation is 6-9pm, Tuesday, October 26, at Mercy Christian Church."

"Samuel was the kind of son for which every mother and father wished; he was loving, loyal, obedient and kind. Samuel was the brother every sibling needs; he was helpful, protective, playful and generous. Samuel was the grandson every grandparent would be proud to have; he was respectful and diligent in all things. Samuel was the friend that would be your friend for life; he was true, easygoing, quick to laugh and a joy to be around. Samuel was an amazing, beautiful boy who would have been the man every boy wants to grow up to be."

"A natural athlete, there was no sport Sammy could not master. He played baseball, soccer, football, hockey, took gymnastics and tae kwon do. In elementary school, his classmates chose him 'Best Kickball Player.' Samuel's teachers found him to be a pleasure to have in a classroom, and he was on the honor roll in both elementary and middle school. He earned the Presidential Academic award, and the Physical Fitness award for best attitude and effort. He played the viola and hoped to learn how to play the electric guitar. Sammy was an avid Xbox player, and those on 'Hot Pocket's' side felt very fortunate to be on his team. Samuel enjoyed playing with animals, whether it was his dog, Sallie, his favorite stuffed animal, Ratty, or a stray kitten in the neighborhood."

"Samuel wanted to be a firefighter when he grew up. He was very protective of his sisters and his little brother and on several occasions verbally and physically stepped up to the plate to defend them. He was just making the transition from boy to young man, but he still liked to snuggle next to his mom on the couch during family movie time or be carried piggyback by his dad, Jake."

"Sammy Boy, you will be missed by every single person who had the privilege to know you. The world is a lesser place without you in it. We all love you, Sammy, and we take comfort knowing that you were a very happy boy that knew you were deeply loved."

"Samuel was preceded in death by his grandfather."

"Because Samuel loved and was passionate about the responsible care of all animals, donations may be made in his name, Samuel Bradshaw Lagunas, directly to the Humane Society."

As the time drew near for the visitation, I grew increasingly anxious. As anxiety increases, one's perceptual field narrows, and clear thinking becomes difficult. I was trying to finish the slide show, but as the minutes ticked away, I started forgetting how to add more pictures, adjust the pictures, or add the songs. I was getting snippy and agitated, and eventually, I asked Jake to take over (although in his noticeably disconsolate emotional state, I was uncertain if he could finish it either).

Victoria arrived with Lydia, helped her dress, and left to go dress herself. Jake was having some technical difficulties with the video, so while he stayed home to finish, I left with the kids for the visitation. Jake knew the video was important to me, and I would carry lifelong regret if we didn't have it for Sammy's visitation. He knew that however badly I would feel not having him ride over with us to the visitation, I would feel worse if the video was a mess or didn't work.

Upon arriving at the church, we entered the sanctuary. Mementos and keepsakes from Sammy's life were displayed on several long tables in the back. Valerie had been at the church setting things up that afternoon. Sammy's baseball bat and glove, *Halo* and *Assassin's Creed* Xbox games, and his Buzz Lightyear toy box, among many other things, were spread across the tables. Seeing his red and green Christmas stocking that looked like an old-fashioned ice skate, the one he picked out for himself when he was 4-years-old and used every year, made my already throbbing heart scream. I looked away from the tables and headed toward Sammy in the casket at the front of the church. He was dressed in blue jeans, one of his favorite t-shirts, and his white hoodie. I sat down on the front pew, and the kids sat next to me. It felt surreal: the church, the ex-husband, the flowers, the casket, and my son's body. We sat dazed, and, eventually, Jake rushed in.

As the start time drew near, Lucas, his parents, his brother Bruce and Bruce's wife, lined up along the front of the church. Jake, the kids and I went to stand in front of Sammy's casket. My mother came to the front of the church and headed over to stand between my ex and his parents, and Victoria followed with a stool on which Mother could sit. Walking over to Mom, I whispered, "Why don't we move your stool and you can sit by me?" I would have liked to have her near me; I craved familial comfort.

"No, I'm fine here," she said. I nearly started crying.

"It's no big deal, Mom, and I would like to have you by me."

"No, I'm fine," she firmly told me. I wanted to say, "But Mom, I'm not fine." I said nothing. Blinking rapidly, I tried to remain composed and not start crying already as I walked back to my spot. I wish she would have moved by me, or at least offered an explanation. Her decision hurt me, and her lack of comfort or any tenderness cut me.

Ten minutes before the official beginning of the visitation, the funeral director asked if we could start early. A large group of people was outside waiting. Jake started the video, and a huge line of people streamed into the church. Many of Sammy's classmates, teachers, and counselors from school had come, as well as friends of my family, Lucas' family, and Jake' family. While they waited in the long line, everyone watched the video on the two big screens in the front of the church. Most of the students were wearing the blue Sammy bracelets we had ordered and taken to the school. They signed the casket cover board, hugged me, Jake, the kids, and the others, and gazed sadly at Sammy. I was surprised so many made the effort to attend. After they said goodbye to Sammy, many of them sat around in the pews, staring at the big screens and crying. One boy who came through the line with his father said to me, "I was a new to the school, and Sammy was the first person to talk to me. He was my first friend. He was nice to me every day and made being in a new place easier." I was glad the boy came to pay his respects to Sammy and to share about Sammy's kindness with me.

Of course, it also tore at my heart. Why Sammy? Why couldn't some mean bully kid have died instead of my nice kid?

The girls were a mess. Lydia kept coming up and standing by Sammy, touching his face and hair, leaning over him crying. Several times, Victoria or Jo took her away somewhere private to soothe her. Sarah kept rotating from standing right next to me leaning on my shoulder, to disappearing entirely. She was wearing Sammy's hockey jersey, which made her feel a tiny bit closer to her beloved brother. A large group of her friends came through the line. Most of them had met Sammy when they attended Sarah's birthday parties at our house over the previous several years. She stepped to the side with them for a while, and they surrounded her with hugs of love and support. Adam seemed to be in another world. He was zoned out, which was not surprising. Adam's way of dealing with unpleasant and stressful things was to compartmentalize. I thought it was a gift that his brain operated in that way. Neither Jake, I, nor the girls had that ability.

Late in the visitation, I realized I hadn't had any interaction with my mother since before it started. I had been accepting condolences from all of the guests coming through the receiving line, and so had she. However, after 9:00 pm, the visitation was technically over. No one was coming through the line anymore, yet Mother hadn't approached me. Other than Tori, I had barely exchanged words with anyone in my family. It was 9:30 pm, and everyone was standing and sitting around talking. Most of the people who remained were extended family members of mine or Lucas's. Looking around, I noticed Valerie and Vince talking to Lucas. What did they need to talk about with him? Why were they not hugging, holding, and comforting my children? Or Jake? Or me? I wish my family had thought to be more affectionate and actively supportive of us. Perhaps no one knew what to do or say, whether it was better to hover or to give space. I suppose no one knows how one should act when a child has died, and particularly in such a confusing, terrible way.

Chapter 12

"Grief is love turned into an eternal missing"

-Rosamund Lupton, *Sister*

The Day We Buried Sammy,
Wednesday, October 27

The crying started the moment I woke up. As it had the day before, it happened around 4:30 am so the kids were still asleep and didn't hear. My chest ached and pounded. My heart felt as if it had erupted like a volcano upon learning of Sammy's death, and it just continued spewing hot lava. That day, the pain was worse. That day, I had to stick my child in a hole in the ground.

I had hardly slept, but I hadn't expected I would. I could *not* wrap my head around what happened. Never in a million years would I have thought one of my children would die prematurely, and in such a horrible way, and under such odd circumstances. I wanted to stay in bed all day. I didn't want to bury my son. I didn't want to do any of it.

I made a brief post on my Facebook wall.

> "Our sweet, precious boy, Samuel, died on Sunday morning. The funeral is today at 2:00 pm at Mercy Christian Church. Some people have asked about donations in Sammy's name, and we are suggesting donations be made to the Humane Society as Samuel was such an animal lover."

The Funeral

"It's time for bed, little mouse, little mouse, darkness is falling all over the house. It's time for bed, little goose, little goose, the stars are out and on the loose. It's time for bed, little cat, little cat, so snuggle in tight, that's right, like that. It's time to sleep, little bee, little bee, yes, I love you and you love me. It's to sleep, little snake, little snake, good gracious me, you're still awake? The stars are out and shining bright, sweet dreams my darling, sleep well, good night."

In spite of being held during the school day, many of Sammy's friends came to both the funeral and the graveside services. I was touched by their attendance, as I had been at the visitation, and was glad so many friends had liked and cared enough for Sammy to attend. It would have felt even more awful if only a few or no school friends had come. It probably is like that for some poor mothers and, had it been a different child of mine, it might have been for me. I should have felt a little grateful at least for that, but I didn't. I couldn't. At that time, and for many years after, I didn't have it in me to feel grateful for anything.

The burial was hideous. I felt like I was locked in a burning building, continuously catching fire, my skin melting off my bones until I passed out. Upon waking from my stupor, the flames of truth—that Sammy was dead, his corpse was in the coffin in front of me, and it was the last time I would ever see his body—licked and burned again. I didn't know the funeral wasn't the final peak in the pain of my child's death. Although burying Sammy was horrendous the missing him, the sorrow that he had missed out on so much, and the learning to live again in spite of the fact that he no longer had that luxury would be a whole different kind of pain.

I felt a slight sense of relief when the last shovelfuls of dirt fell on Sammy's grave, and we were able to leave. Of course, I wanted the funeral services for Sammy to be as nice as I had it in my power to make them, but I wanted to escape from the heinous pain.

When it was over, we headed to my sister's house. I stood alone in a mental fog by a table in the dining room. Valerie, who was always a wonderful host, laid out an enormous amount of food. I later learned that the massive amount of food was because Lucas initially accepted an invitation from Vince and Valerie for him and his extended family to come over following the funeral. He only informed Vince after the funeral that they had made other plans and wouldn't be coming.

The table was spread with all kinds of meats, cheeses, fruit, and sandwiches. I had no appetite. I had no anything. I just stood silently. Jo and her partner Carl came to the table to get some snacks, and Jo began quietly talking to me about the services. When she paused, Carl muttered a few comments about Lucas's behavior and referred to some of his remarks during the funeral service.

From out of the blue, Mother stepped into the room and said, "We aren't going to say things like that. This is a time of healing." Jo and Carl looked at each other and then at the glazed expression on my face. I said nothing. I didn't have the strength to speak. After attending my child's funeral, I felt like I had been burned alive but not granted the mercy of dying.

Vince came over to me a little later and said, "Janie, can we go in another room for a minute?" I was apprehensive. I already felt like the walking dead. What could he possibly need to say to me at that moment? Jake and I moved across the room with him into the master bedroom. "Okay, why don't you sit down," he told us. We sat, perched on the edge of the bed.

"I received a phone call earlier today from Ned (one of my cousins). He said he was talking to one of his construction workers whose daughter Amy is friends with Sammy. And according to Amy, Friday at school Sammy said he was going to pull a Halloween prank on his brother and set up a scene to make himself look like he was hanging." Vince stopped talking. It took a few minutes for the meaning of what he had said to sink in.

"So," I repeated slowly, "Sammy allegedly told his friend Amy, that he was going to pull a Halloween prank and set himself up in a hanging scene?"

"Yes," he said. "I just got off the phone for the second time with Cousin Ned, and that's what he said."

I felt almost nothing, maybe because the story seemed a bit of a stretch. There was no way could it be true. Of course, I would have liked to believe it. I wanted to understand what had happened to Sammy. Yet, something about what Vince said didn't seem to fit. Perhaps, because I had never known Sammy to pull an elaborate prank. As a matter of fact, I had never known Sammy to pull any kind of prank. Vince then said, "Apparently, the cops are over there speaking with Amy now, or they are on their way." That statement gave me pause. In my mind, involvement of the police gave credibility to the story.

With tentative hope in our eyes, Jake and I looked at each other. It had all just been a stupid and terrible accident. Sammy hadn't committed suicide. He wasn't trying the choking game. He wasn't killed by someone, and Peter wasn't guilty of anything. Relief slowly crept through me. While I was slightly skeptical, I knew I could—and would—call the detectives later to confirm the story, and surely Vince knew me well enough to know I would do that (which made me feel more confident that the story was true). "We should call Mother in and tell her," I said.

"Actually," said Vince "I already told her." I felt annoyed at that. I would think info of such an important nature would first be conveyed to the parents, but I tried to dismiss my feelings and focus on the positive news.

"Well, we should call Lucas and tell him," I then said.

"Again, I told him when we were still at the graveside service today, which was when Ned first called me." Another bubble of irritation surfaced. Why had Vince thought it appropriate for him to share that vital information with Mother and my ex-husband, and before he had even shared it with me.

"Okaaay," I said slowly, again trying to push away the frustration that he had made those unilateral decisions. "Well," I finally said, "I guess let's go back into the living room, and you can share the news with everyone else." I considered telling the others myself, but I felt disinclined. Perhaps that was because although I felt a responsibility personally to share that info with my mother and my ex-husband, I didn't feel a responsibility to personally inform anyone else aside from my children. Maybe it was because I felt a little bothered about Vince's choices in delivering the info, and since he had already informed the pertinent people, he might as well tell everyone else. It was also possible that telling others felt a little premature since the information had not yet been verified. I sensed reluctance from Vince, but he didn't say as much and agreed to make an announcement.

We returned to the living room, and Vince called out, "May I have your attention?" The room grew quiet. "I received some information this morning that I think everyone will be glad to know. One of Sammy's friends told her dad that Sammy told her at school on Friday he was planning a Halloween prank for this weekend to scare his brother. He told her was going to set up a scene to make it look like he was hanging. The friend of Sammy's told her dad, who told Ned, and then Ned called me to let me know." When he finished, there was silence for a moment. Then, the whole room collectively exhaled. My friends and family looked at each other and at me with relief on their faces.

Jake and I made eye contact and headed to the bathroom for privacy. "Well...?" I said as we huddled together. "I guess it explains why it happened. What do you think? "I tentatively asked.

"I don't know," he said slowly, "It doesn't sound like something Sammy would say or do."

"I know, but if the cops are over there questioning her that's a good sign!" I exclaimed. I wanted to believe the story because it was the best possible reason to explain what happened. "I will call Detective Higgins later tonight or tomorrow and ask if they have questioned the girl to confirm it," I said as we emerged from the bathroom.

The atmosphere was much more relaxed for the rest of the evening. Everyone was sad our Sammyboy was gone, but knowing it was because of a silly prank eased our minds. I felt lighter. I would no longer have to agonize over what happened. I even felt a twinge of anger at Sammy for doing something so foolish that he had killed himself. Sarah felt that same anger, and had to go in another room to talk about it for a while with Jake.

I was getting a soda from the kitchen when Vince approached me again. "Hey Janie, I was just wondering, do you think Adam would enjoy going to a university basketball game with me sometime soon? I thought it might take his mind off everything."

"I'm not sure. He might?" I said. Adam was not a huge sports fan, but he did like getting out of the house and going places and doing things. "Yeah, he probably would think it was fun."

"Okay," Vince said, "Sometime, in the next week or two, I'll do that."

"Okay, thanks, Vince. That's nice of you," I said.

As soon as we left Valerie's house, I dialed Detective Higgins's number. She didn't answer, but I left a message. "Hi Detective Higgins, I am calling because tonight I was told that Friday at school Sammy told a friend he was planning to pull a joke on his brother and set up a hanging scene. I was told the police had been informed of this and were questioning the friend of Sammy's who said it. I just wondered if this is true. If you could call me back to let me know, I would appreciate it."

Part 2

"How will I survive this missing? How do others do it? People die all the time. Every day. Every hour. There are families all over the world staring at beds that are no longer slept in, shoes that are no longer worn. Families that no longer have to buy a particular cereal, a kind of shampoo. There are people everywhere standing in line at the movies, buying curtains, walking dogs, while inside, their hearts are ripping to shreds. For years. For their whole lives. I don't believe time heals. I don't want it to. If I heal, doesn't that mean I've accepted the world without her?"

-Jandy Nelson, *The Sky is Everywhere*

Chapter 13

"And often the worst thing wasn't the victims--they were dead, after all, and beyond any more pain. The worst thing was those who loved them and survived them. Often the walking dead from now on, shell-shocked, hearts ruptured, stumbling through the remainder of their lives without anything left inside of them but blood and organs, impervious to pain, having learned nothing except that the worst things did, in fact, sometimes happen."

-Dennis Lehane, *Mystic River*

Thursday, October 28th
Four Days After Sammy Died

In the early morning hours, I awoke crying again and then fell back asleep. When I awoke the second time, I was exhausted, deflated, and full of sorrow. Detective Higgins called while Jake and I were getting dressed. She had no information about Sammy telling anyone he had planned a prank. I was puzzled. Maybe the girl's dad just hadn't told the cops yet. However, Vince had said the cops were at the girl's house talking to her, or on their way to talk to her. Maybe he had misunderstood Ned, or Ned had misunderstood the guy who told him. Surely, Vince hadn't made up the whole story. I was confused and disappointed. The Halloween prank story had been such a great explanation!

We had to go back to the funeral home again to pick up flower arrangements, pay the bill, and start looking at headstones. Sarah went with us, and Adam and Lydia stayed home with Jo. Before we went into the funeral home, we visited Sammy's grave. We parked by the big cypress tree, orange with fall leaves, that was right next to Sammy's grave. After watching him being lowered into the ground the day before, I knew on which side of the grave Sammy's head was positioned. My gaze dropped to that place, then shifted to the other end where I knew his feet rested, and then lifted to the empty place where his headstone would be erected (which was evident by the placement of other headstones already in the same row).

"Wait," I said slowly, a bad feeling growing in my stomach. "Sammy's head is here. His feet are there. That is where the headstone will be. Isn't his head supposed to be on the same end as the headstone?" His head was at the other end of the grave. His feet were resting on the end where the headstone would be set. A feeling of dread gripped me and my stomach tightened. "They put him in the ground backwards!" I cried. Jake and Sarah were speechless and kept looking from the side of the grave where we knew his head was positioned, to the other side where the headstone would be.

"Oh my gosh, Momma, they did bury him backwards," whispered Sarah.

"Let's go inside and speak to someone about this," I said anxiously. Sammy's burial suddenly felt like a bad joke. I ached with sorrow for my innocent boy. My screaming heart thrashed and shook at the absurdity of him being buried backwards. Good grief! We hadn't even managed to get him buried properly.

Lucas and Bruce were inside the funeral home retrieving the flower arrangements sent by their friends and acquaintances. Lucas would be just as bothered about the mistake as we were. "Lucas!" I said, as the tears started. "They buried Sammy backwards! His feet are positioned at the front of the grave where the headstone will be. He's backwards," I cried. Reaching out, I placed my hand on his forearm to share with him the pain of the ridiculous backward burial of our son. He stiffened and looked at his brother.

"Well," he said, as he continued to look at anything but me, "there must be an explanation, some reason they put his feet at that end." Filled with scorn and anger, I dropped my hand from his arm. He didn't care that Sammy's headstone would be placed at his feet. He was confident the funeral home had a reason (what kind of reason was good enough to place a person backwards in their grave?) Lucas didn't like to cause scenes, but I thought surely Sammy being buried backwards would matter enough to compel him.

"I don't care what reason they give! It's not right! His head should be by the headstone!" I said loudly to the side of his face as he persisted in looking away. He remained deaf and mute. "What?" I yelled. "Are you thinking 'what does it matter which direction he's lying, he's dead?'" He was silent. "Sure, and it's only a child. It doesn't matter. It's just Sammy!" Without a glance or a word, Lucas walked away. Jake was there immediately and pulled my face into his chest. He got it. He understood. We both felt the same, as we nearly always did. After crying a few moments, I whispered, "Just take me home, and then will you come back and handle this?"

"Yes, Sweetheart," he said.

I thought about the situation as Jake drove me home. Could I live with letting it be? To make it right, they would have to dig up Sammy's casket, lift it and turn it around, and rebury it. Just the thought of that tore me up, but so did the thought of leaving him in the ground backwards. Leaving him felt like I was saying it wasn't worth the effort to fix. It wasn't worth the hassle. Sammy wasn't worth the hassle. Insisting they correct it though, felt a little... dramatic. He was deceased after all. I imagined what Sammy would say if I could ask him. My traditional little boy would want to be buried correctly. He wouldn't like being backwards. I had to insist on correcting it. Fixing it might feel bad for the moment, but leaving it would feel bad forever.

After Jake dropped me off at home, he immediately returned to the funeral home. He found the funeral director and informed him they had to dig up Sammy's casket, turn it the correct direction, and re-bury him. The director pulled out a map of the burial plots and explained that (for some bizarre reason) everyone in that one specific row (and only in that row) in the cemetery was buried with their feet by the headstone; they were uncertain as to why. Jake was surprised and told him we were not informed of that information. The director consulted the man who sold us the plot who confirmed he had not told us. The funeral home agreed to turn

Sammy, and they would do it immediately. Jake came home and told me, and we felt pained and sad, but relieved.

It was Friday, and Jo—who had been with me since Sunday—needed to get back home. She was a soothing and strengthening presence, and really I didn't want her to leave. As we hugged and cried, she told me she would be back Sunday to be with me for Halloween.

Laura called and told us her husband Hank was going to the funeral home to supervise the entire process of Sammy's excavation and reburial. Hank said he wanted to "make sure nothing hinky happens." Gratitude swelled inside me for my noble and upright brother-in-law. He was not the sentimental type; he simply was a good person who always tried to do the right thing. "Will you have him call us when they are ready to lift out the casket and turn it? We want to be there from that point on." I called Lucas to let him know what was happening, but he said he wouldn't be coming.

Forty-five minutes later, Laura called. She was at the cemetery with Hank. "You should come now."

Jake, Sarah, and I were numb as we drove back to the cemetery. A tractor with a big claw lifted Sammy's casket out of the ground and into the air. I had a sickening fear there would be a mishap, the entire vault would be dropped, and Sammy's body would roll out into the dirt. I wanted to witness the actual turning of the casket so I would know, for certain, he was lying the correct direction, but I was too afraid of seeing his body accidentally dumped in the dirt; I looked away. "Tell me when they have turned him," I said quietly to Jake.

"It's done," Jake whispered a minute later. They lowered Sammy into the ground, again. Jake got up and grabbed a shovel, again. Jake buried Sammy for the second time, his tears rolling down his face and sprinkling the soil.

That evening, Sarah came upstairs upset about something and sat next to me on the couch. She had learned through her friends and on social media sites that school kids were talking, saying Sammy had committed suicide. "There is no way Sammy killed himself!" she said, crying. "And he would be totally upset for people to think that about him. And it's even worse if Peter or someone is responsible for his death, but people think he killed himself."

"That is frustrating, Sweetheart. It makes me angry too, but, I don't know what we can do about it," I said. "Maybe you could post something on your Facebook wall?" She promptly wrote a post.

Sarah's Facebook-

"This has been a horrific week, but I just wanted to thank everyone who has offered comfort to me and my family. Because so many people have asked about the nature of Sammy's death, I thought I would share that the detectives have told us this was not a suicide. They are still interviewing people and have several theories about what happened but have not made a definite conclusion yet."

I didn't know if the Facebook post would make a difference in the gossip, but it did provide a small amount of relief to Sarah. She felt she had at least tried to set the record straight. It made me feel a little better too.

Lying in bed later, I felt like my heart was broken, missing a chunk, and spewing blood. I could hardly breathe. I knew my children needed a strong momma. They were spinning in a confusing, dark world. They didn't understand how Sammy could be dead. They were sad and didn't know how to feel better. Normally, when one of them was lost, scared, or wandering, they would come to me, and I could give them a road map or provide insight or take their hand and lead them. I had no road map for this. I had no insight. I couldn't lead because, not only did I not know which direction to go, I could barely walk. I was crawling in the dirt scratching my nails into the earth trying not be swallowed into my own abyss. The agony was almost unendurable. I didn't know how I could keep going on let alone assist my children. None of us, Jake and I included, had the strength to stand up straight under the grief, let alone carry another at the same time.

Chapter 14

"No truth can cure the sorrow we feel from losing a loved one. No truth, no sincerity, no strength, no kindness can cure that sorrow."

-Haruki Murakami, *Norwegian Wood*

Friday, October 29
Five days after Sammy died

Again, I woke up as a dreadful sob pushed up and out of me. Again, I rolled toward Jake, and we held each other. It was becoming a daily early morning ritual. Before I opened my eyes or had formed a thought, out came the first huge wail. It was like when you are sick and wake up with vomit already coming up your throat, and you barely get your head over the side of the bed to the trashcan in time. The grief was coming out, and there was no stopping it. Pressing my face into Jake's chest so I wouldn't wake the kids, I sobbed for 20 or 30 minutes until—with the aid of a Xanax—I fell back asleep.

That morning, we went to the funeral home yet again. We had to meet with the lady who would assist us in selecting a headstone. I was exhausted. I felt like a zombie, but it needed to be done so we just kept going. I looked in a catalog at several options, and some of the headstones had photos on them. Generally, I wasn't a big fan of headstones with photos, but with the death of a child the idea of including pictures seemed right. We walked around the cemetery to see other peoples' headstones and what we thought looked nice, and finally selected one from the catalog that was black with gold flecks. Sammy would like the smooth black stone. We next had to figure out what we wanted engraved and what photos we would like to use, but we needed more time to think about it.

I was already out of steam by then and could do no more, so we left and returned home. We spent several hours selecting and emailing the photos we wanted on Sammy's headstone and when it was finished, I lay down to rest.

Our sleeping situation needed some attention. Starting the night before the funeral, when Jo went to stay at the hotel with her family, Sarah had slept with us. Adam and Lydia were taking nightly turns, with one in our bed and the other on couch cushions on our floor. More so than even the little ones, Sarah needed closeness and comfort for a while, especially at night. I suspected what image filled her mind when she closed her eyes to sleep. It was the image that came to my mind every night, and I hadn't actually seen it. Our bed was a little crowded, though, and I thought the kids might be sleeping with us for a long time. Our room was large enough to accommodate a futon, so I asked Jake to go buy one. While I rested, he and Sarah went shopping.

That evening Laura and Hank came over, and we all sat out on the back deck. Hank told us he had talked to the guy who supposedly told my cousin Ned that Sammy had been pulling a prank. Hank said the guy, with whom he was friends, denied it. "So," I said, a little disgusted, "Vince made it up, or your friend is lying." Hank felt certain his friend was being straight with him, which meant the story had been fabricated. I didn't know my cousin Ned very well, but I knew he did a good deal of business with Vince and Mother, they had weekly meetings together, and he and Vince seemed to be pals. I wondered if I talked to Ned if I could figure out if the hanging prank story possibly had been a miscommunication issue, or if it really had just been a blatant lie.

Up to that point in time, I had purposely avoided (as much as I could) expending *too* much thought or energy on figuring out what exactly had happened to Sammy the night he died. I just couldn't deal with the questions, the possibilities, or the implications while trying to handle all of the funeral details. But, Sammy had been properly buried, and I was ready to start to slowly and meticulously working through what I knew.

My brother-in-law Hank was a retired fire fighter and had some medical knowledge and death scene experience, in addition to being a logical, cool-headed individual. I trusted him and knew he was a good person with whom I could talk.

"I have given a lot of thought to Sammy's appearance when he died, and there is something that really bothers me. When a person is hanged, the noose around their neck will occlude, or block, the veins in the outer part of the neck, the jugulars. The jugulars drain the blood from the brain so when a person is hanged, blood is trapped in the head. The carotid arteries, which carry blood to the brain, are situated deeper in the neck, so whether they are blocked or not in a hanging depends on several factors, such as the weight of the victim, the presence or absence of well-developed neck muscles, and the width of the strap. If the carotids are blocked by the noose, blood cannot enter the brain. The person will pass out in six to ten seconds due to oxygen deprivation to the brain, and the person will appear pale, with no blood coming from his nose, eyes, or ears, no tongue engorgement, no bulging eyes, and no herniation of the brain down the spine. If the carotids are not blocked by the noose, they will continue to carry blood into the brain, where it will be trapped because it can't drain out through the blocked jugulars. The blood will start coming out of the eyes, nose, and mouth. Capillaries in the skin will start bursting causing petechiae, or little red dots in the skin. The tongue will become engorged. Eventually, there is no more room inside the skull, and the brain will herniate down the spinal cord resulting in sudden death. The thing that keeps bothering me is that I don't think Sammy weighed enough for the indirect pressure of the strap to have blocked his carotid arteries. He only weighed 100 lbs., plus he had well developed neck muscles, and the strap was nearly an inch wide. So, the carotids wouldn't have been blocked, and blood should have continued to be carried to his brain. His appearance, however—pale, no leaking blood, no bulging tongue—tells us blood didn't continue to flow into the brain. If he didn't weigh enough for the strap to block the blood flow through the carotids, how did Sammy have the appearance he did?" Hank and Laura said nothing but continued to listen attentively.

"There are some other things of note from the last year. About eight months ago, when Sammy came home from weekend visitation at Lucas' house, he was upset because he said Peter kept choking him. Peter didn't usually hold it very long, but it really bothered Sammy. I explained to Sammy that it should bother him, and that choking him was something neither Peter, nor anyone else, should be doing. I explained how by squeezing his neck, Peter could accidentally kill him or cause him to have a stroke. I told Sammy he might then spend the rest of his life paralyzed on one side of his body, drooling out of the side of his mouth, and unable to speak clearly. Naturally, the thought of living as an invalid horrified Sammy, and I was pretty certain he would be doing everything possible to prevent anyone from squeezing his neck in the future. I called Lucas and informed him of what Peter had been doing and explained the serious risks. I implored him to talk with Peter. Lucas never got back with me to let me know if he had discussed the issue with Peter. However, I assumed he did because after that, whenever Peter provoked or did something to Sammy, he would say, 'Oh, are you going to go home and tell Mommy now?' Sammy, Sarah, Adam, and Lydia had all heard him on different occasions and had told me."

"Next, two or three months ago over at Lucas's house, Peter and Sammy were playing Xbox downstairs, and they got into a fight. Peter pushed Sammy, and Sammy pushed him back. They started hitting each other, and then Peter climbed on top of Sammy, pinned his arms down with his knees, and started choking him. Sammy was strong, but Peter was four years older, probably 50 pounds heavier, and a foot taller than him. Sammy couldn't get Peter off of him. Sarah was downstairs reading and yelled for Peter to stop, but he didn't, so Sarah jumped up, ran over, and pulled Peter off Sammy."

"Here's the last thing. About three weeks ago, when the kids came home from the weekend at Lucas's, Sammy told us that Peter said he knew of a wrestling move called the sleeper choke hold that could take someone out in six seconds. The reason the victim passes out in six seconds is that the perpetrator's arm is hooked around the victim's neck with the inner elbow in front of the neck creating a fulcrum. When the elbow is squeezed by the perp., it puts direct pressure on the carotid arteries on each side of the victim's neck. Although it takes a significant amount of weight to indirectly block the carotids (for example, if a strap is pressing across six inches of neck), it takes very little when the pressure is applied directly to the carotids, as in this sleeper hold. With the sleeper hold, the pressure blocks the carotids, interrupting blood flow to the brain, and the victim will pass out in six to ten seconds. What if Peter tried the sleeper hold on Sammy, accidentally held it too long, and Sammy died? Then, Peter freaked out and hung him to cover it up?" I finally stopped and looked at Hank and Laura to see what they thought.

There wasn't a trace of surprise on Hank's face. He just said, "The day Sammy died, I looked at Peter's arms when we were over at Valerie's house to see if there were any scratch marks, but I couldn't tell because he had on a long sleeved shirt." I was a little taken aback that Hank had suspected Peter right away, but I shouldn't have been. Hank was very street smart and very observant, and he didn't miss much. Also, I knew Hank would never discuss lightly something so potentially incriminating unless he had serious suspicions.

"You were suspicious of Peter from the first day?" I asked, surprised, then validated, then horrified.

"He was acting strange, and I didn't believe Sammy would take his own life," he said simply.

"Well, we know that blood wasn't flowing to Sammy's brain. Either Sammy's carotids were blocked by the strap, or he already had been choked out when he was hung. That also explains why there were no kick or scuffmarks on the door. If blood flow to the brain had continued, he would have had a minute or two of residual oxygen in his lungs. He would have kicked and struggled to get free. If blood flow to the brain had continued, there would have been kick marks on the door and scratch marks on his neck where he would have tried to get the strap off. And after a minute or two when he passed out and died, he would have had blood coming from his nose, ears, eyes, petechiae and an engorged tongue."

"I have to figure out how much Sammy needed to weigh for the strap to have blocked his carotids. If he didn't weigh enough, then we know he didn't initially lose consciousness by hanging, and someone hung him after he was unconscious." No one said a word as we thought about alternative scenarios.

"Another thing that doesn't seem right," I told them, "is there was nothing for Sammy to climb on or step on to get his head into the strap; not even a piece of trim on the wall. I wondered if he might have shimmied up the side of the door, and knowing Sammy he probably could have, but it would have been tough because the door wouldn't stay still. I tried it. If he did manage to shimmy up, the strap had to have already been looped over the hinge on the opposite side of the door. So, he had to get ahold of it and get his head in it. Even if he did manage all of that, what was his intent? I see no indicators of depression or suicide. Plus, if it was suicide, Sammy was practical and would have used a chair or a stool to get up into the strap. Also, I think the strap would have been tied more like a noose and not just a big loop. So, was he just messing around and fell? That seems highly unlikely. Was he just sort of trying it out to see what it would feel like? It's hard to imagine him doing something like that. He wasn't reckless. I have never known him to try risky behaviors, and again, if he was just kinda trying it out, he would have had a chair in place. Also, if he was just messing around or trying it out, he wouldn't have turned on the bathroom fan or shut and locked his door. Supposedly, Peter had already gone to bed and was sleeping when this happened, but all three of the boys had been staying up late together on every visitation weekend for several months. It seems a little too convenient that this one particular night, Peter went to bed right when Lucas said to and in spite of Sammy being awake right next door in his room."

"To me, the likeliest scenario in all of this is that Peter performed a sleeper hold on Sammy, and then hung him. I don't know if they were trying it out, it went wrong, and Peter got scared, or if Peter got angry, did it, it went wrong, and he got scared, or if

Peter intentionally did all of it. But, if Sammy didn't weigh enough for his carotids to be blocked from the strap, then we know for certain someone else was involved. If he didn't weigh enough, then he was already out when he was hung."

Surely Peter wouldn't have purposefully killed his brother? But, if there was an accident, why hadn't he told the police instead of letting everyone assume Sammy had committed suicide? Unless he was too scared of getting in trouble to say what really happened, especially if he had lost his temper. If he had planned it, of course he wouldn't say anything. Contemplating the horror that Peter might have killed Sammy—accidentally or, God forbid, intentionally—sent my mind screaming in horror and pain.

We talked for a while longer about possible scenarios and reflected on what we knew as we tried desperately to determine the truth. Knowing what had happened wouldn't bring him back, but Sammy's life was over and he deserved for the truth about how he died to be known, especially if his life had been taken from him. Eventually, our hearts and minds were exhausted, Hank and Laura left. Jake and I headed to bed.

That night, our sleeping arrangement was much better. Jake and Sarah had purchased a double-sized futon and set it up in our bedroom. Jake slept on it with Adam, and I slept in the bed between Sarah and Lydia. Sometime during the night, Jake climbed in bed next to me, which was very typical Jake—I-need-to-be-close-to-you—behavior and was a quality I loved about him because I felt the same way and had the same need.

Chapter 15

"If only it were so simple! If only there were evil people somewhere insidiously committing evil deeds, and it were necessary only to separate them from the rest of us and destroy. But the line dividing good and evil cuts through the heart of every human being. And who is willing to destroy a piece of his own heart?"

-Aleksandr Solzhenitsyn, *The Gulag Archipelago* 1918- 1956

Saturday, October 30

Six Days After Sammy Died

I woke up sobbing and wailing. I cried into Jake' chest. I went back to sleep. A few hours later, after I awoke again and cried some more, I lay in bed thinking. Where had Vince's story about Sammy pulling a prank come from? It had to be one of two possibilities. The first possibility was that Ned told Vince the story, but neither one had fact checked it. It could have been one of those word of mouth situations where one person says something like, "I knew Sammy and he wouldn't have killed himself. Maybe he was trying to pull a Halloween prank on his brothers and it went wrong?" Then, the person listening (a girl's dad in this case) tells the next person (his employer who happens to be my cousin) only when the dad tells it, he says, "my daughter says Sammy didn't commit suicide. She thinks he was pulling a Halloween prank on his brothers only it went wrong. The cops should look into something like that." When my cousin tells my brother-in-law, he mentions the dad is going to tell the cops, and then Vince tells me the whole thing. The second possibility was that Vince fabricated the entire story. I could imagine him and my mother—with good intentions—deciding it would be better to tell me that story if they didn't want me (as well as everyone else in town) thinking Sammy had committed suicide. In the past, both Vince and Mother sometimes played fast and loose with the truth. I might have simply accepted the story as fact had I not suspected the involvement of another party in Sammy's death. I did suspect though, and a mother searching for the truth about her child's death is like a dog searching for a bone.

Per our court-issued parenting plan, it was Lucas's year to have the kids on Halloween from 5:00-9:00 pm. Sarah had Halloween plans with some friends, which she had already told Lucas about prior to Sammy's death. Adam and Lydia were supposed go to his house, but they were anxious and felt uncomfortable about going. They said if they *had* to go to Lucas's house, they wanted Jake and me to go with them. Frankly, until we knew what had happened to Sammy, we also felt uncomfortable with them going. I would have to discuss alternatives for the visit with Lucas, but whether we could work something out or not would ultimately depend on him since it was his scheduled time. The kids were traumatized. They were trying to digest the horror that Sammy was dead. The manner and circumstances of his death made it much scarier. The fact that they were peacefully sleeping in their beds, while Sammy was hanging in his room all night made it even more creepy. None of them believed Sammy had taken his own life, so they were trying to figure out how he ended up hanged. They all thought Peter had behaved extremely odd the day of Sammy's death. Hearing Sarah tell the story of how the morning unfolded, and the strange things Peter had said and done before the cops arrived, increased their suspicion that Peter had played a part, and that made them reluctant to be anywhere near him. They also didn't want to be near Lucas' house or even Lucas for that matter. They said he didn't listen to them, and they didn't feel safe with him because, after all, look what had happened to Sammy.

I dreaded communicating with Lucas about an alteration to the visitation schedule. It wouldn't go well. It rarely went well when I asked him for anything. However, with Sammy's strange death, the police investigation, and the kids wanting to do things differently, I had to discuss some alternative options with Lucas.

I sent him a text asking if we could talk about his scheduled holiday time with the kids for Halloween the following day. He responded that he was planning to pick them up at 5:00 pm. I texted him back and said we needed to talk about the visit. About ten minutes later, Lucas called.

"Okay," I said to him, "Obviously, the kids are not in the best place emotionally right now. They are freaked out. They have been sleeping with me every night, and they don't seem to want to be too far away from me or from home."

"Well," he said, "they will be with me so they will be fine."

I continued, "They are afraid to go in your house and -."

"I have no plans to take them back to my house tomorrow," he cut in.

"Okay, great. Well, I was wondering if we could all do something together for Halloween this year?" I asked tentatively. Silence. "We could all take them door to door. Or, we could go over to your brother's house and hang out there? Or whatever you want to do, maybe we could just tag along?"

"No," Lucas began clearly irritated, "It is my visitation time with my children, and I don't need supervision."

"It's not because I think you need supervision," I said, an edge growing in my voice, "It is because the children are scared and upset about Sammy, and they said they would feel the best if we all went together."

"Well, it's been a week, and they are going to have to get used to it sometime. So, no. I plan on picking them up at five o'clock per the court-mandated holiday schedule."

"Lucas, you're right. It has been a week. It has *only* been a week! In time things will get back to some kind of normal, but we just buried Sammy on Wednesday and then again on Thursday!" I had no reservoir of patience into which I could tap to deal with his determined obstinacy.

"Yes, and I haven't had my children alone for a week!" He yelled.

"Of course, you haven't" I yelled back. "The only scheduled visit that you didn't get to have was on Wednesday and that was because we were burying Sammy!"

"I will be picking up the kids tomorrow at 5 pm, and if there's a problem, I will call the sheriff," said the father of my children, the good minister, as he hung up.

I cursed loudly at the backyard.

"What did he say?" asked the ever patient Jake. I relayed the conversation to him

"Maybe it would be better if you talked to him?" I suggested. He and I always clash, but you are more patient and slower to anger."

"Okay," he said. "It's worth a try."

Jake stepped out into our backyard and called Lucas. He explained that the kids were fearful and would feel the best if we all went together. It seemed to go well until he said, "In general, I think it is just better for kids to be with their mother when they really need comforting, and this is one of those rare periods of time."

"Well," Lucas retorted, "I am their father and I can comfort them just fine. And another thing, the kids don't need to be upset right now by Jane causing a scene tomorrow when I come to get them."

"If you really feel that way, Lucas, why would you call the sheriff? I mean, that's really going to cause a scene."

"Because it's my allotted time to have them," Lucas said tersely, raising his voice.

"If you think calling the sheriff rather than us all just going together is better for the children, then you are clueless," Jake said, finally feeling exasperated. Lucas dropped a few colorful words and then hung up on Jake.

Laura stopped by later, and I told her about our morning. "So, what are you going to do tomorrow?" she asked.

"I guess if he is unwilling to do anything differently, we will stay here and the kids will go with him," I said, in frustration. "I was hoping he would be willing to work together over the next several weeks and months. I doubt this is going to be the only time this comes up. The kids are freaked out. They are in shock. They are scared. He has got to be sensitive to them and work with me to help them deal with this and that might mean we will need to do things a little differently for a while, at least while the police investigation is ongoing." I should have called my attorney and asked him to get us into court ASAP to get some temporary visitation order while the investigation was on-going. Unfortunately, it was a Saturday and I didn't think I couldn't get ahold of him.

"Well," Laura said, "I could ask Hank to call him and try to talk to him?" I didn't think it would make a difference, but it was worth a shot.

"Okay, thanks. I don't see what it can hurt." She called Hank, who called Lucas, and then called us back.

"Hank says that when Lucas answered, he said, 'Oh, hey, Hank. I just got off the phone with Vince.'"

"What?" I snapped. "Why was Vince talking to Lucas?"

"I don't know. Hank was a little confused for a moment thinking we might have already asked Vince to call Lucas, and therefore another call was unnecessary. Regardless, Hank said Lucas wouldn't listen to him at all or hear what he had to say once he started explaining why he was calling. He said Lucas became quite rude."

"Lucas must have called Vince about our conversation this morning. If Vince, Valerie, and Mother didn't go to *such* efforts to make Lucas feel so comfortable, perhaps Lucas wouldn't feel he could so easily call them!" Why hadn't Vince called to tell us Lucas had phoned him. I felt like my brother-in-law was repeatedly withholding information or excluding me from conversations he was having with my ex-husband. Also, why did Lucas initiate a discussion about our children's Halloween visit with one of *my* family members?

Since our separation in November 2004, I had never asked Lucas if we could do something together. Did he not understand that how we handled our children over the following months would be instrumental in their coping and healing? Why was he so unwilling to adjust the evening's plan and let us all go together? Yes, he was within his legal rights to refuse to alter the plan and to insist the kids go with him, but could he not see that in so doing he would be hurting the children and his relationship with them by being insensitive to their emotional needs? They would be upset that he hadn't listened to them? Sorry, kids. Apparently, Sammy being hanged to death is not a good enough reason to adjust the visitation schedule.

Over the previous week, I had suppressed my anger about so many things. I felt like a boiling kettle ready to blow my top. Sammy was dead. He had died horribly. The reason for his death was not clear. Lucas was telling others it was a suicide. Why was he telling people Sammy committed suicide when we didn't know what happened? Why was he so willing to accept what didn't make sense? Why wasn't he considering other causes of death? Why was he unwilling to discuss anything with me about Sammy's death? Why was he unwilling to talk about or acknowledge Peter's strange behavior? Why was he unwilling to work together as we tried to help the kids get through this? And why was he calling my family members? Since our divorce, I had made it a point to *avoid* most communication with his family, because they were *his* family! He needed to be able to rely on them, trust them, talk to them, and lean on them, just like I needed to be able to with *my* family! Why couldn't he reciprocate the courtesy? Worse, why wasn't my family respecting appropriate boundaries regarding interactions with him? I wish I could have called a family meeting and said, "Everybody, knock it off! There is an active police investigation because the police don't believe Sammy's death was a suicide! That means they are checking out Lucas and Peter to determine if they were in some way responsible. So, stop worrying about Lucas and Peter, stop having private contact and communication with them, let the investigation proceed, and please pour your love and energy into Jake and the kids and me!"

I called Valerie to find out what Lucas had discussed with Vince, but she didn't know anything. She was in Dallas, Vince was in Reno, and he hadn't told her about speaking with Lucas. She could tell I was angry, and she became defensive. I informed her that her husband might consider keeping his nose out of my family business.

I then called Vince and asked him when he was planning to call and tell me he'd had a conversation with my ex-husband about something regarding our children, and everything went downhill from there. Vince was on the defense and started by telling me it would be unwise to deny Lucas his visitation; that ill-informed comment was the last straw. His statement was a perfect example of why my family needed to distance themselves from Lucas. I hadn't told Lucas I was going to deny him his visitation. I had suggested having a more inclusive Halloween with all of us together. I had held my tongue several times over the previous five days as I observed Vince, Valerie, and Mother's odd over-involvement with and concern for Lucas throughout the funeral. Vince taking phone calls from Lucas, and failing to communicate with me about their conversation further exacerbated things. That Vince assumed whatever Lucas told him was accurate and was so presumptuous as to advise me without first talking with me snapped my remaining bits of restraint, and I unleashed on him; I gave Vince a piece of my mind and then some. I probably used enough curse words to make even *The Wolf of Wall Street* blush. Had Dad been alive, he might have told me that some of the things I had said would have been "better left unsaid." Had Dad been alive, the conversation wouldn't have taken place because my family wouldn't have been interacting as they had with Lucas! Exasperated and aware that more words would cause more harm than good, I handed the phone to Jake.

Jake explained to Vince that we would handle our family issues with Lucas, and we preferred Vince and other family members not engage if/when Lucas contacted them. Lucas should be contacting and working through issues regarding our children with us, not my family. Jake plainly said we preferred Vince and my other family members simply maintain polite, public interactions with my ex-husband, not personal, private conversations.

"Okay," said Vince.

For many reasons following my divorce, my dad advised the family to have minimal contact with Lucas. For the most part, the family complied. As a result, there were infrequent problems. However, when Dad died the winds had changed. About a month after his death, Mother came to our house and made some stern pronouncements, including telling us, "there's a new sheriff in town" and that Jake and I needed "to get our butts back in church." She also informed us she would be doing some things differently than Dad. Over the next 18 months, one of those things was she had more contact with Peter; Peter lived with Lucas so that meant more interaction with Lucas. Mom, Vince, or Valerie would contact Lucas about various things, arrange visits, and even plan vacations with Peter. I didn't love all of their interaction with Lucas and involvement with Peter, but I had to accept it if I wanted to keep the waters calm with my family. Also, I could understand my mother's desire to maintain a relationship with Peter, although it did seem strange to me that during those same 18 months she had very little interaction with my other four children who lived with me.

In the week following Sammy's death, Mom (and therefore Vince and Valerie) seemed to be continually in contact with Lucas, while, conversely, being less in contact with and more distant from me. I was uncertain as to the reason. Perhaps, they thought I would be less than fair to Lucas throughout the funeral, but that didn't make sense as I knew they felt I was more than fair to him throughout our divorce. I hoped their behavior wasn't a passive aggressive response to me snapping at Mother the day Sammy died (although my gut was telling me that was precisely the reason.)

I made efforts to be fair to Lucas throughout the funeral—regardless of his non-reciprocity—because it was the right thing to do. I called and included him regarding every major decision. I didn't have to invite Lucas over to my sister's house the day Sammy died, nor did I have to call and tell him what time the detectives were going to the Sprint store the following morning. I didn't have to suggest and be willing to allow his brother to officiate the funeral, notify him of the time of the appointment with the funeral home director, or order a flower arrangement for him to display beside Sammy's casket. I tried to achieve some parental solidarity for the funeral when I asked Lucas if the three of us, Jake, Lucas, and I could alternately read aloud from the book, *Time for Bed*. (Fifteen minutes before the funeral, Lucas had informed me he would be reading aloud by himself from a different children's book and not reading *Time for Bed* with us.) I also didn't have to notify him of Sammy's reburial. Did my mother not recognize I had behaved graciously to Lucas in all of those ways despite the fact he didn't return the courtesy? Perhaps, she was unaware. Nevertheless, from my perspective, Mom, Vince, and Valerie had given more consideration to Lucas during the previous week than they had Jake, the kids, and me. My angry phone call and conversation with Vince certainly wouldn't improve family relations, but my days of more level-headed consideration during conflict had died along with my child.

Chapter 16

"The whole world can become the enemy when you lose what you love."

-Kristina McMorris, *Bridge of Scarlet Leaves*

Sunday, October 31st
One Week After Sammy Died

For Halloween, Adam decided to wear Sammy's Hercules costume (the one Sammy had picked out four days before he died) since Sammy couldn't wear it himself. The costume wasn't something Adam normally would have selected, but he missed his brother, he felt bad Sammy's life was over, and he thought wearing Sammy's costume would be a way to honor and remember him.

I had no desire whatsoever to take the kids trick or treating. None. It felt completely wrong to do what we would normally do since Sammy was dead. It felt wrong that other kids got to go trick or treating, but Sammy couldn't. It felt wrong for us to go around collecting candy and laughing and having fun, but, oh yeah, sorry you can't go, Sammy. You're dead. What was the right thing to do? I didn't know. Jake and I talked about it. Disregarding what we wanted or desired, we tried to think only about what was the best for the kids. They were suffering every day. It wasn't as though they didn't fully feel the loss of Sammy. For their sakes, we felt the need to take them trick or treating. We hoped it might do them some good to have a pleasant, maybe even fun, evening. We would take them when they returned from their visitation time as we had the other years when Lucas had them.

I received a text from Lucas saying he would be picking the children up at 6:00 pm and returning them at 8:00 pm. He had decided to shorten the time which was great, but he wouldn't agree to Jake and me going with them. Perhaps he thought I was exaggerating the emotional state of our children. Maybe he felt getting them back on the schedule we had used fairly rigidly since the divorce was the best thing for them. If so, I disagreed. Normally, yes, routines are good for kids, and typically, I loved routine. However, Sammy's sudden and unexplained death had changed everything. Our routines had to be adjusted for a while according to the children's needs; it was not the time for being rigid.

Jo arrived with her partner Carl and two of her daughters. Adam and Lydia got dressed, and when Lucas pulled up outside at the pickup time, Jo walked them out to his car. He didn't come to the door for pick-ups, and Jake and I were both so frustrated that we couldn't stomach seeing him that day.

Victoria showed up which was a pleasant surprise, and we all ate supper and had drinks. I was antsy and mostly quiet while the little ones were gone. The heartache I felt over Sammy took all of my energy and attention, and I marveled that people could talk about things besides his death. Obviously, other people were going to talk about other things, but *I* couldn't do it. How does a mother just go on with life, just shootin' the breeze with friends, when one of her children died a week before?

Victoria asked to speak to me privately, so we stepped out onto the deck. "Okay, Bennet (Tori's fiancée) and I have been talking. When we were at Mom and Dad's house the other day, I was looking at the family photo taken at the last family wedding. Two people from that picture are now missing, Papa and Sammy. I really don't want anyone else to be missing from the family photo at my wedding." She then said they were tentatively planning on moving their wedding date from February 2012 to February 2011. I was surprised, but not totally shocked. Only two months before in August, when Victoria and Bennet had first gotten engaged, she had wanted to set the wedding date for 2011. For several reasons at that time, I advised her to wait (as had her parents.) However, when someone dies, a sense of urgency seems to shorten time. I understood that feeling and that Tori was experiencing it. I started to speak, but Tori went on, "Also, I would really love for you to be my Matron of Honor."

"Ohh that's exciting, Tori. I get the whole sense of urgency thing, and I am honored that you want me to be your Matron of Honor. Maybe this will give our family something positive on which to focus. I have to say though, I have absolutely no idea how I will feel in four months. I *want* to be able to do it, and I *hope* to be able to do it. But, I don't know if I *will* be able to do it." If I had any inkling then how I would feel four months later, the date to which the wedding was moved, I would have said something completely different. I would have said there was no way I would be in any condition to attend the wedding, and if her concern was to make sure everyone she loved would be there—and in the wedding photo—it would be best to keep the wedding date for February 2012. I ought to have known; normal, somewhat logical me would have known. However, normal me was gone, and it would be years before I returned to any clear, logical thinking.

If I had expressed to Tori that there was absolutely no way my family would be able to attend should she move her wedding to the new date (which was only three and a half months away) she might not have changed the date. However, she was young and inexperienced with life, and I was one week into grief and unable to exercise good judgement to make major decisions. I had never lost a child before and I had absolutely no clue what the road ahead of me held. I genuinely thought the wedding—and all of the preparations—might be a pleasant and enjoyable distraction from the grief! Tip: never ask a grieving mother for major life advice or use her as a sounding board for at least a year or two after her child's death. If you are the grieving mother, do not attempt to make any major life decisions for a year or two following your child's death.

The rest of my time waiting for Adam and Lydia to return was passed listening to the others chat, drinking cocktails, and smoking. During my divorce, the kids were unaware I started smoking. They each realized it in time, but I never allowed them to actually *see* me smoke. I felt *seeing* me smoke—as opposed to only *knowing* I smoked—would have a stronger negative effect on them, acclimating them to see it as "normal" or as not a bad thing. That rule had gone out the window on October 24, when Sammy died and I ripped off the patch. Not only was I smoking again, I was smoking more than ever. Yet the kids wanted and needed to be near me more. Something had to give, and I didn't want it to be my sanity (if I tried quitting then) or my children's emotional needs (if I didn't allow them to be near me when they needed to) so it had to be my rule. Ideally, I would have quit smoking and continued with the patch. However, things were not, nor would they ever again be, ideal. So, I allowed them to come with me when I went outside to smoke. Psychologically, I knew smoking was a maladaptive coping mechanism. Medically, I was aware of potential detrimental side effects. Emotionally, it had soothed me through some hard times, and I was in no place to quit. It would be years before I was anywhere near ready to try quitting again.

When little ones finally returned home, Lydia had a strained look on her face. She came directly to me, sat on my lap, and put her head on my shoulder.

"Did everything go okay, Schmoo?" I asked. She started crying, and I rubbed her back.

"It was weird, Mommy. Peter was so weird."

"What do you mean, 'Peter was so weird?'" I pressed her

"I mean, he didn't act at all like Sammy just died!" she yelled angrily. "He was like, happy and really hyper. Not sad at all." I silently considered the possible explanations for Peter's behavior.

We left soon after to take the kids trick or treating. As was our annual tradition, we went to Nana's house first. When Mother opened her front door, I was taken aback to see Peter standing right behind her. I was completely surprised. He had been with Lucas during the little ones visit; I had no idea when and how he had arrived at Mother's. Lucas and Mother had apparently talked and arranged something. "Hello, Peter," I said coldly. That was the best I could do. I felt a tangled mess of emotions toward Peter, and irritation and frustration with Mother who had not even let me know he would be there. Peter was exactly as Lydia described: light-hearted and jolly, even friendly. He looked as if the weight of the world had rolled off his shoulders. My mother gave the kids their Halloween treats, we took a few uncomfortable group pictures, and then we made a quick exit. As soon as we were out of her house, I glanced at Jake. He was already staring at me. We were thinking the same thing: Peter was behaving like a person who thought he had gotten away with something and was relieved.

Monday, November 1
Eight Days After Sammy Died

Eight days after Sammy's death, we had an appointment with an attorney. It was the last thing I wanted to be doing. I would have preferred to be at the cemetery lying prostrate on the ground six feet above my boy, weeping until I had no more tears. However, after the fight with Lucas regarding the Halloween plans and his threat about calling the sheriff, I thought it best if I was proactive and contacted an attorney. If Lucas was going to involve the law to help work through visits with our kids, I wanted to be prepared. As for crying until I had no more tears, I was beginning to think there was no such thing. As soon as I awoke each morning, the tears started. All day long, every time I turned around, tears would come. I think the pipeline to our tear source must lie in the heart, and when the heart breaks, so does the tear pipe.

The attorney advised we start communicating with Lucas by email instead of text in case documentation of our efforts to collaborate became necessary. He gave us the name of someone who was a local respected children's advocate and therapist and told us to consult her about helping work through visitation issues with Lucas. He said she was very good, and should we have to go to court she would be an advocate purely for the children (and not for either parent). I felt that was exactly what the children needed. As soon as we left the attorney's office, I called and set up an appointment for a consultation with her the next day at 5:00 pm.

Next, we met with a therapist we were considering for our family. She was very warm and personable and seemed perfect to help guide us through the worst of our grief. I made several appointments with her starting the following day.

When we got home, Jake and Sarah headed back out. The week before, we had noticed our neighbors sitting around a fire pit in their yard. Since I only ever smoked outside and at least one of the kids accompanied me, having our own fire pit would make for a warm and calming ambiance. My birthday was November 3, but I had already told Jake I didn't want to celebrate: what a ridiculous notion. I did, however, suggest he get a fire pit for my present. Then, he wouldn't feel bad for not getting me a birthday gift, he wouldn't feel guilty for spending money on an unnecessary item (since that money would have been spent on my birthday gift), and everyone would benefit. We agreed a fire pit might be a pleasant thing to have over the next several months, and we needed all the pleasant we could get. I thought it might even be therapeutic. Jake and Sarah returned home an hour or two later with a fire pit.

Up to that point, Sarah had been managing decently (not awful, but not great.) That evening, sitting outside around the fire she was particularly antsy. She looked miserable. She kept getting up and sitting back down. I have dealt with anxiety before, and that is what she looked like: anxious.

"Sarah, are you okay?" I asked.

"I'm fine," she answered shortly. She was, of course, not fine, and she was not okay. It was a stupid question. We were experiencing a tragedy foreign to us. Regular lingo was not going to cut it. I needed to learn the vernacular of grief.

"Are you just missing Sammy?" I asked. Good lord, but I was clumsy.

"Yes!" she yelled, and jumped out of her chair. "I am going for a drive," she announced and rushed off to get her keys. I hopped up and followed her inside.

"Wait, honey. I don't think that's a good idea," I said. She wasn't listening. She grabbed her purse and her keys and charged out the front door. "Sweetheart, it probably isn't safe for you to be driving when you're upset," I said, following her.

"I'm fine!" she yelled,

"Honey, let's just talk," I said.

"*Mom*! I need to go for a drive and be alone!" she yelled, and got into her car and took off. I could have told her no, that she was too upset to drive, but honestly I was caught a little off-guard. In her entire life, Sarah had never had an irresponsible moment, nor had she ever been the least bit belligerent or rebellious. Knowing how different her behavior was from her norm, I didn't try harder to prevent her leaving. I knew she was struggling. Our previous parent-child-respect-obedience construct would no longer be effective. My children needed complete understanding and gentleness for a while. We were all only a step away from flipping life the bird and running wild and naked through the woods—or, in other words, going nuts.

I watched her drive off. A very private person, Sarah despised breaking down in tears in front of anyone and did her best never to let it happen. The tears were running down her face when she got in her car, which (if I hadn't already noticed) communicated to me how upset she was (usually she controlled her tears in until she was in private). She knew she shouldn't be driving while she was so upset; she didn't care. I got it. I felt it, too. Sammy was dead. Who cared about anything? If I die, I die. But good god, I didn't want to have to try to live through another child's death. I was a nervous wreck and called Laura. When I told her what happened, she was just as nervous about Sarah driving as I was, which somehow helped a little. Twenty minutes later Sarah pulled back into the driveway. "See, Mom. I was fine," she proclaimed. She no longer seemed as anxious, but I felt a bite in her voice. She was dealing with anger.

"You were, Honey. This time. But you're smarter than to drive when you're upset."

"Well, I had to do something! I felt like I was going to jump out of my skin!" she said, defiantly.

"Yeah, I do understand that. I'm sorry, Sweetie. I was just worried. I love you."

It was not the last time she would go for one of those drives. They became a regular coping mechanism for Sarah. After the first few times, I asked if she just drove around or if she went anywhere specific. She told me she went to Sammy's grave, which about gave me a heart attack. Generally, she went at night. I was scared to death for her to be in the cemetery alone at night. Frankly, I was surprised she wasn't afraid, but she said visiting Sammy soothed her. I asked her not to go alone at night anymore, because I worried it wasn't safe. A week or two later, she came to me, upset, and asked if she could resume her visits to the cemetery whenever she felt the need. "Mom," she implored me, "it is probably safer for me to be sitting in the cemetery crying than driving around crying." She was probably right. It made me nervous, but it was important to her and she found it helpful. Besides, who knew if any of my efforts to protect my children even made a difference? I had always been considered over-protective, but that hadn't helped Sammy. So, I told her it was okay. If it was something she felt helped her, I understood. Over the next two years, her spontaneous drives would become a regular occurrence.

I was glad I had an appointment for her to start counseling with the therapist the following day. Sarah needed to be able to talk about her feelings with someone independent of the situation, someone who had the strength, training, and insight to assist her.

Tuesday, November 2

Nine days after Sammy died, Jake drove Sarah and me to the therapist's office for our first session. I still hadn't driven at all (except once to the visitation). I was entirely too jumpy, weepy, dazed, and distracted—a bundle of high-octane emotion—to feel I could drive safely. We had our sessions, and Sarah and I both bonded well with the therapist. It was a relief to say anything I wanted regarding my feelings about Sammy, his death, the funeral, Peter, my mother, to someone with whom I need not worry about weighing down with the heaviness of my grief or fret about depressing with my tears.

After therapy, we had a family appointment with our astute young physician, who never seemed to have a problem with my nurse-mode tendency to diagnose my family's ailments. I wanted him to be aware of what had happened in case we had any resulting health issues. In fact, we already had a few problems. Both girls and I were having daily stomachaches. Before we ate, our stomachs burned, and after we ate, we had digestion issues. I asked if we were over-producing stomach acid because of the stress, and in need of Prilosec or Nexium. He confirmed we did. I described the previous night when Sarah had been agitated and anxious. I told him it looked like anxiety and wondered if she had been on the verge of a panic attack. I said I'd been struggling with anxiety also, and I still had some Xanax from after dad died that I had taken the previous several days. I described how my stomach would begin to feel tight, and I would feel antsy and nervous. He confirmed that both my symptoms and Sarah's sounded like anxiety. He told us not be surprised as anxiety was normal after the death of a close loved one, more so with the death of a child, and even more so with a traumatic, unexpected, sudden death. Unable to hold myself together, I wept as I told him what we knew about Sammy's death. I was leaving a trail of motherly tears throughout my beloved hometown, but I had little to no control over the crying. My doctor asked if I still was taking the anti-depressant/anti-anxiety med Effexor I had started following Dad's death. I was. He told me not to be surprised if I needed to increase my dosage. He prescribed Nexium for Sarah, Lydia, and me for our stomachs, and Xanax for Sarah and me for anxiety. Jake and Adam needed no medication, but he said to keep an eye out specifically for depression in Jake and anxiety in Adam and Lydia.

At 5:00 pm, Jake and I met with the child advocate therapist. Upon our arrival, a little tuxedo cat sat outside the front door of the therapist's office. She looked right at us and stared as we got out of the van. She then walked straight to us—while maintaining her steady gaze—and rubbed up against our legs, purring affectionately. Being huge cat lovers, Jake and I instantly were taken with her. Samuel had been highly allergic to animals so we had never been able to have any (although we had tried). Unable to resist the pretty kitten, Jake picked her up, stroked her black fur, and had a little conversation her. She looked about six months old, appeared well cared for, had been spayed, and her front claws were removed. Assuming she belonged to someone who lived nearby, we reluctantly put her down and stepped inside the office.

Our meeting with the child advocate therapist went well. I told her about Sammy's death and briefly gave the history of the divorce, the visitation schedule, and the general story about Peter. I told her I was concerned that the children's biological father was not, and would not be, sensitive to the kids' changing needs during the next several weeks, months, and years, and I told her about what happened over Halloween as an example. I also talked with her about my concerns regarding Peter—his possible involvement in Sammy's death, if he might have an empathy disorder, and if she could and would evaluate him (yes, she could, and yes, she would.) I filled her in on everything I thought might be helpful to her as she assisted the kids in working through the issues, as well as things that would be important for them to address with Lucas.

When we exited the building two hours later, Miss Tuxedo Cat was perched outside the door as if she had been waiting for us the whole time. Once again, she made and sustained direct eye contact with us. We held her and loved on her one more time before we left.

Later that evening, I started thinking about a subject I hadn't given much thought over the previous ten days: sex. Following my dad's death, Jake and I didn't engage in sexual activity for six weeks. I was too sad and had no desire. About a year later, Jake talked with me about that period of time; he shared how difficult those six-weeks of no intimacy had been for him, and not merely on a physical level. We had always appreciated that when we shared consistent, regular intimacy, we felt more closely connected, and some of our emotional needs were met. Generally, we both felt that if one of us desired intimacy, the other should lovingly engage. Jake told me abstaining for that six-week period had made him feel less secure, less loved, less needed, and less connected to me.

With Sammy's death, I knew his need would be even greater. He also was very emotionally wounded. Over the previous five years, Sammy had grown closer to Jake than he had even to me. They were kindred spirits. They thought alike, acted alike, and shared a close connection. Regular physical intimacy would be imperative for Jake's healing, and I would come to see it as instrumental in my own healing as well.

It had been ten nights since our last encounter on Saturday, October 23. We had received the tragic wakeup call from Sarah the following morning. Jake hadn't mentioned the topic to me, because that wasn't his way. Not wanting me to feel obligated in my fragile state, he wouldn't bring it up. He wouldn't want me to do what I might not feel ready to do, and for that I loved him more. I loved him for his generosity, his consideration, and his self-sacrificing heart. I determined I needed to take initiative in this area.

With the kids sleeping in our room, we had to find a different location in the house. We utilized one of the kid's bedrooms. For me, that first post-Sammy experience was neither pleasant nor fulfilling. I kept turning my head so Jake wouldn't notice my sadness. I knew if he saw any tears he would feel awful and stop, putting my feelings before his own needs as he always did. I adored my sensitive husband. My mildly conflicted emotions about our activity didn't compare with my love for him, my desire to do what I could for him, and my appreciation for his un-selfish heart. I held him close so he would be unaware of my tears, and struggled privately with my horrible thoughts. *Sammy is dead in the ground and this is what we are doing? Sammy will never experience sex, or any of life's greatest gifts. Are we seriously trying to have pleasure while across town Sammy is dead in a grave?* I felt like throwing up. With the next two encounters, the nausea and unpleasant thoughts decreased a little, but it wasn't until the fourth time we had sex that I was able to appreciate the closeness with my husband unencumbered by unpleasant thoughts or feelings. I was finally able to feel that bond of oneness, totally connected with my best friend and to take comfort in our intimacy. From that fourth time on, I felt no more internal conflict during sex.

I mention this topic because it seems to be a huge problem among bereaved parents. Had either one of us been unwilling to engage, we both would have been denied what was ultimately a healing and comforting balm to our battered psyches. Had I acted only on cues I received from my body, it would have been a very long time before any kind of sexual activity resumed between us. We wouldn't have had that unspoken closeness that comes with regular sexual intimacy. Our gentle lovemaking would be the one thing we could both look forward to at the end of each long and difficult day. It was not like some of the more passion-filled nights before our son died, but it was tender and sweet, a holding and sharing of ourselves with the other to love, soothe, and comfort during the darkest nights of our lives.

Chapter 17

"There is only one way to achieve happiness on this terrestrial ball, and that is either to have a clear conscious or none at all."

-Ogden Nash

Wednesday, November 3

Ten days after Sammy's death, the kids returned to school. When they were gone, I lay in bed sobbing and crying and finally took a Xanax to get a little sleep. Lydia called me after lunch to come get her. Someone had said something to her about her brother "killing himself." I had told her if she got upset about anything during the day, to go to the counselor's office. She did, but she still felt weepy and bothered and wanted to come home. I understood. I knew it had to feel so weird to be going back to school again—back to the normal activities of daily living—when for us, nothing felt "normal".

Later in the day I spoke with Detective Higgins and asked if they had gotten any new information from Peter. A day or two after Sammy's funeral, they had called Peter into the police station for a third interview. She said no. Peter continued to say almost exactly the same thing in every interview. I asked her if that was not evidence in itself. I had read that in a true accounting of an event, things changed a little as more details were recalled. To that, she didn't have much to say.

I decided to invite Peter over to our house to ask him some questions myself. For many, many years, Peter and I had been close. I never even had a single worry about him having difficulty with the divorce. In fact—for various reasons that I won't go into—I had anticipated he might be *glad*. Regardless, we did have the history of our years of deep, candid talks from before all of the unpleasantness, so I felt I should at least try to get him to talk about Sammy's death.

On my birthday that Wednesday, I called Peter and invited him to come over. Surprisingly, he agreed to come. I have no idea why he agreed. Perhaps, because he was guilty and wanted to find out what I knew. Maybe he wanted to try and convince me he was innocent, or he wanted to confess. He *didn't* agree to come over because he missed me. I figured it would probably accomplish nothing, but I still had to try. Although Peter was not street smart—he had very little common sense—he was very book smart (as my dad would have said.) He seemed to have an almost photographic memory. It was possible he had the highest IQ of all my children. He was very good at games of strategy and rarely lost to anyone at chess. He was also very unemotional (with the exception of anger), so he wasn't easily rattled. I desperately wanted to know what happened to Samuel, and there were too many things about his death—the scene, the intent, Peter's demeanor, and Peter's responses—that, in my mind, pointed to Peter. I felt certain Peter knew more than he was saying and fairly confident he was at least partly responsible. I didn't know if it was purely an accident, if Peter lost his temper and in the heat of the moment did something, or, god forbid, if he had planned the entire thing. I probably had no chance of getting him to open up about what happened, but I would try. For everyone's sake—including Peter's—I would try. In part, I wanted Peter to tell me what had happened because I hoped I could better process it then and have a little more closure (as could Jake, the kids, and everyone else.) I also felt like there was a small window of opportunity when Peter might talk, and if he didn't talk soon about what happened, I feared what it would do to him. Also, if we didn't clear the air soon—meaning, either he convinced me he wasn't involved or he told me what really happened—I had serious doubts about whether Peter and I could ever have any kind of relationship again. If he was in any way responsible, he certainly would need professional help getting through the aftermath of emotions. In fact, regardless of whether or not he had any responsibility in what happened, he would need professional help, just like the rest of us! My guess was if the boys had been messing around and had an accident, he *might* tell me. If he had lost his temper and done something, he probably wouldn't tell me. If he planned the whole thing, then, of course, he wouldn't tell me anything.

I was nervous when he arrived; nervous, because I wanted to say the right thing so he would open up and talk, nervous about how I would react seeing him given what I thought, and nervous in general. When he arrived, I knew that he knew what I wanted to talk about. We went out on the back deck, and I got straight to it.

"Okay, Peter, the reason I asked you over is because I want to hear from you about the night Sammy died, with all the details."

"Okay. Dad told us to go to bed at 11:00 pm. I went to bed and slept until 9:00 am. I went to wake up Sammy, and I found him," he finished, looking at me blankly. He knew me well enough to know what I meant when I said I wanted all the details. Apparently, he didn't want to give me any.

"Okay, let's go through that again but with more detail. Start from when you and Sammy and Adam were playing Xbox downstairs the evening before and Lucas left at 5:00 pm to go tailgating and to the football game," I said (details I knew because of Sarah's account of the night.)

"Um, okay. We were playing Xbox. Dad got home around 11:00 pm. I went to bed and...." Perhaps, he had memorized a script (so to speak), and he didn't want to stray too far from it and accidentally give away something.

"Aren't you leaving out at least one thing?" I interrupted. He looked at me with a raised eyebrow. "A movie. Sarah and Adam said you guys were watching a movie," I told him.

"Oh. Yeah. We were watching a movie for a while," he said. "Um, Legion. Yeah. Dad got home, and we went upstairs."

"Did Sammy go upstairs with you and Adam?" I asked.

"I ...think so, but I'm not sure," he said.

"Well, Adam and Sarah say Sammy didn't come upstairs, but Lucas says he did," I said.

"Yeah, I think he did," he said. "We talked with Dad for a few minutes and he told us to go to bed. So I went to bed."

"Didn't Lucas tell you guys you could sleep in the following morning and skip Sunday School. And that you should wake everyone up and drive them to church?"

"Yeah," he said.

"And didn't he tell Adam he could sleep with him?" I asked.

"Yes." He answered. I took a deep breath, trying not to feel aggravated. These were all details he could be telling me, only he wasn't.

"So I went to bed, and I slept pretty hard," he told me, preemptively stating the depth of his sleep. Interesting. He was already on the defense, or that statement was also part of his mantra about what happened.

"You heard nothing?" I asked, though I don't even know why. Obviously, that was his intended point in saying he had "slept pretty hard."

"No. Like I said, I slept pretty hard that night." His words sounded completely scripted. Then, he said, "I was tired because I took the ACT that morning." I had been told that exact same thing by Lucas as an explanation for why Peter went to bed so early—early for Peter—and why he had slept so long, 11:30pm-9:00 am. Peter had always required several hours less sleep than everyone else. Nine and a half hours of sleep? Peter hadn't needed that much sleep since he was a toddler, and since the age of four, he had required many hours less. I didn't buy it. I stared intently at Peter.

I said, "I find it interesting that for the past several months, every weekend when Sammy and Adam came home from Lucas's, they were exhausted. When I asked them why, they told me they were up with you until 2:00, 3:00, or 4:00 in the morning on both Friday and Saturday nights. Lucas told you all to go to bed at 10:00 or 11:00 pm, but you guys weren't tired. Since you all were downstairs, and Lucas was upstairs and couldn't hear you, you stayed up without him knowing. But this one particular night, you just happened to go to bed at 11:00 pm, right when Lucas told you to?"

"Yeah," he said, "I went to bed." He stared at me. He was lying.

"Sammy was awake in his room, but you went to bed?"

"Yeah," he said. He went on. "I woke up around 9:00 am and went to wake everyone up. Sammy's door was locked. So, I got a coat hanger and picked the lock."

"You didn't knock on the door and call his name first?" I asked.

"Yeah, I did." He paused and then said, "He didn't answer."

"Obviously," I said, "then what?"

"I went in his room and saw him. I went upstairs and got Sarah."

"Wait," I interrupted. "You saw him hanging there, and then you just went and got Sarah? Why didn't you freak out?" I asked.

"I don't know. Even Sarah thought it was a joke when she first saw him." In fact, Sarah's first thought was that Peter had killed Sammy and might kill her next. And why had he automatically jumped to Sarah's reaction instead of explaining his own? *Because he is trying to normalize his response*, I thought.

"Okay," I said, "go on."

"So then Sarah went to look with me and when she saw him, she said, 'Very funny' and went back upstairs."

"That is because you were acting so calm and normal she didn't think it could be real. Also, you left out the part where you picked up the hatchet off the floor and were tossing it around."

"Oh. Well, yeah, I did that."

"Okay, go on. Sarah said, 'Very funny' and went back upstairs, and then…?"

"Then, I poked him with a stick, and he didn't move. Sarah came back downstairs, and I told her that. We went back into the room, and Sarah started crying. She wanted to call 911, but I thought we should call Dad."

I jumped in, "You mean when you grabbed her phone from her?" (Obviously, I was not a great interrogator.)

"Well, yeah, she had her phone. I said we should call Dad, and she wanted to call 911. I took her phone and tried to call Dad, but he didn't answer. Then Sarah called 911 and handed the phone to me."

"Wait," I said, "Didn't Adam come into the kitchen before that?"

"Oh, yeah, he came in, and Sarah told him to sit on the couch."

"And then she asked if you were going to tell him what happened?"

"Yeah, and I did."

"Yeah, you looked at him and said, 'Sammy's dead.'"

"Yeah."

"Okay, so you are on the phone with 911. Tell me about that."

"They are asking 'What is your emergency?' I tell them my brother is hanging. They ask if any adults are home, and I say 'No.' They tell me to cut the strap that is holding him up. I get out my pocket knife and cut the strap. He sort of slides down the door and then falls over to the side toward the closet." My heart let out a loud, horrified screech, and I momentarily caught my breath.

I clarified, "He slid down the door and then fell over? Was he stiff? Did he bang his head against the back of the closet?"

"Yes, he was kind of stiff, and yeah, he did hit the back wall of the closet," he said. I felt a stab of pain as I thought of Sammy falling over and smacking his head against the wall because someone who was supposed to love him, his big brother, didn't handle him with care. Why didn't Peter catch him? Why didn't he carefully lay Sammy on the floor?

"Okay, then what?" I asked.

"They said to lay him on his back. Well, you know I am kind of weird, so I got the comforter off his bed to move him."

"Wait, what? You got his comforter off his bed in order to move him out of the closet area and get him on his back?" *He didn't want to touch Sammy*, I thought. *Either he was grossed out, or he was being really careful not to leave any skin, hair, DNA, etc., on Sammy.*

"Yeah," he said. "They told me to begin mouth to mouth, and I told them there was this gross brown stuff coming out of his mouth. They said to scoop it out, and I said 'With what, a spoon?' They said 'No, with your finger.' And, again, I am weird, so I went to get a towel." I was flabbergasted by his responses. Where had been his feeling of urgency to revive Sammy? Also, he seemed different while talking about the phone call, more relaxed, and his memory definitely seemed to have sharpened. He was freely offering more detail. Why was that? Probably, because he knew there was a copy of the 911 call. Perhaps, because he thought by being detailed on the part that could be checked for accuracy, he could increase his credibility for the whole story. Regardless, he was very detailed about the 911 call, which could all be fact-checked, as opposed to everything that had happened before the call, which could not.

"Okay," I say, "go on. You didn't want to use your finger, so you went to get a towel."

"I wiped off his mouth with the towel, and then they told me again to start mouth to mouth. I said, 'Without vomiting?' Then, I explained to them that his jaw was stiff. Then, the paramedics came in the room."

I was astounded by his coldness. There *had* to be something wrong with him. I had always known was different, but the complete lack of feeling, sensitivity, or empathy as he recounted finding his little brother dead, hanging from his closet, was shocking and disturbing. Unless, the response I was seeing wasn't a true response of a boy who suddenly found his little brother dead, hanging, but the response of a boy who had *faked* finding his brother but in reality knew exactly what he would find—because he was responsible. Then, his behavior made sense. Then, it was the behavior of someone who was guilty and wanted to appear innocent, someone who knew Sammy had been dead all night, so he wasn't surprised, someone who knew Sammy had been dead a while and was a little grossed out by his brother's very dead body, (a body he knew couldn't be revived,) and possibly someone who was paranoid and wanted to leave as little DNA on Sammy as possible. From Peter's own account, he never touched Sammy.

Either Peter had something wrong with him that explained his inappropriate responses, or he was guilty of something and faking innocence—or possibly both. Those were the only two explanations that made sense. Otherwise, I couldn't reconcile his behavior. For example, even if Peter had been perplexed and unsure when he found Sammy, would he not have shaken him? Would he not have rushed to get Sarah instead of being so casual about it? Would he not have said something to his sister such as "Sarah! Come here! Something's wrong?!" And was it possible that he was so completely unaware of what had happened that he would pick up a toy hatchet off the floor and casually toss it around with his brother hanging from his neck, pale and still, four feet in front of him? To me, that action was entirely too cool for that moment to be believable. To me, that was the action of someone trying way too hard to look casual and innocent in a critical moment, but over-playing the act. I was almost certain he was lying. I wasn't sure about which parts, but my gut screamed at me that Peter was lying.

If he had played a part, why had he not just fessed up to whatever had happened? His lack of claiming any responsibility, in spite of all the things that indicated otherwise, only caused me to fear the worst: either he had lost his temper and in a fit of rage had killed his brother, or he had planned the entire thing.

Thursday, November 4

After supper the next evening, we had a family therapy session with the child advocate therapist. She talked with all three kids and asked them questions about what they wanted and what they were feeling. Sarah told her she no longer wanted to continue visits with Lucas, at least for a while, and she wouldn't be going anymore (a few days before the appointment she told us she had come to that decision). She explained that both she and Sammy had already been feeling that way for a while before Sammy died, and since his death, she felt much more strongly about not continuing the visits. All in all it was a good first meeting.

When we had arrived at the office, the tuxedo cat we had seen two days before was still there! She sat beside the front door watching us as we parked. Like she had two days before, when we got out of the van, she came over and rubbed up against our legs, all the while continuing to make direct eye contact! Jake picked her up and petted her, and, of course, the kids fell in love. They took turns holding her and didn't want to put her down. Finally, we took her inside the therapist's building and asked if we could keep her with us during our session. To the kids' delight, the therapist said yes! Lydia had recently watched the film, *The Golden Compass*, and from that story picked up and liked the idea that everyone had a spirit animal.

"Maybe this is Sammy's spirit animal!" she exclaimed, referring to the kitten.

I looked directly at the kitten sitting on Jake's lap and said, "Are you Sammy?" The kitty—who had not yet made a single noise—took two steps toward me, looked me straight in the eyes, and meowed! We decided right then we were taking her home and keeping her (the therapist's secretary told us they were planning to call animal control the following day). In the van on the drive home, she kept walking around rubbing up against each one of us. For a while she hopped up in the van seat next to Adam—where Sammy would have been sitting had he been there—curled up in a ball and let him pet her. Then, she walked back to the front of the van and sat down under Jake's feet. She hadn't meowed again since the one time in the therapist's office, so I tried the name experiment again. "Are you Sammy?" Again, she looked right at me and meowed, convincing Lydia she *was* Sammy's spirit animal. So, we named her Samantha.

While we sat outside around the fire pit that night, I called my cousin Ned and asked him about the Halloween prank story. He told me he had received the information from a guy who worked for him whose daughter had been friends with Sammy (the same man with whom Hank was friends and who had denied everything.) I told Ned that not only did the cops know nothing about the Halloween prank story, his worker had denied saying anything. Ned continued to say he had only repeated what the guy had told him. "Ned, someone is lying. Your worker is adamant he never told you this. So, either he's lying, or you're lying." Ned just continued to stick to the story.

After the phone call, we continued sitting with the kids around the fire pit talking about whether the Halloween prank story had been a bad misunderstanding or a lie. We had all been so relieved when Vince told us the story at his house the night of Sammy's funeral (although Jake and I had been somewhat skeptical.) The kids were just as frustrated and disappointed that the story wasn't true as Jake and I were, and they were upset that Vince had said it. Something of note about grief is that anger is often mixed in among all of the volatile emotions swirling inside a bereaved person, and that anger seeks people toward whom it can funnel itself.

Chapter 18

> "Every time you see me, Momma, you look at me like you want some doctor to perform a retroactive abortion."
>
> -Pat Conroy, *The Prince of Tides*

Friday, November 5

My therapist scheduled me for a session at the same time the kids were scheduled to have a session with the child advocate therapist and Lucas. I considered rescheduling my appointment time but decided maybe it was for the best. Perhaps Lucas would be more relaxed, more willing to listen to the kids said without me being there.

After our sessions, we all returned home at the same time. The kids, upset and keyed up, started talking all at once trying to tell me what had happened. First, the therapist had Jake sit out in the lobby during their session. The kids were alone with her and Lucas, and they didn't like that one bit.

"She probably thought Lucas would be more comfortable and would hear what you guys had to say better without Dad in the room." I told them. "And she knows that the problem is between you guys and Lucas, not Dad."

"We are the ones she should be making more comfortable!" exclaimed Sarah. "It's hard to say some of the things we want to say to Lucas without you or Dad or someone we trust in the room with us."

"Okay, I will speak with her and explain that you guys don't want it to be like that again." I told them.

"Another thing," Sarah said, "When she did let Dad come in the room, she kept referring to him as 'Jake' and Lucas as 'Dad'!"

"Hmm, I'm not surprised she referred to Lucas as 'Dad', since he *is* your biological father, but I am a little surprised that she didn't also refer to Dad as 'Dad' since that's what you guys call him. I'll tell her that you guys want Dad referred to as 'Dad 'also. She can refer to them as, 'Your dad Jake,' and 'Your dad Lucas.'" I couldn't remember when they had started referring to Lucas as "Lucas" at our house. I knew when they were with Lucas, they called him "Dad" and referred to Jake as "Jake". I think they began referring to Lucas by his first name when they weren't with him, as a clarification around the time they began calling Jake, "Dad." If they were discussing something with me about "Dad", it became cumbersome to specify if they were talking about Jake or Lucas, so they simply started referring to Lucas as "Lucas" when they weren't with him. Of course, I also think they were looking for an excuse to call Lucas by his first name instead of "Dad", because they were upset and angry with him.

"And she made me go sit right next to Lucas," said Lydia.

"Well, why didn't you just say, 'No thank you', if you didn't want to sit next to him, Lydia?"

"Because if I had he would have gotten mad at me later!" she yelled.

Before I could respond to Lydia, Adam blurted out, "So, I'm going to a basketball game with Uncle Vince tonight?"

"What?" I asked, confused.

"Lucas told the therapist during the session that he was dropping me off at Uncle Vince's house later because I was going to the game with him. I assumed you had arranged it with Uncle Vince since you asked me last week if I would be interested in going to a game with him sometime."

"Um, no. I didn't talk to Uncle Vince or make any arrangements with him. I know nothing about a set plan, only that when we were at Uncle Vince's house after the funeral, he asked if you would be interested in going sometime, which was why I asked you. He must have called and arranged it with Lucas."

"Seriously?!" Adam said, irritated. "After the whole fight thing before Halloween, he called Lucas again?"

"Adam, you don't need to worry about that. I will have a conversation about that with Uncle Vince."

"I don't want to go to the ballgame with him," Adam said. "I'm mad at him anyway for lying and telling everyone Sammy died because he was pulling some Halloween prank. I just thought you had arranged this so I was going do it."

On top of all the other things that bothered Sarah about the session, she was annoyed because she felt Lucas announced he had arranged to drop off Adam at my sister's house to go to the game, as an affected display of cooperation and agreeableness with my family and, therefore, me. Or, as Sarah put it, "He was trying to make it look like he's all friendly and works with you, Mom." Both Sarah and Adam were frustrated because Vince had called Lucas again after we explicitly asked him not to. In addition, they were angry about the Halloween prank story, and, of course, they had general anger because of their grief over Sammy.

"Okay," I said, "I better call Vince to tell him Adam isn't going to the game with him."

"Mom, I want to tell Vince," Adam said, "I also want to tell him I'm angry that he lied about Sammy." I was a little surprised, as Adam had never before been so bold, but I would soon understand that part of his reaction to our tragedy was to become very protective of our family and much more assertive when he perceived any of us had been wronged. He called Vince, but there was no answer so he left a voicemail. He told Vince he wasn't going to the ballgame. Adam then said, "Also, I think you are a bum." Inwardly, I cringed a little, and Jake and I looked at each other. "I didn't want to go into the whole lying about Sammy's death issue on a voicemail, so I just decided to tell him how I feel about him doing it," Adam told us after he hung up.

"Well, okay," I said. Normally, I would have told Adam that what he had said was rude and the respectful and the appropriate way to have handled the situation would have been to explain why he was upset with Vince. I would have said that regardless of age differences, people should treat each other with respect and dignity. It wasn't right for adults to be rude to children, and it wasn't right for children to be rude to adults. However, Vince had been wrong both in contacting Lucas again and either his fabrication of the Halloween prank story or in failing to confirm the information before sharing it as fact. I understood Adam's frustration (I had just given Vince a piece of my own mind a week before.) Besides, we weren't overly concerned with something as minor as rudeness just then, when one of our family members had recently been hanged to death. We all had so much anger. We were coping, and I recognized Adam was dealing with his feelings. He needed extra love and support, not correction. We were all fragile. One minute one of us was full of sadness and crying, but something minor would happen, and the next minute that same person would be full of anger.

"Okay," I told Adam and Lydia. "Go grab sweatshirts and anything else you two want to take with you. You guys have about twenty minutes until Lucas picks you up."

"I am going over to Susan's for a while," Sarah told me.

"Ok, Sweet Pea. I love you."

"I love you too, Momma, so so much," she said, giving me a long, tight hug. Then she left to go see Susan, her best friend since fourth grade.

I was angry that Vince had contacted Lucas yet again, even after our phone conversation with him that previous Saturday. We had been very clear about him not interfering in our family matters or communicating with my ex-husband. I had never made such an issue of it before, but none of my children had died at Lucas's house before; also, there hadn't been an active police investigation into one of our children's deaths before. Apparently, Jake felt the same way I did because he said, "Will you be upset if I text Vince, Sweetheart? I told him on Saturday if he couldn't stop communicating and interacting with Lucas, we would have to discontinue interacting with him."

"Go ahead," I told him. Jake texted Vince, saying we had asked him to discontinue private contact with Lucas, he had ignored our request, therefore, he (Vince) was no longer welcome in our home. He also said it appeared Vince had learned nothing about loyalty from my dad. Frankly, I was a little surprised at Jake's text. Jake is very patient and even-tempered. Nevertheless, as a father he felt it was his job to protect Sammy throughout life, and he had failed. If Vince couldn't respect our wishes regarding no private interaction with my ex-husband, at least during the investigation, then Jake would do what he felt he had to do for the good of our family.

Later that night, when Lydia and Adam returned home from visitation with Lucas, we were sitting out by the fire pit. After they walked over and sat down with us, Adam made an announcement: "I am done going for visits with Lucas."

Saturday, November 6th
One Week Six Days After Sammy Died

The next morning, Adam remained insistent he would no longer be going for visits with Lucas. He was angry that Lucas simply assumed Sammy committed suicide and was doing nothing to seek out the truth. He was angry that Lucas was being so difficult during such a terrible time for our family. He was also angry about some issues from before Sammy's death, particularly one incident when Lucas lost his temper with Sammy. I didn't have it in me to insist that he go. I wouldn't have encouraged him to stop his visits, but I wouldn't force him to go if he chose to stop, not after what had happened. Before Sammy's death, I would have talked with Adam as I had with Sarah and Sammy on several occasions when they mentioned they wanted to discontinue their visitation times with Lucas (unfortunately, desire to discontinue visits with one of the biological parents is not an uncommon thing for kids from divorced homes.) I would have explained to Adam the importance of having a healthy relationship with his biological father. I would have told him that while his father wasn't perfect, no parent was, and Lucas was better than many. However, everything had changed. Adam had suffered a terrible loss. He needed security, love, understanding, and to feel he had some element of control in his life. He didn't feel he had any of those with Lucas. For my part, I was uncomfortable every time the kids had to be with Lucas because that meant they also had to be around Peter. I would no longer be pushing or insisting Adam continue that relationship, at least for a while. He could discuss his feelings with the child advocate at our next appointment.

I dreaded sending an email to Lucas about Adam's decision, but I had to do it right away as he was due to pick the kids up that morning at 10:00 am. It didn't matter how nicely I cushioned the news of Adam's decision, Lucas would be (understandably) upset. He would be angry and would blame me (shocker). I had tried to convey to him that the kids were freaked out. I had tried to work with him in spite of feeling anger with him for simply accepting and promoting Sammy's death as a suicide. I kept the email brief and to the point. We were supposed to be addressing the visitation issues with the child advocate anyway, and it would be better if we addressed it all with her in the room to help us work through it.

When Lucas arrived to pick up Lydia, Jake walked her out. Lucas told him, "This isn't how the next visitation is going to go. If we can't work something out, I'll have to go in a different direction." That was precisely the reason I had already spoken with my attorney and had set up sessions with the child advocate therapist.

That evening, Laura stopped by. While we were talking, she mentioned Peter had gone deer hunting at my brother's house that afternoon. I was speechless. Considering the circumstances, I found that to be very disturbing behavior. I would think that shooting and killing a deer would feel wrong after the trauma of your brother dying, and of you being the one to find him dead, and of finding him hanging. Apparently, my family members hadn't thought it strange though, as they had allowed and facilitated it, and, apparently, had contacted and interacted again with Lucas.

Sunday, November 7

Two weeks after Sammy died, Jake and I were sitting by the fire pit in our back yard one evening talking with Hank and Laura. They had come to visit and to check-in on us, and we were talking through Sammy's death and what might have happened to him again. Unexpectedly, Mom and Valerie came around the side of the house to the back yard. I hadn't seen Mom since Halloween or Valerie since the day of the funeral. I stood to greet them. "Hi, Mom, Hey, Valerie," I said, walking over to them. My Mom went right up the deck stairs and into my house without a word or glance in my direction.

Valerie wouldn't make eye contact with me and looked like she was in a hurry as she said, "We came by to pick up our coolers we left here." They were both visibly frosty toward me. Presumably, Valerie was mad about the—"you're a bum"—voicemail to Vince from Adam, the –"you're no longer welcome"—text to Vince from Jake, and the –"stay out of my family business, and stop the buddy treatment with my ex, you blankety-blank, blank—phone call to Vince from me the previous Saturday. Those were all the reasons Mother must have been mad too, and of course, because of what I said to her the morning Sammy died. With a sigh, I went inside to find her.

She was collecting the dishes from when she and Laura had brought over the sandwich platters and tidied the kitchen on the 25th. I walked over and hugged her stiff, unresponsive body. Then, she then stepped away to carry on collecting her things. She was definitely angry with me. I left the kitchen and made my way to the back deck. After grabbing the coolers, Valerie came up the stairs to the deck, and I followed her inside. "Here is your birthday present," she said handing me a small box.

"Oh, thank you, Valerie." It was a 14 ct gold charm bracelet (both Valerie and Victoria had identical charm bracelets which I had previously admired—and yes, nearly everyone in my extended family was wealthy, except Laura and Hank, and us.)

"Ohh, it's beautiful, Valerie. Thank you so much," I said. She then turned and moved into the kitchen where Mother was still busily doing something.

Just then, Lydia came in through the deck door. Lucas had dropped her off. She heard Mother saying something to Valerie in the kitchen and asked, "Is Nana here?" I nodded my head. Lydia leaned toward my ear and whispered, "Lucas and Amber (his girlfriend) took me to Cracker Barrel for lunch, and Nana was there eating at a different table, and she was really nice when she saw Lucas and hugged him and talked to him."

Lydia's comment irritated the crap out of me. I knew Vince would have told Mother and Valerie what Jake and I had said to him on the phone regarding the family's interactions with Lucas: polite and civil, not warm and engaging, at least for the time being. I heard Mother and Valerie leaving through my front door without saying goodbye. Jake came through the deck door, and I told him what Lydia had just told me. "Okay. Enough is enough," he said and went through the kitchen and out the front door to speak with my mother. I turned to Lydia, "Brush your teeth and go get in my bed. You can read until I get there to tuck you in." I suspected the talk Jake was having with Mother and Valerie wouldn't go well. When Mother got angry with a person for something, it generally took her a long, long time to move on from it and no amount of talking ever seemed to make a difference.

I went to sit by the fire pit in the backyard with Laura, who asked, "Where did Mother go? And Valerie?"

"They are leaving I think. And Jake just went out front to speak to them," I said, dully. I was deflated by their cold and aloof treatment. Laura looked at me, then jumped up and went to the front yard. A few minutes later, she was back looking nervous.

"Hank, will you go out front and try to help," she said. He silently got up and went to the front. I didn't even ask.

The situation in the front yard didn't go very well. Jake tried to explain we would appreciate it if my family members could be only civil and polite to Lucas, but not engage in hugging and chatting, sharing family information or having phone conversations.

He tried to explain that Lucas was unwilling to have even a courteous relationship with us, and it was irksome for us to see my family take such a friendly and warm approach with him. Further, Jake told them, we didn't trust Lucas, and we didn't want him to have access to information about our family. Jake tried to explain that this wasn't how Dad had handled family relations with Lucas, and things had gone much smoother then. He didn't tell them there was an ongoing police investigation regarding Sammy's death, and the two people that didn't need any information about it were Lucas and Peter.

Mother and Valerie were very irritated by Jake's words, and they flatly refused to agree to anything he asked. Then, Valerie told Jake that on the day Sammy died, when they arrived over at Lucas's house, I had "behaved like an ass," toward Mother (regarding the Mother-Hugging-Ex-Before-Daughter incident). And *there* it was. I knew Mother was pissed about that, but I had no idea just how pissed. Jake exploded, "Of course she was upset about that, Valerie! Who wouldn't be? She had just found out her son was dead. She wanted to be comforted by her mother, not see her mother comfort her ex-husband?" Hank attempted to help the situation by being a peacemaker and suggesting some compromises, but it was no good. Nothing was resolved. Valerie and Mother said they could talk with whomever they liked, whenever they liked. They would agree to nothing, and they left very angry.

Jake came back to the fire pit and told us what happened. I was completely overwhelmed, and I lost it. I had a major meltdown. I just wanted to mourn the death of my son, and I could barely hold myself together under the grief. I couldn't handle anything else. My heart was broken into a million pieces, and I needed my family more than ever. I would like to have completely dissolved and for my particles to have soaked into the earth.

Chapter 19

"And what if—what are you if the people who are supposed to love you can leave you like you're nothing."

-Lydia Scott, *The Unwritten Rule*

Monday, November 8th

Fifteen Days After Sammy Died

    Jake took Adam and Lydia to school, came back home, and got back into bed with me. He knew I needed him. I slept very little the night before. If a photo could have been taken of my heart, it would have resembled Edvard Munch's painting, "The Scream." I didn't want to accept that I would never see Sammy again. I desperately wished I would have had at least a few moments with him before he died to tell him how much I loved him, what a privilege it was to be his mom, that I would love him till the day I died, and that I would never let him be forgotten. Why did his death have to be so sudden? It was just like when Dad died. Everything was normal: no warning of impending doom. Life was great. Then, boom, Dad was dead. Things had finally returned to a better place, the dark cloud of sadness that covered me for about 15 months after Dad died had *finally* dissipated and been gone a few months, and then, boom! Sammy was dead. The horrific suspicion that Peter played some part in Sammy's death only made it completely heinous. With my family behaving as they were, I felt like the final rug had been jerked out from under me. I needed them. I didn't know if I could make it through the long road ahead without their love and support. It hurt me that they couldn't just love me and Jake and the kids, that they couldn't just embrace us, comfort us, and help us, in spite of our rough edges, even if they disagreed with some of our decisions. Was that not part of the wonderfulness of having family?

After a while, I started thinking about Adam no longer wanting visitation with Lucas, and what Lucas meant when he said, "This isn't how the next visitation is going to go. If we can't work something out, I'll have to go in a different direction." That had to mean he would be seeking some involvement of the court. Lovely. I had tried to be as open as I could with him regarding what the kids were feeling and what they were wanting. If he had been willing to work through the kids' grief together with me and be a little more flexible, we probably could have gotten through it all without the kids hating him. However, Lucas wouldn't listen to me, and they were growing increasingly frustrated. They had some major grievances with him about a few things that had happened before our tragedy, and they were upset about his response to and his assumption about Sammy's death. Their natural anger at their brother's death was being stream-lined right back at Lucas. For my part, if he would have been willing to hear my concerns about Peter, I would have felt ten times better. I was very concerned that Peter was involved or at least knew more than he said. Lucas either staunchly believed Peter was innocent, was covering for Peter, was covering for himself (though I really didn't think Lucas was in anyway responsible), or—the most likely reason—thought it easier and much less messy to assume Sammy had done it on his own rather than dig any deeper. Anyway, I had to contact Lucas to discuss Adam's feelings about visitation and to address the coming visitation times.

I emailed Lucas, and asked him if he had any thoughts about how to handle his visitation times for the coming weekend and for Thanksgiving. Lucas did return a vague response to my email, but he didn't talk about his thoughts with me, ask my thoughts or engage in any brainstorming together about the kids. Lucas didn't see that his lack of openness and cooperation was seriously working against him.

Wednesday, November 10

Every day, I busily sent and received emails to and from the kids' teachers and counselors, to and from the funeral home (regarding the headstone and the flower candles), and very sparingly to and from Lucas. Every day, at least one of us had a therapy session. Several days, one of the kids had special tutoring sessions with one or another of their teachers. They all missed a week and a half of school initially, and although they were attending class again, they were dazed and in shock. They were trying to learn new material as well as learn and makeup what they had missed. Every day started with me sobbing in the early morning hours, and crying episodes throughout the day and night. Every evening I spent sitting by the fire pit with Jake, drinking Coke Zero and vodka, thinking, and talking through every possible scenario to explain what had happened to Sammy. As a person who naturally likes closure, always finishes a book, and watches an entire movie even if it is bad (a J on the MBTI), the lack of an answer was maddening. I couldn't appropriately manage an emotional response to the why and how of Sammy's death since I didn't know why or how he had been hung. I couldn't even begin to work through the subsequent appropriate emotions. The five most likely cause of death possibilities each had vastly different emotional implications: 1. Sammy committed suicide. 2. Sammy had a stupid accident; either he was messing around with the strap and fell into the loop, he thought he would temporarily hang to see what it would feel like, or he was trying the choking game. 3. Sammy and Peter had a stupid accident; they were trying the sleeper hold and something went wrong and Peter, in fear of getting in trouble, made it to look like suicide. 4. Peter lost his temper and performed a sleeper hold, which accidentally killed Sammy. 5. Peter intentionally murdered Sammy. That last possibility, number five, brought a whole new kind of horror. I didn't think my first-born was a sociopath, but I recognized that as his mother, I might not always have seen his behavior objectively. Also, Peter was 17 ½; I hadn't spent much time with him since he was 12-years-old and I didn't know all of the ways he had changed through puberty. The pre-12-year-old Peter was not capable of cold-blooded murder, so it was also difficult for me to see the 17-year-old Peter in that light. As for the first possibility, I knew Sammy well, and unless I saw or was made aware of some new info indicating a depression problem, then I couldn't believe he committed suicide. This was a kid who still slept with his baby blanket at the end of his bed and with an enormous stuffed animal. Regarding the number two possibility, I didn't believe Sammy, by himself and on his own initiative, would have done everything he would have needed to do, to have accidentally killed himself—turn on the fan, shut and lock his door, locate and remove a duffle bag strap. Honestly, he wasn't that creative and he was a little lazy. Removing from the possible scenarios a murder by Peter, a suicide by Sammy, and an accident by Sammy alone. I was left with the likeliest scenario being Peter put Sammy in a carotid sleeper hold—either when they were horsing around, or if he lost his temper—something went wrong and Sammy died, and Peter made it look like a suicide because he was afraid of getting in trouble.

Sarah was having a difficult time controlling her anxiety. In addition to dealing with the sorrow and sadness of losing Sammy, she felt angry with Lucas and unsure and very troubled about Peter. She was also trying to catch up with the schoolwork she missed when she was out. She was an extremely driven student. She was a member of National Junior Honor Society, made all A's, and had aspired to attend an Ivy League college since she was 11-years-old. Sarah would feel very anxious and take a Xanax, and although it relaxed her and relieved the anxiety, it made her mind very sluggish so she couldn't think to study. It also made her sleepy. If she didn't take a pill, her anxiety would keep increasing, narrowing her perspective and making her so anxious and jittery that schoolwork became impossible. I told her we just needed to adjust the dosage to find the correct amount for her body. "Take only half a pill, Sarah. That may relieve the anxiety without putting you to sleep," I suggested. "Then, at bedtime, take a whole pill."

In addition to a small prescription for Xanax, my go-to remedy to help with my own anxiety was vodka. Every evening, I poured a shot or two into my Coke Zero—several times. Not only did it quiet the horrible, anxious feeling, it numbed the worst of the gut-wrenching pain. My anxiety was bad and seemed to be worsening, but the pain was heinous. Every moment of every day was filled with pain, overwhelming grief, and anxiety. Every moment of every day my heart retained the same appearance: open mouthed, large empty eyed, hands holding horrified face, and screaming. Every night, Jake and I took thirty minutes to lie with Adam and Lydia. As I had done since the first night after Sammy died, I continued giving them Benadryl a few hours before bed; it helped with their allergies since we had taken in the cat, it helped them to fall asleep as it has a sedative effect, and it helped with the small amounts of anxiety they exhibited because it is a mild anxiolytic. While Adam didn't have the more obvious symptoms of anxiety like Sarah, he was having problems focusing in general. He would be in class, and wouldn't hear anything the teacher said. The class would finish, and he would have no idea what had been taught.

When Sammy died, both he and Adam had been attending the same middle school. I couldn't stand dropping off or picking up Adam at that school without Sammy. So, Jake took the kids to school and picked them up every day. Poor Adam—three weeks before, he had been riding in the van to and from school every day with Sammy. Since his brother's death, Adam rode in the van to and from school with an empty seat. He also had to walk the halls at school where he used to see Sammy during the day. It was no wonder his mind was fuzzy, and he felt inattentive.

Thursday, November 11

Each day when I got up, I pulled on my black sweat pants and hoodie, then my Ugg boots, and that was my preparation for the day. There was no selecting what to wear, choosing of shoes, or putting on makeup. I hadn't given those kinds of things a second thought since my boy died. Every day, I forced myself to get out of bed. Once out of bed, I felt like I was walking through five-foot-deep mud. Every step and every movement took tremendous strength and energy. It was exhausting.

Late in the afternoon, Victoria came over and we sat on the porch swing outside. With excitement, she told me about her wedding plans, and I tried not to feel resentful. Of course, her life was moving on. Life was moving on for everyone else, but not for me, not for my family, and not for Sammy. I talked to her about the investigation but asked her to please have discretion and not discuss it with the rest of the family. I shared with her my frustrations and disappointment with the family, and she listened but didn't say much. I didn't expect she would. She was planning her wedding. She was having daily interactions with her mom, her dad, and Mother/Nana. She left after a brief stay.

Later, I phoned the child advocate to set up another appointment. If the relationship between the kids and Lucas was going to be salvaged, certain issues had to be addressed and discussed with them all together. Their feelings toward Lucas were going downhill fast. I would do what I could to facilitate healing, but if he wouldn't humble himself and apologize for some things, and at least open his mind to consider options regarding Sammy's death other than suicide, I didn't think the relationships would improve, at least, not for a while.

Since the day after our nightmare began, we had all been wearing black clothing. The thought of wearing anything other than black felt wrong. After Dad died, I had worn black mourning clothes for six months. I was fairly certain it would be longer with Sammy, and I wanted the kids to be able to wear black as long as they wanted if that helped them. So, we went to Old Navy and loaded up our carts with black jeans, t-shirts, sweaters, and everything else. We would all wear those mourning clothes for a long time, in fact, it would be several years before I could wear any other color again.

Friday, November 12

Almost three weeks after his death, I had my first Sammy dream. In the dream, I was lying in a bed in a hotel room, crying hysterically and screaming. In a corner of the room, Mother and Valerie stood talking to Jake. "She has to get a hold of herself! She can't just keep sobbing like this," Mother was saying. Still crying in the hotel bed, I then fell asleep—I was having a dream within a dream. In that second dream-state, Jake and I were lying together in the same hotel room and bed as in the first dream. There was a knock on the door, and Sarah, Adam, and Lydia rushed into the room, followed—to my amazement and delight—by Sammy! He was alive! He had on his blue hoody and his hair was a little long, as he had worn it for several years. I shouted, "Oh my god, Sammy! I thought you were dead! I just had a dream that you were dead! I can't believe how real that felt. It was awful." Flooded with relief and joy, I ran my fingers through his silky, blonde hair.

He looked at me, his sweet, hazel eyes twinkling, and in comical pretense of exasperation, groaned my name with two syllables, "Mo-om."

"Really!" I told him, "I just had a horrible nightmare you were dead!" He flashed me a grin and started running around the room with the other kids. I looked at Jake and said, "I had the most horrible dream. It was so real! I seriously thought he was dead!" I watched my beautiful boy goofing around with Sarah, Adam, and Lydia.

I began to hear faint laughter from somewhere, which sounded like a group of girls. Looking around, I couldn't spot any girls. The laughter kept getting louder until... My eyes snapped open, and I was awake (from the second dream-state, but still asleep within the first dream-state) and lying in the hotel bed by myself again. The group of laughing girls was standing outside of my ground-level hotel room; their laughter had awakened me because they were congregated right outside my window, which for some reason had no glass in it. I suddenly realized that I had been sleeping and only dreaming Sammy was alive. The girls had awakened me and Sammy really was dead! I was enraged. I wanted to be back asleep where Sammy was alive, and I screamed at the girls, "Get out of here! My 13-year-old son is dead!"

An old friend I had known since childhood named Mike came into the room wearing a white t-shirt. Mike approached me to offer his condolences, and having just realized that Sammy was still dead, I clutched at Mike's t-shirt and started sobbing on his chest. Jake came up behind me, put his arms around me, and we all three cried together.

In the midst of our sobbing, I dozed off to sleep again and my legs buckled; I had slipped back into another second dream.

This time in the second dream-state Sammy was still dead. I floated out of the hotel room through the window with no glass and followed a balding man of about 30. Somehow I knew the bald man had an important piece of information about Sammy's death. I floated down street and followed him as he turned left, but something happened, and I awoke from the second dream state. The bald guy had disappeared, and I was devastated that I had awakened before receiving the man's important information. Although I had only been dreaming I was following the bald guy, I had physically floated out the window and down the street, and when I woke, I fell into the grass. Curled in a ball on the ground, I lay there crying. I was sad about Sammy and frustrated that I hadn't gotten the info about Sammy's death from the bald guy. Jake came running, picked me up, and carried me back to the hotel room. Mother and Valerie were talking to a big group of people beside the big picture window outside our room. We didn't want to talk to anyone though, so ignoring them, we went into our room.

Our hotel room had changed and become a house perched on a hill. Three loud, snarling dogs, which strangely, all looked like Lucas's dog, began digging under the ground of the house as if they were trying to get inside. Jake became angry and chased away two of the three dogs, but they kept coming back. The biggest of the dogs got very close to where I stood near the picture window (which, as it had in the hotel, held no glass). I was scared, but the dog only started gumming my finger and then wouldn't let go of my pinky. It seemed he wanted, or was trying, to tell me something.

The next thing I knew, Jake and I were laying in a bed in the house. I had realized and told Jake that when we were in a dream, we could see Sammy. So, we were in bed trying to fall asleep. We dozed off, and, lo and behold, wearing his blue hoodie and smiling at us, we saw Sammyboy! He was standing on a large rectangular floating skateboard, similar to the hover boards in *Back to the Future 2*, only bigger. Holding hands, Jake and I gazed at our slightly translucent son. Sammy reached toward me, and I grabbed his hand and stepped onto the huge hover board. From somewhere I heard knocking on a door. Jake stepped onto the hover board, but he turned his head toward the direction of the knocking. He faded and disappeared, and I knew he had awakened. Fighting to stay in the dream world, I looked back at Sammy, but I already could see myself disappearing. Then, Sammy was gone, and I was back in bed (but still in the first overall dream). I started crying and got upset with the kids for banging on our bedroom door and waking us when we had succeeded in seeing Sammy. I feared I might be losing my mind, but then I realized if my mind cracked, even though seeing Sammy might only be a hallucination, I didn't care. I would get to see him, and I felt peace with that possibility. Then, I awoke from the overall dream to someone knocking on my bedroom door. I was no longer asleep or dreaming.

I opened my eyes to see Jake leaning over me. "Time for dinner, Sweetie," he said. The whole dream within a dream state, in which my sub-conscience had been engaged while I was sleeping, seriously messed with my head. I was disoriented and confused. I felt like I had just experienced the most vivid, awful dream in my life. I had dreamed that Sammy was dead! I felt like I had been asleep for several weeks. I thought, *God that was long and awful. It was like Sammy was really dead.* I felt tremendous relief to be awake again. Straining to clear the fog from my brain, I thought, *Wait, is Sammy really dead?* I looked at Jake and asked, "Is Sammy dead?" Before he answered, I already knew. I broke down as all of that goddamn pain flooded my heart and mind. When I calmed down, I explained the dream to Jake. I told him about how near the end of the dream, when I was still in the first dream-state but thought I was awake, I had wondered if I was losing my mind; but I had felt okay with that because if my mind cracked, I would be able to see and be with Sammy. Of course, I wouldn't really be seeing Sammy, it would be a hallucination. But, unable to differentiate hallucinations from reality, I would believe Sammy was real. I was okay with that if it was my only opportunity to see Sammy anymore. It was true, I told Jake. I was fine with losing my mind in real life if it meant I would still get to see and be with Sammy.

Tuesday, November 16

On November 16, we had a pivotal therapy session with Lucas, mediated by the child advocate therapist. The kids clearly verbalized their anger and frustration about a few things, one of which was an incident that happened at Lucas's house a few months before Sammy died. Lucas had told Sammy to take out the dog, and Sammy had done so. A little while later, Lucas became angry because he thought Sammy hadn't worn his shoes to take out the dog. Sammy told him that he *had* worn his shoes. Lucas started yelling and saying Sammy was lying. Sammy insisted he was not lying. Lucas then pushed Sammy up against the wall, picked up Sammy's backpack and smashed it down on his back, and then opened the front door and shoved him out. All of the kids were upstairs by the front door watching it happen, because it was time for Jake to pick them up. He was outside waiting in the van.

Sammy was crying when he got in the van. At 13-years-old and well into the changes of puberty, Sammy rarely cried anymore. When Jake asked him what was wrong, Sammy told him. Jake, angry with Lucas, stepped out of the van and onto the street. Lucas was standing by his open front door as Sarah, Adam, and Lydia came out and walked to the van. An unpleasant exchange took place, which included Jake telling Lucas never to lay hands on Sammy like that again, Lucas telling Jake to get off his property, Jake pointing out he was on the street not Lucas's property, and Lucas cussing out Jake.

Over the next two weeks, Sammy stated he was never going to Lucas's again. We talked with him about anger, about what was and was not appropriate behavior from a parent, and about how to handle such a situation if it were ever to happen again. I told him Lucas had been in the wrong, and if he really felt strongly that he couldn't continue visits with Lucas I would support his decision. However, if he could continue, I thought he should try. I explained that parents weren't perfect. Lucas loved him but sometimes he struggled with his temper and this had been one of those times. When it was time to go to Lucas's again two weeks later, Sammy had calmed down and was fine with going. I will always regret encouraging Sammy to resume the visits. Because this particular incident happened shortly before Sammy died, it was still pretty fresh in the minds of the kids. In a way, I think they blamed Lucas for Sammy's death. Lucas struggled with his temper and wasn't a good example for Peter, and they all thought Peter had lost his temper and accidentally killed Sammy.

Sarah brought up and retold this specific incident during the therapy session. Lucas *denied* remembering it had happened. The kids—who had witnessed the entire thing—were *infuriated* by Lucas's response. They were certain he was lying about not remembering.

Adam then mentioned another instance from the previous few months that the kids were upset about (which, if I recall, was about spilled milk and Lucas yelling), but Lucas said he couldn't recall that incident either. The kids were livid and didn't even bother to bring up anything else, including their frustration that Lucas assumed Sammy committed suicide. That was the end of their willingness to give Lucas a chance. They could forgive mistakes. They would not forgive lying, evasiveness, lack of accountability, or inability to acknowledge and apologize for wrongdoing.

For reasons unknown to me, Lucas cancelled the next session. I never scheduled any more sessions and neither did he (nor did he ever again bring up the topic with me), and that was the end of therapy with the children's advocate to try to repair things between the children and Lucas. Maybe Lucas was embarrassed by what the kids had said during the last session and didn't want them bringing up more incidents of that nature. Perhaps he thought I was negatively influencing the kids against him, therefore it was a losing battle. Had he asked for my thoughts or input regarding how to mend fences with the kids, I would have suggested he hear what they were saying, humble himself, and apologize for mistakes. Also, he had to stop saying Sammy committed suicide and look at the events of that awful night and following morning more objectively. Regardless, we didn't have any more sessions, Adam and Sarah didn't resume visits with him, and although Lydia continued daytime visits through May 2011, she then also chose to discontinue all visitation. They never resumed visits or a relationship with Lucas or Peter.

Thursday, November 18

  The night before Sammy died, I purchased online tickets to take the kids to the November 18 midnight premiere of *Harry Potter and the Half-Blood Prince*. We always went to the midnight premieres of the HP films, and we often dressed up, made Harry Potter snacks, and showed up early to save our place in line. It was the evening of the newest film release, but there was no way I could attend. I had noticed that leaving the house was becoming increasingly difficult. It made me feel too anxious. My stomach would get tight, I would feel jittery, I would get sweaty, and I usually ended up crying. No, I always ended up crying. It was too much for my nerves. Going to *Harry Potter* would have been way too challenging for several reasons. First, I had to leave the house. Second, there would be a huge crowd, which made my anxiety even worse. Third, although Sammy was not nearly the HP fan that Sarah, Adam and I were, it would still feel horrible to go without him. Were he alive, we would all be going together. I couldn't do it. I told Sarah she could invite her best friend to use the extra ticket. The kids had been planning their costumes for weeks. Sarah was going as Hermione after she drinks the Polyjuice potion with the cat hair in it, Adam was going as a Slytherin boy, and Lydia was going as Moaning Myrtle. They excitedly got dressed, we took some pictures, and Jake took them to the theater. I took a Xanax, climbed into bed, and cried. I missed Samuel. I wanted to see his face and brush back his silky hair. I hated that he was missing out on *Harry Potter*. I hated that he would miss out on everything. He had barely lived. I cried hard until the pill kicked in, and I finally fell asleep.

Chapter 20

"He had the look of one who had drunk the cup of life and found a dead beetle at the bottom."

-P.G. Wodehouse, *Love Stinks*

Wednesday, November 24

One Month After Sammy Died

November 24, 2010, marked the one-month date since whatever happened to Sammy, happened. We decided to remember and honor him by going to eat at Waffle House; it was one of his favorite restaurants.

After we left Waffle House, we drove downtown to one of the tattoo parlors, where Jake, Sarah, and I would be getting tattoos. Sarah had wanted to get a Sammy tattoo since October 25. I had suggested she wait, and we could all do it on Sammy's one-month memorial. It would give her time to make sure it wasn't something she would later regret, and she would have time to decide exactly what she wanted. Over the previous month, she hadn't changed her mind. She wanted a tattoo as a way to pay tribute to her beloved brother.

We each were taken into different rooms to get our tattoos, so I asked Adam to stay with Sarah. When my tattoo was finished, I rushed into Sarah's room. Adam was standing behind her with his hands on her shoulders. He was encouraging her, supporting her, and letting her know he was with her. It made me cry. There was a time when she would have had three brothers surrounding her. Only one brother remained in her life: her baby brother, the youngest of my three sons.

November 25, 2010

On Thanksgiving Day, I didn't feel the least bit thankful. I was full of anger that Sammy was dead. I was pissed at the world, and my grief was raging. Why was *my* child taken? I was no saint, but I thought I was a good mother and a good person. It should have been the child of a selfish, lying, mean, bad person. I hadn't heard from my mom or Valerie since they left my house on November 7, which only fueled my anger. That hurt. A lot. I was enraged that my family members had just stopped coming to see us, calling us, or doing anything to help us through the pit of hell (except for Hank and Laura who were still regularly calling and checking in on us). What kind of people did that to their family members? Who did that to people they were supposed to love?

We were calling the day, Fucksgiving. In the past, I wouldn't have allowed the kids to use that kind of language so freely. Sadly for us, it was no longer the past where Sammy had been alive. It was the present, where Sammy was dead and we didn't understand how or why. We weren't thankful, and we didn't give a fuck what people thought about our mourning choices. It was irritating to call the day "Thanksgiving" when we didn't feel thankful. We made barbecue chicken pizza, Sammy's favorite, and took it with us to eat at Sammy's grave.

I was also angry about and could not stand to hear any more people tell me they were praying for me, nor could I stomach reading anymore comments on my Facebook wall about trusting God, having faith, believing it was part of God's plan, that Sammy was in a better place, or that everything happens for a reason. There *was* a small bit of comfort in the love and sympathy of others, regardless of how they chose to word their condolences. Somehow, knowing they were thinking of our family made the pain feel spread out a little instead of only resting on my heart, like others were helping to carry a little of the enormous weight of the grief. It was just that the religious nature of some of the comments was becoming wearisome.

CAVEAT - Skip the next part if you are a religious person and a grieving parent. The last thing I would want to do is to heap more pain or uncertainty on the shoulders of fellow suffering, bereaved parents. The next part is simply my non-believing response to some of the typical comments (many of the religious nature). The comments were irritating, in part, because I was no longer a believer, and, in part, because even if I *had* still a believer they seemed trite.

1. ***"He is in a better place."***

Really? Because I think the best place for a child is with his mother! If Heaven is a better place and God really loves us, then why are we all not there already with him.

2. ***"God needed another angel."***

Well, if that is the reason then screw you, God. I needed my child. He was my angel. You are supposed to be all-powerful. Make your own damn angel.

3. ***"God doesn't give us more than we can handle."***

First of all, what does "handle" even mean?! I am still alive. Does that mean I could handle it? If it does, then I suppose, yes, I could handle it—for the time. I haven't offed myself yet anyway. However, I can assure you, my son being hanged to death was definitely more than I could handle. It broke me and left an empty shell of the former me (although I am still breathing and have a beating heart)

Second, that statement—"God doesn't give us more than we can handle"— implies that God either gave us the tragedy, Sammy's death, or at the very least allowed it to happen. If he could not prevent it, he is impotent. If he could have prevented it, but chose not to, or if he planned it, he is a jerk. If that is how God treats his friends, I don't need the friendship.

4. ***"God allowed this to happen in order to bring you back into the fold."***

To that I say to God, the family Bradshaw does not negotiate with terrorists.

5. *"Everything happens for a reason."*

God allowed the tragedy to happen because one day Sammy would have grown up to become a murderous psychopath. Or perhaps, one day he would have developed a horrible disease which would have caused him to suffer miserably for months before he died. Were there no better options for God to have handled it? Couldn't God have just not let Sammy be born? Wouldn't that have been easier on everyone? We wouldn't all be broken-hearted and suffering. Whatever the supposed reason for it happening, had there really been no gentler way? If the hideous pain with which we all had been afflicted and were living with was the reason, then God is a masochist and I have no interest in that kind of relationship. Also, I don't buy the answer of, "I can't understand it now but in time I will, because everything happens for a reason." That sounds like poor reasoning to me: bad logic. It sounds like a circular argument

Essentially, God, or why God allows bad things to happen, cannot be proven, so you must just "believe," or you must "have faith." In order to believe "Everything happens for a reason and therefore there is a reason Sammy is dead," you have to first accept many things which have no proof. You must believe: 1. God exists. 2. God is all-powerful and all-knowing. 3. God is loving and merciful. 4. God loves you and has a wonderful plan for your life (except, apparently, he didn't love Sammy or didn't have a wonderful plan for his life. Unless, somehow being hanged to death was part of the wonderful plan for Sammy's life.) Why should I just decide to believe in all of those things without any proof? In order for me to believe "everything happens for a reason," I must first have scientific evidence that God exists. For far too long and with no scientific proof, I swallowed evasive evangelical Christian lines. For example, "if I really loved God, I would trust in him and his plan," which apparently, included my son being hanged to death; that sounds like an abusive relationship to me—"baby, you gotta believe that I love you" says the wife-beater). To date, I have not seen or heard any hard evidence proving God exists, but I continue to be beseeched by friends and family (and strangers too) to "have faith." Honestly, I would rather "have faith" that Sammy could rise from the dead if I am going out on a limb to believe something with no proof.

6. ***"I am praying for you."***

Even among my mostly religious grief group, this feels empty when not accompanied by anything else (although it is acceptable for social media friends). It feels like others think if they say they are praying for you, they feel they have done their part and don't feel they need to do anything else. While grieving mothers who are religious might appreciate the prayers, they *need* much more. "I am praying for you," feels like a cop out to me. By saying "I am praying for you," you essentially are saying, "I feel bad for you and sorry for you, and saying I'm praying for you (and possibly following through and truly praying) makes me feel better, like I am doing something without really having to do anything." So, if you tell a grieving mother you are praying for her, support your words with actions. Do something for her. Then, you have earned the right to tell her you are praying for her.

Here's the other problem I see with praying—Don't you think if God already made the decision to kill my child, or to allow my child to be killed, that he will do whatever he wants? Is he really going to do anything differently because people ask? Doesn't it seem to show a lack of trust in God to ask him for things if you believe everything happens for a reason? If he is all-knowing and all-powerful, and if he chose to kill Sammy or allow him to be killed, don't you think he already knows if he is going to give strength or peace to my family? If your prayers are doing anything, then people should be praying all the time asking God to not kill their loved ones. If he still kills the loved ones, then the praying is pointless. Another thing, if God really loves me, why must I ask for things from him? I don't wait until my children ask me before I do what is best for them. I simply do what is best for them.

7. **"At least you have other children."**

While I am very grateful that I have other children and I love them with all that is left of my damaged heart, that doesn't take away the pain of losing this specific person: Sammy. Sammy was a unique person. Neither Sarah, Adam, nor Lydia are Sammy. My children are not just non-unique, non-specific beings to keep me busy. I have a relationship with each member of my family. I'm not grieving because one of the five children I birthed is dead; I am grieving because my precious and highly individual son Sammy is dead. I miss Sammy's soft skin. I miss Sammy's pretty, puffy lips. I miss Sammy's little jokes, his laugh, his randomness, and his face, not just some generic spot that was child number three. Although, having the privilege of knowing and loving three of my four other little humans I birthed is still something I am able to enjoy, it in no way lessens how much I miss Sammy.

8. *"You are so strong. I couldn't have done it."*

Just because this tragedy happened to me doesn't mean I'm strong. I'm just like everybody else. If I survive the loss, and am able to move back into the land of the living one day, then perhaps, you can tell me how strong I have been. Right after I have lost my child, which to me means in the first four years or so, telling me I am so strong has no meaning, even if you are trying to be encouraging.

In summary, the religious comments were pushing all of the wrong buttons for me. I finally wrote a message on my Facebook wall and told everyone I didn't want to hear any more about God's will, prayers, or glass half-full crap. I only asked for love, sympathy, and human kindness, and to leave religion out of it. Besides, from everything I had seen throughout life, good deeds had less to do with someone's religious beliefs and more to do with a person's inherent goodness. Even the Bible supported the truth that words without actions are meaningless.

"What good is it, my brothers and sisters, if someone claims to have faith but has no deeds? Can such faith save them? Suppose a brother or sister is without clothes and daily food. If you say to them, 'Go in peace; keep warm and well fed,' but do nothing about their physical needs, what good is that? In the same way, faith by itself, if it is not accompanied by action is dead." James 2:14 NIV

Friday, November 25

The day after Thanksgiving, we drove two hours for a holiday dinner with Jo and her family. She had invited us, I had heard nothing from my family, and we had no strength to cook food at home. It was a nice distraction to be away from the house and to be with people who were not dripping with pain and sorrow. If I thought leaving town would allow me to escape from the some of pain, I was wrong; all of the pain and misery went with me. It was a lesson—I couldn't run from the pain, at least not during the acute phase (I assumed and hoped I would not always be in an acute phase). Where I went, so did the heartache. Eating the Thanksgiving meal was miserable. It had always been a large family event, but Sammy wasn't there with us and we weren't with family. I struggled with eating a big, delicious meal, while Sammy lay cold and alone in the ground in the cemetery. I ended up in the bathroom having a meltdown. Later in the evening, it was Sarah having the huge, sobbing meltdown. The pain of my own broken heart was heinous, but to try to comfort my grieving child was pure hell. I had no good advice with which to soothe her. There was nothing I could do to bring back Sammy. He was forever lost to us. The only thing to do was to just keep going on, to keep putting one foot in front of the other (as Dad would have said.) We had to continue to live, breathe, and keep walking on with our lives, in spite of the awful, awful, pain.

Jo organized an activity for everyone, in which each person was to sing, act, dance, or give some small performance to earn their dinner. She exempted me and our family, but I wanted to participate and wrote a dark poem for my part, called "Letter to Death."

> I do not apologize for what I am about to read, but if you are uncomfortable with cursing or violent thoughts or would prefer not to hear the ranting of a broken hearted mother, then by all means, excuse yourself.
>
> To Death,
>
> Fuck you very much for stealing my sweet, precious, 13-year-old boy, Samuel; my son, my Puffy, my Sammy the

Body, my Hot Pocket, my Puffmeister, my ray of sunshine; my studly, handsome, kind, funny, loyal and loving child.

Fuck you for being such a coward as to snatch him when he was away from home and not under my watchful eye and protective care.

 Fuck you for taking him in such a violent way and without leaving any clues, reasons, or answers.

Fuck you for robbing my sweet boy of the excitement of his first kiss, the thrill of driving a car, the infatuation of first love, the pleasure of sex, the buzz of a beer, the nausea of getting drunk, the honor of becoming a fireman, the satisfaction of earning his own money, the joy and peace of finding his soul mate, the love and beauty of a happy marriage, the miracle of watching his children be born, the pride of seeing his children grow up, the joy of being a grandpa, and the wisdom of growing old.

Fuck you, Death; you piece of shit, you motherfucking asshole.

If I could find you, I would spit on you, laugh at you, and dismember you limb by limb until you were merely a torso and a head: then I would stop.

Chapter 21

"There are ships sailing to many ports, but not a single one goes where life is not painful."

-Fernando Pessoa, *The Book of Disquiet*

December

Five to Seven Weeks After Sammy Died

Concerned about a few things with respect to the medical examiner, I sent an email to our attorney. The most important thing was that I discovered when the medical examiner had moved to town 15 years before, he had briefly attended the same church my ex-husband and I attended (and where my ex had been an associate pastor). During one of our phone conversations, the M.E. made a statement that was concerning to me, and I wondered if his judgment might be biased. I was concerned that knowing Sammy and Peter's father as a minister, he might brush aside minor peculiarities with Sammy's autopsy (because he might not believe Peter—or for that matter, Lucas—could have played any part in the hanging). The M.E. told me he "did not feel Sammy's death was a suicide, but possibly a terrible accident, and whether Peter was involved or not, no one needed to be prosecuted here." While it might be true that, "no one needed to be prosecuted here," I thought that was an inappropriate comment from the medical examiner (besides the fact that he made the statement in complete ignorance of the history of choking, sleeper hold, ect., between Peter and Sammy). I also was not pleased when I discovered the M.E. had failed to scrape under Sammy's fingernails for skin, did not initially perform a histamine test, and said he couldn't give me an exact time of death. He did tell me that, in his opinion, based on the appearance of the edges of the ligature mark, Sammy's heart was still beating when the strap was applied to his neck. I asked him if with the evidence he had, if he could rule out if a sleeper chokehold was performed on Sammy prior to his hanging. He said, "No, it could not be ruled out, but it was very difficult to prove; almost impossible without a confession." I asked my attorney if I should get a second opinion on the autopsy. I had already called the St. Louis Chief Medical Examiner's office and spoken briefly to them, and they advised me to speak first with my attorney.

My attorney promptly responded, "The local medical examiner's office is excellent. If it is "difficult" to prove for them, it will be difficult to prove for anyone anywhere. The only way a medical examiner is likely to conclude "homicide" is if there is some evidence (confession) of criminal agency." On the death certificate, the M.E. selects one of the multiple-choice options as the cause of death: suicide, homicide, accident or unknown. He had marked Sammy's cause of death as "unknown."

I continued to think through every single possible scenario that could explain Sammy's death. The police were still investigating, and I occasionally called Detective Higgins to ask if she had anything new. Something that had bugged me from the very first day was that I didn't think Sammy weighed enough for the strap to have occluded, or blocked, his carotid arteries. His appearance indicated they were blocked. If he didn't weigh enough, then they had been blocked before he was hung.

Before our lives were tragically altered, I worked on the neurology floor at the hospital for a year and a half. I frequently cared for the patients of an outstanding neurosurgeon who is considered the best in the Midwest. He is brilliant, hardworking, and honest, and I have tremendous respect for him. I had no idea if he would remember who I was, as I had moved off the neuro floor to a different unit about a year before Sammy's death, but I called him and left a message. I was hoping to speak with him about Sammy's death appearance. I was surprised and appreciative when he returned my call later that evening.

I explained to the doctor that Sammy was found hanging. I told him I wanted to describe Sammy's appearance and then hear any thoughts he might have. I explained that Sammy had no blood coming from his eyes, ears, or mouth, his tongue was not engorged, he had no petechiae on his face, his facial color was pale, he had no uncal herniation, and no midline shift. I also told him there were no scuffmarks or any kind of marks on the wall or door from which Sammy was hanging, Sammy was 5 feet tall and weighed 100 pounds, and the strap used in the hanging was about an inch wide.

"Hmmm," he said, "Okay, not to fan the flame or anything, but something doesn't add up. The carotid arteries need a certain amount of pressure to be occluded. Now, if a person was to apply direct pressure, they could easily do that with a thumb and forefinger without even leaving a mark. But, for the carotids to be occluded by the indirect pressure of a strap..." Pause, and then, "He weighed 100 pounds?...." A long pause.

I spoke up, "Sammy didn't weigh enough for his carotids to be occluded by the strap, right?" That was exactly the question the doctor was considering. I asked him what he would have expected Sammy's appearance to be and he said; engorged tongue, petechiae, blood coming from eyes, nose, and signs of kicking and struggling, because blood should have still been traveling to the brain. The fact that he didn't have that appearance told us that blood wasn't traveling to the brain, meaning either the carotids were occluded by the strap, or the blood flow to the brain had already stopped when he was hung. Three times during our 45-minute conversation, the doctor said, "Not to fan the flame, but..." and then went on to describe the difficulty he had with the facts he was given adding up to Sammy hanging himself. He did say that it wasn't impossible, but with the information I had given him, unlikely.

When the phone call was finished, I felt a little vindicated. I had suspected the same thing all along. Could the detectives do anything with the information? I didn't know. I organized my lists of all of the possible death scenarios and the problems with each scenario, both for my own benefit, as well as to email to the detectives.

A few thoughts before jumping into the possible scenarios:

Although he was not as book smart as Peter, Sammy had much more common sense and street smarts. If for some strange reason, he behaved contrary to his normal behavior and attempted one of the following scenarios, I am almost positive he would have used a chair. However, I could easily imagine if Peter (my abstract thinking, absent-minded son) killed Sammy, and then hung him to make it look like a suicide, he very possibly might have overlooked the need for a chair.

I talked with Sammy's friend, Trever, who had been at Lucas's house with Sammy on Saturday, Oct 23. He stated that Sammy was totally normal that Saturday. He said they had never tried the choking game and had never even talked about choking game. He also denied playing with or even seeing any neon duffle bag strap that day. (I was curious as to where the strap came from, and if, perhaps, they had been playing with it that day. It would have made more sense to me that Sammy might have used the strap for something if he had been messing with it that day—or ever.) I also talked with Kyle, Sammy's best friend; he said they had never tried the choking game and had never talked about it.

Sammy had only been allowed to start attending overnights the summer before his October death. He had spent the night at a friend's house and had a friend over to our house to spend the night, a total of one time each (both times it was Kyle.) He didn't go to other people's houses to hang out either; he was always at school, at an activity, somewhere with us, at home, or at Lucas's house. He didn't have many opportunities for the privacy expected if (contrary to what his friends reported) he had been trying out the choking game.

Cause of Death Scenarios: Only Sammy

These potential scenarios assume it was even possible for the strap to have occluded Sammy's carotid arteries (that Sammy weighed enough).

1. Suicide- Sammy showed no indicators or history of depression, had no known problems at school, was not bullied, had friends, and appeared happy. Plus, there was no

chair, the strap was a loop not a noose, there was no note, and could he have gotten into the strap alone and with nothing to climb on?
2. Autoerotic asphyxiation- Sammy was fully dressed, and there were no materials at the scene, in his room, or anywhere else to support this theory. Plus, there was no chair and no safety release (no way to release pressure on neck when desired.)
3. A prank- Samuel had not ever pulled a prank. Pranks were not his nature. If it was a prank, it much more likely would have included Peter. Plus, there was no chair, no safety release, and why would he turn on a fan or lock his door if it was a prank?
4. The choking game- prior to death, Sammy showed none of the signs to look for in teens privately experimenting with the choking game: no bloodshot eyes, no frequent, severe headaches, no disorientation after spending time alone (he didn't spend much time alone; he never was in his room except when we told him to go to bed at night and for his final six months at our house he didn't even have a door on his bedroom—and didn't complain about it—because I removed it to paint and had not yet rehung it.) There were no ropes, scarves or belts tied to bedroom furniture or doorknobs or found knotted on the floor. Again, there was no chair and no safety release, and why turn on the fan?
5. An accident- If it was a complete accident then why was his door shut and locked and why was the fan turned on.

A few thoughts, including what I think is the most likely theory: The medical examiner stated that the ligature mark on Sammy's neck indicated Sammy's heart was still beating—either normally or erratically—when he was hung.

So, 1.) he was hung from the strap when his heart was beating normally, which would seem to indicate he was a lone actor or a willing participant;

Or 2.) he was hung within 25 minutes after being choked out, before his heart had completely stopped beating.

To my mind, the most likely cause of death scenario:

1. Sammy was choked out, and whether accidentally or intentionally, someone held the choke hold too long.
2. Sammy didn't regain consciousness (which usually happens within 10-20 seconds after release of choke hold). He remained unconscious, but his heart continued to beat erratically.
3. Within 20-25 minutes someone hoisted him up his closet door so he looked like he hung himself.

Notable Things Regarding Peter

1. Peter did not have a verifiable alibi for the time of the incident- "I went to bed at 11:00 and slept pretty hard. I got up at 9:00."
2. Peter had choked Sammy in the past on several occasions when he had gotten angry and sometimes when he was joking around and playing too hard.
3. Peter's behavior upon "finding" Sammy was outside of normal.

Questions for the Detective

1. Did anyone look or take pictures of Peter or Lucas's arms the day of or days after the death, to check for scratch marks?
2. Was the strap used fingerprinted to make sure Sammy's fingerprints were on the clips? If they were not, wouldn't that tell us something?
3. Were pictures taken of the downstairs tv room that morning so that Adam and Sarah could look and see if things appeared different than the night before or if they had been disturbed?
4. Did anyone asked Lucas where the duffle bag was located prior to that night?

<u>Additional Thoughts</u>

Sarah, Adam, and Lydia state that they never saw Peter or Sammy messing around with a neon strap on Friday or Saturday at any time. Trever said that he and Sammy did not play with nor did he ever see a neon strap when he was over on Saturday.

Was it not odd that two weeks after your brother's death by hanging, and particularly when you were the one who found him, to go hunting and to kill a deer.

Lydia was very upset after seeing Peter on Halloween, one week after Sammy died, because she said he was very hyper and acted as if nothing had happened.

When we saw Peter at Mother's house on Halloween, we also observed that he was oddly cheerful and definitely seemed as if the weight of the world had rolled off his shoulders.

Why didn't Peter cut him down right away when he first found him? Possibly because he wanted someone else to see the scene.

Was Peter lying about his bedtime, and if so, what was his reason for lying. He never went to bed at 11:00; he certainly wouldn't have gone to bed if Sammy was still awake. It would be more believable if Peter had said he and Sammy were playing Xbox until 3:00 in the morning and then they went to bed.

Was it a coincidence that the incident occurred on a night that Adam wasn't sleeping downstairs and Peter and Sammy were alone down there?

Was it part of a plan to invite Sammy to a movie, the only time that Peter had ever done so, one week before the incident occurred to make it look like he and Sammy were buddies?

Why was Peter so reluctant to call 911?

Why was Peter so reluctant to touch Sammy's body?

Was it a coincidence that Sammy mentioned to his dad, Jake, shortly before the incident that Peter told him he knew how to take someone down in six seconds by performing a sleeper hold?

Where was the duffle bag that the strap came off located prior to this evening? Lydia said she was playing hide and seek with the kids two weeks earlier and she did not see the duffle bag in Sammy's closet.

Sammy never just hung out in his room; the only time he ever went into his room was to go to bed. If everyone were going to bed, he would have gone to bed.

If Peter was involved, the fact that the medical examiner believed the strap was applied prior to the heart while it was still beating might indicate they were messing around with the strap already, or Peter had the strap already to use prior to the sleeper hold, which pointed to pre-meditation.

If they were fooling around and Sammy went unconscious, why had Peter not run upstairs and gotten Lucas or Sarah? Either he was afraid, or this was premeditated?

If Sammy were just goofing around, he would not have locked his door. He never locked his door.

The only reason the door might have been locked, would have been if he was really attempting suicide, the autoerotic asphyxiation, or the choking game, none of which seem plausible to me. Or, if someone hung him there and locked the door on the way out of his room to make it look like a suicide.

The fan in the bathroom was on. Sammy *never* turned the bathroom fan on after he used the bathroom. And if he was goofing around, he wouldn't have turned the fan on. Peter and Sammy were the only ones downstairs. One of them turned on the fan. Sammy was very simple, not strategic; Peter, the chess wiz, was the strategic one.

The first week of December, I emailed these lists to the police department. I didn't know if they would be at all useful, but they couldn't hurt. Then, I waited. I would later discover that because of a tight filter on incoming emails at the police station, the police didn't receive the lists.

Part 3

"My sister will die over and over again for the rest of my life. Grief is forever. It doesn't go away; it becomes a part of you, step for step, breath for breath. I will never stop grieving Bailey because I will never stop loving her. That's just how it is. Grief and love are conjoined; you don't get one without the other. All I can do is love her, and love the world, emulate her by living with daring and spirit and joy."

-Jandy Nelson, *The Sky is Everywhere*

Chapter 22

"Disappointment is a sort of bankruptcy - the bankruptcy of a soul that expends too much in hope and expectation."

-Eric Hoffer, *The Passionate State of Mind*

Friday, December 10

Six Weeks Five Days After Sammy Died

Nearly seven weeks after Sammy's death, Detective Higgins called with the police report. My heart rate quickened in anticipation when I saw her name on my caller I.D. Finally, we would have some answers. "Hi Detective Higgins," I answered. She got right to the point and informed me Sammy's case had been made inactive. They would no longer be actively investigating. I was speechless. For five full seconds the phone was silent.

"Soo, what happened to him?" I finally asked. They didn't have an exact answer. Their unverifiable conclusion was that Sammy had an accident. If they received new information, the case would be made active again, and they would investigate further. They were switching the case to inactive rather than closing it, because they didn't have a conclusive answer as to what happened. For the time, there was nothing more they could do.

I felt like a helium-filled balloon that has been untied at the bottom so it hisses and streaks back and forth through the air and then falls flat on the ground. If the police and professional detectives couldn't figure out what happened, who could?

Detective Higgins invited us to the police station to review things and ask questions. When we arrived, we were led to a small room where we took a seat across from Detective Higgins and another detective. They showed us pictures they took of Sammy's room the morning of his death and pictures of the neon orange nylon duffle bag strap. Then, they gave us a quick summary.

"Okay," Detective Higgins said, "What are your questions?"

I spoke up, "Is it even possible Sammy could have gotten into the strap by himself?"

"Yes, we believe he could have," she answered. "We took a strap that was similar to the one used and went to the house and into Sammy's room. We hooked it over the hinge of the closet door. Since I am 5'2", I am only two inches taller than Sammy. If I stood with my back against the closet door, I could jump up in to the strap," she finished.

I tried to imagine what she meant. Sammy's back would have been against the inside corner of one of the closet's double doors. The strap would have to already have been hooked over the hinge. Then, he would have to have held the looped strap out in order to get his head into it when he jumped. The strap wasn't very long; could he have reached that high? If he could even reach and hold onto the strap, could he have gotten his head through the loop with the door swinging around? If you tried to open the door all the way, it opened into the walkway area in front of Sammy's bedroom door. It opened up to about 190 degrees, and then—because the hinge wouldn't allow it to open further—it started to swing back the other direction. In other words, the door couldn't be braced against a wall so jumping into the strap would have been tricky. Since he would have been holding the strap out in order to jump up and get his head in, how did he get his head in the loop without trapping his fingers under his chin or by the sides of his head? It didn't seem plausible to me. Had Detective Higgins *literally* jumped up into the strap herself, or had she merely stood with her back against the door holding out the loop and *thought* she could do it? In addition, one had to assume that for whatever reason, Sammy intended to do it—get his head in the strap/loop. In my mind, there was no scenario in which Sammy acted alone that made sense.

"What was his intention?" I asked. (A stupid question, which she obviously couldn't answer.) She said they weren't sure.

They didn't think it was suicide, and they had no physical evidence to support any of the other things—the choking game, auto erotic asphyxiation, foul play—which they had looked into. They did think it was possible for him to have jumped up into the loop by himself, so with no hard evidence they were left to assume he did it by himself. "Maybe he was just messing around?" she offered.

Again, I was speechless. I didn't even know what to ask. "Sammy wasn't stupid," I said. "He wouldn't have just decided he would try and jump up and see if he could get his head into a noose," I said, "or do it to see what it would feel like. He had too much common sense." Also, if he was just fooling around, he wouldn't have locked the door or turned on the fan. To me, those two things pointed to someone doing something with intention, like a suicide or a cover-up, and a cover-up made much more sense than a suicide. I could never see Sammy being so strategic as to lock his door and for him to have turned on the fan for any reason was not believable. That wasn't how he operated. Maybe, if he was attempting suicide he might have shut and locked his door, but to have gone and turned on the bathroom fan? No way. Also, suicide wasn't in Sammy's genetic make-up. He wasn't a hypersensitive boy. He was simple, easy-going, and funny. He might occasionally lose his temper, but if that had happened and he was really mad at Peter or Lucas, he wouldn't have then decided to kill himself. If anything, he might have left the house, walked to the gas station, and called me. *Could* he have just been messing around with the strap? Possibly, but then he wouldn't have turned on the fan or shut and locked his door, and Peter wouldn't have passed by his room to go to bed with Sammy still awake. If the door had been shut and locked, Peter definitely wouldn't have passed by. He would have wanted to know what Sammy was doing and if Sammy hadn't opened the door for him, he would have picked the lock with the hanger.

"Any other questions?" asked the detective, drawing me away from my thoughts. Their job was to investigate the death for evidence of foul play. They had no physical evidence of foul play, just suspicions and theories. I was devastated. I had been certain they would get to the bottom of what happened to Sammy.

Until that moment, I hadn't realized I had been holding myself together with faith that the police would discover the answers to Sammy's death. My hope that whatever happened to Sammy would be figured out dissolved. There would be no answers. I wouldn't find out how or why my child ended up hanging from his neck by a duffle bag strap. I would receive no understanding as to how that became my son's end. There would be no sense of closure. I simply had to live with the fact that Sammy was dead, with no understanding of why.

The shock, incomprehension, and intermittent numbness I had experienced since October 24, receded, and I was left with only the raw gaping wound. The pain was acutely intense. My chest ached all the time. My heart collapsed on her knees, rocking forward and back with outstretched hands, palms up to the sky, screaming "Why?!?" at the universe. The pain in my chest and the screaming of my heart, throttled up in intensity and became almost unbearable.

Although I had been struggling with the grief over the previous seven weeks, I had managed to maintain a sense of purpose. Without the investigation and not having any answers about Sammy's death, I quickly deteriorated. I had been having two or three drinks a day, but I began to drink all day. I threw a shot or two of vodka into each of my six to ten glasses of Coke Zero, because without it, the pain was utterly heinous. It was impossible to go through every minute of every hour of every day with that burning, shrieking pain. I could barely make it through each day; it was daunting and completely overwhelming to think I might have to live the rest of my life in that amount of pain.

Several hours every day, I looked through my pictures of Sammy on our computer. I put together online photo books of his life: his childhood, his sport endeavors, pictures with me and/or with Jake, or all of the kids. I made picture slide shows with music— when he was a baby, over the span of his life, the last two years of his life—and every night I watched one of those picture movies, sitting in his favorite recliner, weeping. It was slightly soothing to sit next to our brick fireplace, watching, warming, and sleeping by the fire. Jake cut down some of the lower limbs from the trees in our yard to chop up for firewood. The tree limbs needed to be cut down anyway, and it provided wood, which we couldn't afford to buy. In spite of his own pain, Jake did anything he could think of to try to alleviate mine.

Our new kitty Samantha also soothed me a tiny bit. While I lay on the couch, Samantha reclined on me. She was persnickety, had to be stroked in a certain way, and ran off if I moved too much, but she was nice to have around. Her presence, the weight of her warm body on my legs, and the silkiness of her soft, black fur, ever so slightly mollified my pain. Samantha was my daily companion.

In mid-December, I realized I needed to make Christmas plans. I had to do something for the kids, although drinking myself to oblivion would have been my preference. I didn't, and couldn't, leave the house but shopped from my laptop. Buying presents for Sarah, Adam, and Lydia, but not Sammy, was utterly wretched. I uploaded a few pictures of Sammy and made some photo memorial jewelry for Christmas presents: keychain, charm bracelets, picture necklace charms. Then I uploaded pictures to Walgreens and made ornaments and a few blankets with Sammy's picture on them for each of us.

There was no way we could go out to the Christmas tree farm and cut down a tree, not without Sammy. He had loved going to the tree farm each December and had been our only child who could cut through the tree trunk with a hand saw. I didn't want to cut down a tree. I didn't want to put up a tree either, but I felt I had to do something to make the house at least a little festive for the kids. The only way I could tolerate a tree in the house was if, somehow, it was also an acknowledgement of Sammy, which I decided meant it had to be a metallic blue tree. I don't know why that made sense to me, except I thought Sammy would have liked metallic blue.

We found, purchased, and set up a blue Christmas tree, but the tree remained bare with no ornaments or decorations. Normally, every year I took the children to each pick out a new ornament that reflected their current interests or hobbies. Consequently, I had a big box of their ornaments from the past 17 years (since Peter's birth). Just the idea of seeing Sammy's ornaments—his Buzz Lightyear, Superman, Spiderman, his *Wizard of Oz* Lollipop Guild Boys, the fireman, or the baby booty with his baby picture and birth date on it, among all the rest of his ornaments collected through the years—was intolerable, so there were no ornaments. It was all I could do just to put up the blue tree.

Our Christmas was subdued. We didn't video the kids coming out of their bedrooms to the den to see what Santa had delivered; they all were still sleeping in our bedroom anyway. Santa did visit, and we took a few pictures. Everyone liked his or her Sammy charms and other gifts, but the wrongness of Sammy's absence was salient. I had to use all of my will power just to get out of bed. I strained to offer any smiles for the kids. My sweet, beautiful boy had lived such a short and incomplete life, and it wasn't fair.

Christmas afternoon, we went to visit Sammy's grave. It was snowing and very cold which felt like the appropriate weather. The snow covered everything making the cemetery look like one big grave. The only distinction between the graves was the headstones, and we didn't like that. Although the snow felt right, the lack of contrast between the graves did not. Sarah and Jake decided to build a snow wall around the perimeter of Sammy's grave. I stood back and watched with my drink in one hand and cigarette in the other. As I observed my husband and children lovingly pile snow around Sammy's grave that afternoon, I gave the Invisible Man in the Sky the bird. In fact, I think it was the double bird. Of course, I didn't believe in a supernatural being in the sky anymore, but just in case, I wanted him to know how I felt.

Later in the day, Laura came for a brief visit, and Tori sent a text. Aside from that, I heard nothing from my family. I had heard nothing since November 7. I guess there was still a small part of me that hoped surely on Christmas they would reach out. They didn't.

Over the holiday break from school, Jake and I watched a few films with the kids that included, in part, the topic of families experiencing the death of a child. I sensed my remaining three children were looking at me with increased worry in their eyes, and I didn't want them to fret. I wanted to help them understand that what I was going through was, for lack of a better word, "normal" for a grieving mom. They had observed that I was smoking more than ever and was regularly consuming alcohol. They had noticed I rarely showered and wore the same clothes for days. I knew I was struggling, but I knew I would make it through the quagmire of sorrow, if for no other reason than for *them*- my living children. I could make no promises as to how intact—or not—I might be once I survived the worst of grief, but for my babies, I would at least survive. Watching the movies helped them to see my reaction to Sammy's death was normal, and, in time, I would likely get better.

Jo suggested I watch the film, *What Dreams May Come*, starring Robin Williams. In the story, a couple loses their son and daughter in a car accident. The wife is completely devastated and becomes depressed, hopeless, and suicidal, slicing her wrists open and landing in a psych ward. She barely pulls through the tragedy. There is much more to the plot, but after Sarah, Adam, and Lydia saw the agony of that grieving mother, it seemed to help them have a better understanding and to look at me a little less anxiously. We watched *Rabbit Hole* with them next, and a few days afterwards Lydia said to me, "Mom, I am glad you don't do drugs to make yourself feel better (*Rabbit Hole*), and you still love Dad (again, *Rabbit Hole*), and you aren't suicidal (*What Dreams May Come*). You are doing just fine. It's okay that you mostly stay at home and don't wear make-up and are sad." Her mind, all of the kids' minds, seemed more at ease.

Another thing the children noticed was that I hadn't returned to work. I didn't know if I would ever return to work. The day after Sammy's death, the hospital gave me a leave of absence. They were very patient and understanding of my situation, and said they would hold my position for a period of time should I want to return. However, near the end of December they notified me if I wasn't going to return to work very soon I needed to resign so they could hire someone else. I had to make a decision.

I loved being a nurse, and I really liked the hospital where I had worked, especially the neurology and general medicine floors. Going back to work would keep me busy and possibly prevent me from obsessing too much over Sammy's death. It would help our family return to some kind of normalcy, and it would certainly be the right decision as far as easing our budget. Fortunately, I hadn't used many of my vacation days since I started at the hospital, so with those accumulated days I was still receiving paychecks. Unfortunately, I had finally used all of my Earned Time Off, and if I didn't return to work soon we would begin to have serious financial problems. Even when I was working we lived on a modest budget. Another consideration was that if I resigned and took more time off, going back later might be even more difficult. On the other hand, I had never been a person who could compartmentalize well. I had difficulty with the concept of collecting all of my thoughts, feelings, and emotions regarding something so enormous—such as my child's sudden death—and sticking them in a box on a shelf to deal with at a more convenient time. I was struggling with accepting and adapting to life without Sammy. I was angry all the time. I was mad at fate, the gods, and the universe that Sammy was gone. I was mad at my ex for not watching over Sammy better and for accepting Sammy's death as suicide. I was mad at my family for abandoning me during the most heinous period of my life. I was frustrated that the police made the case inactive. I was in a constant state of sorrow. I was a bawl bag. I was anxious. I was taking Xanax several times a day to help with the anxiety, and, honestly, I thought I was taking too much to be able to function safely in a nursing capacity at the hospital. In addition, there was the vodka in my Coke Zero. That also had to stop before I could go back. As a nurse, people's lives literally were in my hands, and I didn't want—on account of my distressed state—to administer drugs incorrectly and accidentally kill someone. Returning to work at that time would have been reckless and irresponsible.

We had a very long road ahead of us. My primary responsibility was my emotional health and mental stability, and then my husband's and children's. The life insurance money we received due to my father's generous foresight was nearly gone, and subsequently, we had just discontinued therapy. I had to be as available for my children (as much as I was able) anytime they needed me. They were trying to get their heads around the horrible reality of life without Sammy. They, especially Sarah, were also attempting to maintain their grades at school at the same time. Most importantly—as my dad used to say—I had to do what was right for me, and in the end that would be right for everybody. When I was younger, I thought that particular statement of Dad's sounded selfish. I realized as I grew older, his intent was not to promote selfishness. His intent was that if one didn't evaluate and address his (or her) own needs first, he would find himself too powerless, too poor, or too exhausted to be of any use to anyone. If returned to work because others thought that was best or because I thought I should for Jake or the kids, but it wasn't what I thought best for me, and I ended up falling apart/having a nervous breakdown/causing a major medical error/etc., *no one* would be better off. I had to do what was right for me to be the healthiest and best me, which would then be the best for others. I resigned.

Shortly after resigning, and as part of my attempt to distract myself from the hideous pain, I turned to one of my favorite pastimes: watching potential award-winning films. I made myself go to our local independent theater to see *The King's Speech*. It was a big step for me to be out of the house at the theater. Feeling anxious shortly into the film (in spite of my Coke Zero with several shots of vodka I had brought with me), I used my phone as a light to search my purse for my bottle of Xanax. An uptight woman sitting behind me called out for me to shut my phone. Surprised and a little irritated, I turned to look at her but didn't say anything. I carried on trying to locate the pill bottle lost in the bottom of my enormous purse. A different lady behind me then told me to put away my phone. *Seriously?* I thought, continuing my hunt for the bottle, *my son is dead and you women are so bothered by the minuscule amount of light from my cell phone that you have rudely called out for me to put it away?* I was anxious, looking for my Xanax. I felt the eyes of the two ladies on me and heard their disgruntled muttering. The scant lighting from my phone wasn't truly distracting from their viewing experience. They were likely just older, white, female, self-important, self-righteous rule-followers, who apparently didn't have enough going on in their lives so they knit-picked (I had experience with many of those throughout my decades in church). I grew increasingly irritated and flustered by their very audible continued murmuring, and I finally turned to the second lady and suggested she go fuck herself. The disgruntled woman's indignant husband got up and exited our theater. Soon an usher came and told me I had to leave. I stood, turned to the women, and through the tears choked out, "My 13-year-old son died two months ago, and I was looking for my Xanax!" Sobbing and dejected, I waited outside for Jake to pick me back up. People sucked. Life sucked. Everything sucked.

Chapter 23

"I no longer feel any allegiance to these monsters called human beings"

-Suzanne Collins, *Mockingjay*

January 2011

Two Months After Sammy Died

On New Year's Eve, I was completely abject. All I could think about was how the last year Sammy had lived was ending. He would never see 2011. On New Year's Eve the previous year, our decorations were up, we were eating strawberry cake from The Upper Crust bakery, and we were all playing Twister. In the middle of one Twister round, it was down to Sammy, Lydia, and me. I was straddling the mat, with one foot on one side of the mat on a red circle, the other foot on the other side of the mat on a green circle. It was all fun and games until Sammy said something hilarious, and I accidentally tinkled on the mat. In my defense, I *have* given birth to five babies, and I was standing in a completely spread eagle position. We all started cracking up, but Lydia was completely disgusted. Even after I thoroughly disinfected the mat, Lydia would not play anymore that night. Sammy jumped right back on the mat where he had been before the tinkle incident. He wasn't going to let any potential pee germs stop him from victory! Naturally, Sammy won. He was so flexible and strong and had such great balance none of us could ever beat him.

For New Year's Eve 2010, I didn't put up decorations. There was no strawberry cake. There certainly was no Twister. Instead, I was looking at pictures of Sammy's funeral on my computer and watching my Sammy videos. I made no resolutions. I would probably never again make resolutions; they had become a waste of time in my mind, as did planning of any kind. Who knew if you would even be alive tomorrow, so why waste time planning? It would be many years before I could bring myself to even purchase a daily planner, and several years more before I would be able to write in one.

January 14, 2011

One day in mid-January, after dropping the kids off at school, I drove to St Louis to see a few Oscar nominated films with Jo. I was uptight about the drive and being among all of the people in the theater, but at least there I wouldn't see anyone I knew and my best friend would be with me. The total disinterest in my personal grooming was still a problem and had worsened. My showers had become rare. I regularly wore the same sweats and t-shirts for days or weeks. I slid the pants off at night and climbed into bed in the t-shirt. The next morning, I pulled the sweats back on, slid my feet in my Uggs, and that was it. Before Sammy died, every day I would put on make-up, a clean outfit, and usually something small and sparkly, a pair of earrings or a bracelet. At bedtime, I *religiously* removed my make-up, washed and moisturized my face, and brushed my teeth—every single night. Over the years, when Jo would bring her children and come to town to visit me, she always found it amusing that no matter how late we might stay up talking, I didn't forgo my bedtime routine. The following morning, no matter how tired we might be from our late night chat, when I appeared to make breakfast I would have on a fresh outfit and make-up. But the old me, the one who gave care and attention to those kinds of personal grooming details, was gone, and the me who still lived was being decimated by grief and couldn't care less. I didn't care about anything, except Jake and the kids. I loved them. But I had nothing to give to them. I was alive, but that was all I had for them.

January 15, 2011

As of January 15, it had been 12 weeks since my precious boy was taken, and for the last ten of those miserable weeks, Mother and Valerie hadn't called or come to see me; it was unforgivable. I could not comprehend how, at such a horrible time, anyone could completely ignore family. I began to hate them. I seriously doubted whether I would ever again be able to enjoy any kind of relationship with either of them. How could they leave me alone in such a fiery pit of hell? I cried every single day, many times. My life felt like a complete disaster. One of my children was dead and one was... Well, he was out of my life, to say the least, but I was heart-broken over both of my older two sons. We were barely making ends meet. My house was a dirty mess. I looked like I was aging years overnight, and I had started gaining weight like crazy. I felt like I was barely alive. I spent most of everyday either asleep, or sitting outside sipping my coke and vodka, smoking, and listening to audiobooks. I didn't know how to help myself. I didn't know how to get through all of the pain. I didn't know anything.

January 29, 2011

On January 29, there was a bridal shower for Victoria for which I had zero desire to attend. In order to make myself go I had to muster all of the will-power, determination, and concerted effort I could. I didn't want to go anywhere or do anything much less dress up and socialize. I couldn't stand the thought of chitchatting about trivial things with people I barely knew, or with those I knew but with whom I was disappointed and angry.

"How have you been doing, Jane?" an acquaintance at the shower might ask.

I would want to answer with something like, "Well, my 13-year-old son, Samuel, died three months ago; his brother and sister found him hanging from his bedroom closet. So, life has been complete hell. We have no idea why he was hanging, but there were all kinds of odd details at his death scene that didn't seem to add up, so the cops investigated for two months. They couldn't determine exactly what happened, but to make it all sickeningly worse, they suspected my oldest son was involved and questioned him several times. I also worry that he was involved. He was acting very weird on the morning Sammy died, but we don't have any answers. On top of all that my mom and sister got mad at me because on the day

Sammy died I said something rude to Mother. And then I asked the family if they would stop having so much communication with my ex-husband, with the investigation into Sammy's death going on and all, but they got mad about that too, refused to respect what I asked, and haven't visited or called me in nearly three months. I have been so wracked with grief that Sammy is dead I can hardly make myself go on living. How are you?"

I was completely let down, disgusted, hurt, and angry with most of my family (with the exception of Laura who dropped by to visit every few weeks). It was the end of January, and I had last seen Valerie and Mother on November 7. Victoria had come by a few times after Halloween and texted very sporadically, but she was busy with her wedding plans. To make the situation even more challenging, I was fairly certain Tori had told Mother and Valerie about the incident at the independent theater (I had heard they were both aware). Someone let me know that Tori's wedding photographer was at the theater that night and had told Tori what happened. How Tori thought sharing such information could be helpful in healing the family rift, I couldn't understand. I was so angry with my mother and sister I wanted to scream at them for abandoning me. Whenever I thought of them, I felt like crying. I had believed in their love. I had trusted in them, and in my darkest hours, they had completely let me down.

I didn't want to leave the house. I didn't like being around other people anymore. If my own mother and closest sister wouldn't come to my aid during the most horrible time of loss and despair in my life (regardless of their anger), who would? So what was the point of cultivating relationships? My grooming (or rather lack of grooming) issue also presented a problem. The event was a bridal shower, a very social gathering and at which my family and many people who knew them would be present. I barely had the energy for the basic things required for living, much less doing my hair and makeup. I had gained 15 pounds since December 10 when Sammy's case was made inactive. So, there was a two-fold problem: 1) I looked overweight and gross, and 2) my clothes no longer fit. In spite of all of the reasons which inclined me to stay home and not attend, I did think going would be good practice to see if there was even a remote possibility of my attending Tori's wedding in February. So, I drank a little extra vodka, showered, found something in my closet that happened to have an elastic waist, and went to the shower.

When I walked into the partitioned room at the restaurant, my mother said loudly, "Well, there's my baby girl!" She might have been genuinely happy to see me, but—because I no longer trusted her—I didn't trust the motive behind her uncharacteristically warm and friendly demeanor. Her joyful greeting was probably one of the friendliest I had ever received from her in my life, but it roused not a flicker of warmth from me. What was left of my ruptured, hemorrhaging heart, felt no trace of life or love. Out of courtesy to those around me, and a sense of duty and obligation to the one who gave me life, I walked over and gave her a curt, "Hello, Mother," and a perfunctory hug. I then walked to a side table and sat next to Laura. Valerie wasn't there due to a schedule conflict. I made it through the shower, but it was neither pleasant nor easy.

I have always had a hard time brushing aside arguments and/or misunderstandings without discussing them with the involved parties. Whether I have been wronged, or I have wronged someone else, I cannot ignore it, act like it didn't happen, and move on. I must talk it out with the person. Pretending everything is normal without talking it out is not in my DNA. There was no way I could have faked pleasantries with my mother at the shower. I felt completely justified in my anger and didn't know if I could ever forgive her or Valerie, even if they asked, which they hadn't.

January 30, 2011

By the end of January, it had been 14 weeks since my sweet, funny boy was snatched away. I started having conflicting emotions when I caught glimpses of my broken heart necklace in the mirror. Some days, it comforted me to know that where he rested, in his satin bed with his blankie and lambie, Sammy wore the other half of the heart, and we shared a connection. Other days, it made me think about him being cold and alone in his casket deep down in the ground. When that thought flashed into my mind, I could hardly stand it, and my stomach dropped like it does when you go over a big hill in a fast car. Then, my aching heart would feel as if it had just scraped against the gritty asphalt, and then slowly strained to pull itself back into position.

Daily, I wondered why death had taken *my* son. I was a conscientious mother. I used to read to my children every day and tuck them in every night. I sang to them, scratched their backs, and prayed for them. I had been a stay at home mom and even home educated them for many years. I didn't take my children for granted. I invested all of my best stuff into my children. I adored my children. And yet, Sammy was gone. It wasn't fair.

February 13, 2011

Three and a Half Months After Sammy Died

A few weeks into February while I was on my porch swing listening to an audiobook (*Beach Music*, by Pat Conroy), chain smoking, and sipping a Coke Zero and vodka, a police car pulled up and parked right smack in front of my house. My stomach immediately clenched and knotted, my pulse began to race, and I thought, *Oh fuck. Oh no. Jake is dead.* As the officer walked up the sidewalk, I think he could see the alarm on my face. He slowed his pace, and lifted his hand out in what looked like a low Heil Hitler motion (which had to be a cop wave) as he approached me.

Feeling quite tense, I stared at him apprehensively. "Afternoon, ma'am," he began, "Sorry to trouble you, but we had a complaint call from one of your neighbors." My stomach loosened a little, and I felt my face start to relax. "Oh, everything is fine." He said, using a kind voice. "I just need to tell you that you aren't allowed to park your trailer unhitched on the street for over 24 hours without moving it," he finished. My eyes filled with tears of relief and because he had been kind. I was at a place when kindness from anyone, even a stranger, reduced me to tears. I shared with him that my son had died 16 weeks before, and consequently, my nerves were on edge and my emotions raw, and when I saw him, I thought he must have come to deliver terrible news. I had to sound like a raging lunatic, but what can I say? By that point, I was a little unhinged.

The officer left, and so did my relief that he hadn't come to tell me about some new tragedy. I was pissed. Really? Which fucking neighbor had the audacity to call the cops on us? And about a fucking trailer?! ? It was a small, white U-Haul style trailer where Jake kept his tools. It was parked on the street in front of our house. How in the world was that hurting anyone? Surely, everyone in our neighborhood knew that our son had just died? Three families from the neighborhood had taken the time to bring my family a meal. The asshole who had called the cops was likely not one of the three. The asshole didn't have the heart to come offer his or her condolences or bring a meal to our family, but could call the police station to complain about our trailer sitting on the street. Well, whoever it was could Kiss. My. Ass.

I made a sign and stuck it in our yard where it would stay for two weeks. I wanted to make sure the police-calling-busy-body saw it, and I didn't give a crap who else saw it. The sign read:

"Thank you to the grand citizen/neighbor for your heroic call to the police to inform them of the atrocity of our trailer being parked unhitched on the street for over 24 hrs. I am certain you must have been among the few kind neighbors who were so thoughtful as to bring a meal to this grieving family whose 13-year-old son was killed 16 weeks ago. We're so glad our tax dollars are being put to such good use."

February 15, 2011

"How do some people sleep in peace at night while their family suffers?" Jo posted on my Facebook wall. She knew the deep pain my family's behavior—inattentiveness, lack of care or comfort, overt callousness—had caused and continued to cause me. In response to Jo's question, the answer I told myself was that some humans were more highly evolved than were others. Some had developed more love, compassion, kindness and empathy, thus further separating themselves from the other animals. That explanation mitigated my pain a tiny bit, because surely no one could cause him or herself to evolve more quickly. In other words, some humans are more evolved—specifically, emotionally—than others. Since one cannot choose their own genetic coding, and with a huge part of who a person not being something which they can control, they—humans—are less intentionally mean-spirited and unkind and more a product of their DNA. The other explanations—they were too haughty and proud to admit mistakes and repair damage, being right was more important to them than their relationships with Jake, the children, and me—were harder for me to stomach, because it meant that love wasn't enough, or specifically, my family's love for me wasn't enough.

    I was still trying to determine if I could hold it together to attend Victoria's wedding. I loved her and didn't want to miss her special day. I was touched she had asked me to be her matron of honor, and I knew she would be so disappointed if I wasn't there. However, I knew myself fairly well, and I was afraid that were I to attend, I would a basket case, spoiling the day for everyone. I didn't want to miss it, but I didn't want to ruin it either. It would be a huge family gathering, and Sammy's absence would soak up all of my energy. I would be thinking about Sammy not being there and how quickly life was moving on without him. I would have difficulty being joyful knowing—at least in my mind—Sammy was still fresh in his grave, while his extended family was celebrating. My feeling that Peter held at least some responsibility for Sammy's death would cause me to struggle when it came time to take the family photograph, and while Sammy, obviously, couldn't be in the photo, Peter could and would. Tori had asked all of her cousins to be in the wedding in some way, and Peter was to be an usher. If Peter was involved with Sammy's death, the thought that he—the guilty party—would be standing up in a tuxedo, smiling for the picture, while Sammy—the innocent party—would remain dead in his grave and not in the picture, was not a scenario I could stomach. I couldn't stand up in the same group with him knowing that was a possibility. The very idea was unconscionable. On top of that, there would be the awkwardness, strangeness, and bitterness of seeing (with the exception of a few) family members I hadn't seen or even had a phone call from since two weeks after my child's death (over three months before). Why would I want to celebrate with them when they hadn't mourned with me? I would have difficulty hiding my anger and disappointment in them, which would definitively put a damper on Tori's day. I had no reserve from which I could draw to subdue my feelings in order to honor Tori. I was hardly alive, my few resources going toward basic survival. I barely had a pulse. I concluded there was no way I could attend her wedding. I considered just sending the children, but they were so emotionally fragile, and I hated to send them to such an event without the presence of Jake or me. (Jake had already told me he wasn't going if I didn't go.) The wedding would be the first large family event since their brother's death. I knew there was bound to be something that could upset them. My family had shown themselves to be unreliable for comfort, and I couldn't stand the thought of my children feeling even a small slight and suffering more than they already were.

February 15, 2011

Three and a Half Months After Sammy Died

I didn't look forward to telling Tori. She would be upset, but in spite of her disappointment, I hoped she would understand. I should have met in person with her to explain and to talk to her about it, but I didn't have it in me. Besides, how long had it been since she had taken any time to come talk to or check in on me? That afternoon, I sent her a text message.

Tues, 12:53- Jane to Tori: Tori, after thoughtful deliberations alone, with Jake, and then with the kids, I am sorry to tell you that our family will be unable to attend your beautiful wedding. We hate to miss it, but our grief is too raw, and we feel somehow that attending such a family celebration would be dishonoring to our beloved Samuel. We have all found it difficult to attend functions where he ought to be as it amplifies his absence. I love you and I hope you have a beautiful wedding.

Tues, 12: 56: Tori to Jane: Ummmm ok… I'm not sure that is something you say over a text. I don't understand your pain but I know you are hurting more terribly than anyone should ever have to. I want you to know that in your pain of losing your son you are pushing away a lot of people who care about you that are still alive. I love you and hope your pain begins to lift soon.

    I should have just dropped it. I didn't. I should have kept silent. I couldn't. I hated my decision. I hated making the decision. I hated that I had to make the decision. I hated that when Tori told everyone she was moving her wedding date up a year, no one in the family had shown the good judgement to say, "We can't have a huge marriage celebration four months after one of our beloved children in the family has died?! That would be insensitive and inappropriate!" When Tori came to me one week after Sammy died to announce her changed wedding date and ask me to be matron of honor, I was years away from being in an emotional state to be giving advice or making decisions. Why had no one in the family counseled her otherwise?

    Tori saying that I was pushing away a lot of people who were still alive who cared about me cut on several levels. First of all, if a person hadn't been frequently calling, regularly visiting, bringing me meals, or doing things to help me get through the worst pain of my life, they didn't get to say a word about how I was responding (and since no one in my family—aside from Laura—was doing those things, that included them!) Frankly, even if they had been doing those things, if they hadn't experienced waking up to find their 13-year-old son hanged to death, they Did Not Get To Tell Me how I should be acting! Second, no one was coming around for me to push away, unless Tori was referring to the things that had happened within the first two weeks following Sammy's death. For her to suggest it was my fault my family members had been so upset with me immediately following my child's death that they had not visited or called me, was astounding and infuriating. Third, even if I had inadvertently pushed people away by being easily angered, highly emotional, and irrational was not the death of my child the one time in life when I should be given an extra portion of grace, love, and understanding, particularly from my family? Fourth, I loved my extended family members, but not more than my own child, regardless if he was living or dead.

    Thus ensued a text exchange. I was broken and bleeding: Tori was disappointed and upset. The worst part of the exchange was that she said my decision not to attend her wedding was the most hurtful thing anyone had ever done to her. That cut and stung me. I was completely torn up about the decision. She knew I valued marriage, enjoyed weddings, and appreciated family celebrations, and I thought she knew I loved her. The text messages between Victoria and I over the following several hours were like heaping spoonfuls of salt funneled straight into my chest. I hadn't thought it possible to feel worse than I already did. It was possible.

If Tori had simply conveyed disappointment about my decision, she would have had my sympathy. I felt horrible. I wanted to be there. I hated to miss out, but I was a basket case. There was no way I could hold it together to attend the wedding. She was fully aware of everything that had transpired over the previous four months, Sammy's death, Peter's potential involvement, the visitation problems with Lucas, the lawyers, the therapists, and the lack of love or care from the family. I thought she trusted me. I had always been there for Victoria when she had a problem, needed to talk, needed help, needed a place to crash for the night, or needed me to talk on her behalf to her mom. Surely she knew I would be there if I could. I couldn't. I was barely keeping myself alive.

I texted Jo to talk about it, but she and her partner were getting ready to move in together, and they were out looking at new houses. They were also shopping to find Jo a new car. Five hours passed and I still hadn't heard from her aside from an initial text or two. I tried not to feel bothered. I knew she was at an exciting place in her relationship, it's just that I was at the worst place in my life.

She finally responded but seemed either unaware or indifferent to the level of my despair, and she didn't indicate she was available or willing to keep texting or to talk on the phone about it. Her brief text was detached and analytical, not empathetic and soothing. We had both been through enough in our lives to know how tough life could sometimes be, and typically, if one of us was upset and hurting, we supported, sympathized, and encouraged the other. Over the decades, many a time I had stepped away from my family, my bed, my kitchen, etc., to listen, comfort, and just be there for Jo, and she had always done the same for me. On this night, it seemed to me like Jo was too busy with her new life—partner, house, car—and was giving me the brush off. Also, I sensed something different coming from my best friend. Judgement? Distancing? I wasn't exactly sure what. In frustration, I sent her a curt and sarcastic text regarding her lack of interest or support. Jo didn't respond well to my snapping at her. She became defensive, stated she had shown support, and yada, yada, yada. I couldn't believe it, but another texting fight ensued, this time between me and my best friend, until at some point, she just stopped texting. I felt like I was coming apart at the seams, and I collapsed in bed. I couldn't sleep, and I didn't hear anymore from Jo.

By the next afternoon, I still hadn't heard back from Jo. I texted her an apology for nipping at her, but she remained completely silent. By that evening, Jo still hadn't responded, and I was beside myself. I had already been in a very bad place before the fight with Tori. The decision not to attend the wedding had been a hard one to make. I knew my family would not understand and would be more furious with me than they already had been. Tori's response had been disappointing and hurtful. The fight then with Jo, and her subsequent radio silence, was almost more than I could take.

Jake, himself exhausted, hurting, frustrated, and trying to hold me and our family together, ended up texting Jo. He told her if I went over the edge because of our fight and her subsequent lack of response to my apology, on top of everything else we were going through, she might end up feeling bad if my funeral was the next one she had to attend.

Jo finally responded after that text, angry because she felt Jake was being manipulative by insinuating I might be suicidal, and if something happened to me, it would be her fault. She wasn't off on her assessment, only on Jake's motives. Jake doesn't have a manipulative bone in his body. His intent was exactly what she thought: "Jane is about to crack, and your fight with her—and the total, unresponsive silence—might be more weight than she can bear." He was trying to convey the message: "Hey, Jo! Jane is losing it, so text her, talk to her, work this out." Jo responded, saying she needed some space from our relationship to reflect on her own stamina, and if he felt I was suicidal, he should take me to a hospital.

I was blown away, flabbergasted, at a total loss to comprehend why my best friend of 19 years would say such a thing. Stunned, Jake and I sat on the back deck. I drank, smoked, and cried. I was completely broken by life.

Chapter 24

"Did you really want to die?"

"No one commits suicide because they want to die."

"Then why do they do it?"

"Because they want to stop the pain."

-Tiffanie DeBartolo, *How to Kill a Rock Star*

February 18, 2011

A few days later, I saw on Facebook that while sprinting down the street, one of Jo's daughters had fallen and cracked her head on the asphalt. I texted Jo some things to watch for following head injuries and suggested she take her daughter to the ER for a head CT. Jo called me to talk about her daughter's accident. We didn't discuss our fight then. It still needed to air out, but we both knew, eventually, we would have to talk it out.

February 24, 2011

Four months After Sammy Died

By the time I reached the four-month mark, I was having a hard time getting through each day. I rarely left the house. I knew too many people in town, and I didn't want to talk to most people. Aside from their large, staring eyes, one problem I had with seeing people was not knowing what to say to them. I figured most people assumed Sammy committed suicide. I wanted to tell people it wasn't suicide because I thought Sammy would hate people thinking that, but I didn't know what the heck happened so what was I supposed to say? Some didn't seem to recognize me, which didn't bother me so much. I knew I no longer looked like my old self. I looked like I had aged 15 years overnight. I had gained 20 pounds since mid-

December, and my face looked puffy all the time. Additionally, I never wore make-up, and my hair was usually dirty and unbrushed.

With every breath I exhaled pain, and sadness oozed out of my pores. I couldn't sustain clear, logical thought processes because my brain, along with the rest of me, was too full of sorrow. Even simple tasks overwhelmed me. I had no daytime or nighttime schedule. I slept when I could no longer stay awake. If I tried to lie down and close my eyes before I got to that point of fatigue when I could no longer stay awake, an image of my sweet Sammy, hanging by his neck, would fill my mind. My child, all alone in death, was all I could see.

February 25, 2011

Fluffy, white, snowflakes appeared, floating down from the endless dark sky, drifting toward my face, and settling on my cheeks and nose. After sitting alone on our porch swing for several hours, drinking vodka and chain smoking, I stood to go inside, lost my balance, and collapsed. I lay on my back in the nearly two feet of snow blanketing our front yard and had not yet found the resolve to get up. Everything in the world seemed hushed and still. Watching the falling snow was soothing. The Smirnoff that warmed my blood or Sammy's rabbit fur, Russian-style hat that insulated my head, or both, prevented me from feeling the frosty air, the icy wind, and the wetness of the snow. Maybe it was the heavy cloak of grief that covered my heart, my mind, my whole self that numbed me to the frigid weather. Regardless, I wasn't cold and all seemed quiet and untroubled. *This wouldn't be such a bad way to go,* I thought to myself. *If I lie here long enough, maybe I will just fall asleep and freeze to death. Dying like this probably wouldn't hurt. I would just fall into a deep slumber: only I would never wake up. I wouldn't have to open my eyes from the dark nothingness to remember Sammy is dead, and I will never see him again. Good god, what a sweet relief.* The faces of my beloved husband and remaining children came to mind as I imagined them finding my lifeless body. Their anguish from our recent, heinous loss would be multiplied by my death; I couldn't do that to them. I attempted to force open my eyes and sit up, but the vodka haze and snowy bed had anesthetized me, and I was relatively pain-free for the moment. *If I could just stay right here, in this place, feeling this way...* I dreaded the passing of that transient reprieve and the brutal heartache I knew would return. I didn't want to live with that burning, consuming, agony that filled my chest and head and body, every moment of every day. *I might doze off before I make a conscious choice. Then, I could be free from this soul crushing misery without having to feel guilt for the additional sorrow my death would bring my people.*

I heard footsteps crunching through the snow, coming toward me, and then right above me, Jake's voice, "Sweetheart, what are you doing?"

I opened my eyes to see my beloved. "I fell and couldn't make myself get back up," I said. My sweet, strong, steady husband pulled me up, and I returned to my dreadful life.

February 26, 2011

The day of Victoria's wedding, February 26, I cried all day.

February 27, 2011

The Academy Awards ceremony was usually a fun night at our house. I love and appreciate great art through film. I gravitate to pictures that convey life truths and realities, and I respect actors who convincingly deliver those lessons. In order to be prepared for the big show every year, I usually see as many Oscar nominated films as possible. With the terrible tragedy our family had suffered, we hadn't seen many of the nominated films, but we still filled out Oscar ballots and watched the show. One film we had all watched together, *Rabbit Hole*, had a powerful impact on me; it was about a woman whose 4-year-old son has been hit by a car and killed, and her struggles living after his death.

One scene, in particular, resonated with me:

Becca is discussing her grief with her mother, Nat. Becca's brother died in his twenties so her mother knew the pain of child loss.

BECCA: Does it ever go away?

NAT: No, I don't think it does. Not for me, it hasn't – it has gone on for 11 years. But it changes though.

BECCA: How?

NAT: I don't know... the weight of it, I guess. At some point, it becomes bearable. It turns into something that you can crawl out from under and... carry around like a brick in your pocket. And you... you even forget it, for a while. But then you reach in for whatever reason and - there it is. Oh right, that. Which could be awful - not all the time. It's kinda...

[deep breath]

NAT: not that you like it exactly, but it's what you've got instead of your son. So, you carry it around. And uh... it doesn't go away. Which is...

BECCA: Which is what?

NAT: Fine, actually.

  I loved the film and particularly that scene. Nat's explanation gave me a bit of hope I would not always feel so bad, that one day the pain would be less raw, less heavy, more manageable. It would be a long time before I would be able to crawl out from under the grief—if I could ever crawl out. It was so big and so heavy I couldn't even see the scope of it all. I had never been one to avoid my feelings or sweep things under the rug, but the loss of my child, and the concurrent web of emotions, was too massive, too intricate, to be easily addressed, and I couldn't have pushed it under a rug if I tried; there was too much. Like heavy, soot-filled smoke, it was all around me, in me. Usually when sad or bothered about something, I reflected on why I had those feelings and what I needed to change, and then I implemented the needed adjustments. With the immense complexity of my grief, that method wouldn't be effective. Besides, there was no fix for the problem; nothing could bring my child back to life. The reality that he was gone forever and I would never see him again, had to be accepted and lived with. Learning to live with it would be a slow, emotionally cumbersome process. In the same way that I couldn't decide to run a 26-mile marathon one day and run it the next, I couldn't face the heartache, the loss, the reality, in one day, or one week, or one month, hoist it over my shoulder, and carry on. I had to build the strength in my legs slowly before I would be able to crawl out from under it, if I would *ever* be able to crawl out from under it. The weight might be too much for me to crawl out from under, let alone carry in my pocket.

The nature of the loss, being like soot-filled smoke, made it impossible to simply gather up. I had to wait for the smoke to clear and the soot to settle. Only then could I even begin to try and sweep it up. All I could do for the time being was *whatever* I needed to do to make it through each breath, each minute, each hour, and each day. Truly, because of the overwhelming pain and sadness that covered me, in order to just make it through one minute, I sometimes literally told myself, "breathe in" (then pause as I breathed out, I didn't seem to need remind myself to breath out, it just happened), and again, "breath in."

The heartache was almost completely debilitating. Nothing seemed to diminish the pain. I felt like I was walking up a steep mountain. It was easier to look at the ground and maybe a few feet ahead, because to try to look to the top of the mountain was overwhelming and made me feel like giving up. Trying to see the top of the mountain (if there even was a top to the mountain) made me want to quit life and lie on the ground on my back, staring blindly up at the sky, out into the universe.

Occasionally, I wondered if Jake and the kids would be better off without me. I wasn't helping them, training them, and benefiting them. I was simply a dead weight they had to carry around. I thought, *if I were gone, they would at least have the life insurance money and be better off financially; oh wait, no they wouldn't if it was suicide.* Usually, I would come back around to my belief that even if I was only a ghost of the wife and mother I used to be and didn't do much for them except exist, I had to at least do that, because *my love* was valuable to them.

Most of the time, I was aware that my children didn't necessarily need me because I cleaned, cooked, or did laundry; someone could be hired to do those tasks (not to diminish the love and effort taken by every parent who sacrifices to fulfill those needs for their loved ones.) The children needed me, primarily, because I-was-Momma. They knew I loved them, they trusted my love for them, and they trusted me to look out for them, guide them, instruct them, and be there for them. In the midst of all the pain and fogginess, it was hard to remember the value my love held for my husband and precious remaining children. Because I was so sad, it was easier to focus merely on the filthy house, the unorganized desks and bookshelves, the laundry piles, the very tight budget because I wasn't working, the over-weight, tired, dazed mother with whom they had been left, and consider if they might not be better off in another situation. In those moments, I would forget that my motherly love was irreplaceable. All of the sacrifices I had ever made for them and all of the love I had poured into them, had knit their hearts to mine, and we were bound together. If I were to die, a section of each of their hearts, where they were grafted to mine, would be ripped and begin hemorrhaging as mine had when Sammy was ripped away. On the tougher days, when I felt more cynical, I would think about how I had made all of those same sacrifices and poured all of that love into Peter, and it hadn't seemed to make a difference.

    I knew nothing could bring Sammy back, yet I suppose I was desperate enough to look at existential possibilities that, prior to Sammy's death, I never would have considered. After watching *Rabbit Hole*, I started wondering and reading (via audiobook) about parallel universes. I wanted to believe that even though Sammy was gone in this universe, he might be alive and thriving in a parallel universe. No longer able to believe or convince myself that his spirit still existed in another place (heaven), I was able to consider things of a more scientific nature. If parallel universes were proven to exist, and Stephen Hawking or some physicist could find a way we could travel to them, I would go. I would find a Sammy from a different universe and bring him back to mine. As I pondered the possibility, I realized that a Sammy from another universe would be sad if I made him come live with me, because I would be taking him away from his real family in his own universe. Even if parallel universes existed, I couldn't get my Sammy back, but the notion that another version, or versions, of him might be living out there somewhere, comforted something in me.

Around that time, I had a dream, which was likely prompted by all of the parallel universe thoughts. In my dream, Jake and I were driving in the van somewhere with the kids, when we parked and got out. As we walked across a grassy hill, I suddenly noticed Sammy was missing. He had disappeared. I began frantically running around looking for him when a small Asian woman approached me. She told me Sammy had been grabbed mistakenly and was in a parallel universe, and I needed to listen carefully to her instructions if I wanted to get him back. To retrieve Sammy, I must go through a special door in a certain alley that she noted, and I would enter the universe where Sammy had been taken. Upon entering, I had to run through all of the alleys looking for him. He would be standing in a doorway in one of the alleys waiting for me.

As soon as the lady was finished speaking, I left and found the door in the alley and passed through. The universe I entered looked like a darker, grayer, gloomier version of Earth. I started running through the creepy-looking alleys searching for Sammy. There were huge, ugly creatures, zombies, and monsters roaming the streets, looking to attack and eat people. I was scared, but I kept running searching for Sammyboy because I wasn't leaving without him. Just when I was starting to feel a little frantic, I saw him, anxiously fidgeting as he stood in a doorway. "Sammy!" I whispered loudly, hoping not to attract the attention of the scary creatures.

"Mom! You found me!" Sammy whispered back, looking relieved. As I ran toward him, he flashed me his huge, beautiful smile. I grabbed his hand, and we started running back through the alleys to find the door back to our own universe. Just then, I saw the small Asian woman again standing on a corner motioning to me.

We ran to her, and she handed me a small gift bag and said, "Take this with you when you cross back over."

"What is it?" I said hurriedly.

"It is the name of another child who was wrongly taken," she answered. "Now go! Quickly!"

"But what do I do with it?" I asked looking over my shoulder at her as we started running again. She said nothing but shooed me away and quickly disappeared around a corner. Soon, we found the door back to our universe and rushed through.

Sammy and I were overjoyed to be back in our own world of bright sunshine, fresh air, and sparkling snow on the ground, and I was bursting with happiness that I had been able to save and bring back Sammy. I noticed we were near Valerie's house, so we ran in that direction. The gift bag the lady had given me was pulled out of my hand, as if by an unseen force and, with purpose, began tumbling and bumping down the street.

When we arrived and entered Valerie's house, all of her furniture and décor was different than it had been for the last several years, yet somehow, it was familiar. Valerie was wearing a craft-sale Christmas sweatshirt with bows all over it, which I remembered her wearing when I was a kid back in the early 80s. From another room in the house, I heard a man laughing and, with delight, I realized it was my dad! Oh my god, Dad was alive! I scratched my head, trying to understand how my dad could be alive again, then all at once, I knew; although I had come back to the correct universe, I had somehow landed in the wrong time. The year was 1984! I woke up then, feeling happy that both Sammy and Dad were alive, until of course, I awoke fully and remembered I was in 2011, and they were both dead.

March 5, 2011

On the morning of March 5, 1997, I met my OB-GYN at the hospital where he broke my water and started a Pitocin drip, initiating contractions. After a relatively easy labor my bald-headed, squinty-eyed, plump baby, Samuel James, entered the world and promptly peed on the doctor as his older brother had done four years before. (Their younger brother, born 15 months later, would be the only son I birthed too polite to do such a thing.) My baby boy, Samuel, made every day of my life sweeter, richer, funnier, and more fulfilling. March 5, 2011, we should have been celebrating his 14th birthday party. He should have been opening presents and eating strawberry cake, not lying dead in a box in the ground. I wanted to dig into the earth, climb into his coffin with him and his baby blanket, and make him come back to life.

Jo came to town to remember Sammy's birthday with us, and we took 14 blue and black balloons to his grave. Laura joined us. We sang a song, released the balloons, and cried. No one else stopped by. No one called.

Jo and I talked about our fight from three weeks earlier. She apologized, and I forgave her. I was still deeply hurt by how she had responded that night, but I didn't think I could make it much farther down the path of grief without her friendship and love. I think I forgave her, in part, because I felt I *had* to for my own survival, but the forgiveness wasn't wholehearted. I felt she had turned her back on me when I was on life support. I was still hurt and angry about it. Regardless, we had the benefit of a long history of a great, enduring friendship, and I hoped in time, everything would be talked out and would heal. Until then, I needed her. Desperately.

It would be three years before I would revisit that incident with Jo, express to her my full pain and disappointment with how she had responded, and tell her I needed to take a break, to step back from and re-evaluate our friendship. By then, I had reached a better emotional place along my grief path. I didn't necessarily feel like I needed her for survival, so I was free to let go for a bit and reflect. Our friendship took a six-month hiatus as I worked through my feelings to find a place of understanding and true forgiveness. Perspective was finally starting to return to me by that point in my grief journey. I recognized that my grief was heavy and she did have to care for her own emotional well-being. It was like I was buried under the weight and breadth of the grief, and Jo and Jake tried holding my oxygen mask on me as I struggled to breathe through the sooty air. In my madness and delirium, sometimes I nipped at or bit those who came near, even to help. Jo had gotten bit and left briefly to tend her wound and reflect on whether she could handle going back under the rock of grief to help me breath again. She did return, after she had a brief rest and some wound care. She returned and stayed by my side until I asked for the friendship re-evaluation break. By then, perspective had returned and I had finally resolved and settled the issue. After the six-month break, we picked back up, dusted ourselves off, and resumed our beautiful friendship.

March 10, 2011

I dreamed of Sammy again. He had died, but I learned a spell that if I performed over his body, could bring him back to life: as a zombie. I didn't care how he came back, I just wanted him back. I chanted the spell, and sure enough, he opened his eyes and stood up! He was alive, only not really. He was a zombie, but he appeared completely normal. He returned to school, and we told everyone there had been a mix-up; Sammy hadn't really died. He continued to go to school and act normal for the most part. He didn't eat regular food, but that was the only obvious thing he did differently from the other kids. I thought everything was going great, until one day his best friend Kyle called and said he needed to talk with me about something. He told me Sammy was being teased at school. I was surprised because Sammy had always been a pretty cool kid. Then, Kyle started telling me some things Sammy had been saying and doing, and I realized what was happening. Sammy continued to look the same, but he was aging backwards in maturity, intelligence, and in social and verbal skills. His behavior had regressed to that of a 7 or 8-year-old instead of a 14-year-old (his correct age for that time), which was why he was being teased. Kyle felt bad even telling me about it. I felt terrible for poor Sammyboy. I pulled him out of school both to protect him and to spend his last few months with him. Somehow, I knew he would continue to age backwards until he reached the maturity level of birth, when he would, die, for lack of a more precise term.

Chapter 25

> "And often the worst thing wasn't the victims--they were dead, after all, and beyond any more pain. The worst thing was those who loved them and survived them. Often the walking dead from now on, shell-shocked, hearts ruptured, stumbling through the remainder of their lives without anything left inside of them but blood and organs, impervious to pain, having learned nothing except that the worst things did, in fact, sometimes happen."
>
> -Dennis Lehane, *Mystic River*

Wednesday, March 23, 2011
Five Months After Sammy Died

Anytime someone has a major life event, a hospitalization, a new baby, a career change, or suffers high levels of stress for any of a number of reasons, that person's body will often begin to over-produce stomach acid. If the person doesn't relieve the stress, alter his or her diet, or take medication, the excess stomach acid will irritate the lining of the person's stomach causing inflammation. If not treated, several unpleasant and serious ailments may develop.

That was precisely what happened to me after my dad died; I developed gastritis, which is irritation of the stomach lining. My doctor prescribed Prilosec, and after nine months my stomach had returned to normal. Shortly after Sammy died, I spoke with my doctor about my stomach and the probable need for a G.I. med, and he put me on a daily dose of Nexium 40mg. In January, in spite of the Nexium, I started having some intestinal issues: constantly burning stomach, nausea, random vomiting, and frequent diarrhea. I wasn't surprised given the amount of vodka I was consuming, the cartons of cigarettes I was smoking, the irregular sleep, the bad diet, and the sorrow and anger. In February, it had worsened, so I called my doctor. He doubled the Nexium to 40mg twice a day. In March, it was still worse, so my doctor scheduled me for an endoscopy.

I had the procedure on March 23. As I was coming out of anesthesia but still in a partial-drugged state, I was a bawl-bag mess and started rambling, "My son died suddenly several months ago, and we still don't know why or what happened," and "My poor boy. My poor son." The nurse was shocked to learn one of my children had recently died and was very kind and sympathetic. Honestly, strangers seemed to be able to offer more sympathy than most people. The nurse was very nice and tried to make me feel better about my weepiness by saying it was common when patients came out of anesthesia.

Before the procedure, I told the doctor about Sammy and my subsequent and continued use of vodka and cigarettes. He was sympathetic, but after the procedure he informed me that my G.I. tract looked like "raw hamburger meat." I had Esophagitis, Gastritis, and Duodenitis, which meant irritation and inflammation of the esophagus, the stomach, and the first part of the small intestines. He told me if I had a colonoscopy, it would probably show Colitis (inflammation of the colon.) He said with the stress of the shock and grief, plus inadequate sleep, and lack of exercise, it was imperative for me to discontinue the vodka and the cigarettes in order for my G.I. tract to heal, or it would develop into something much more serious. He told me to continue taking the Nexium twice a day and gave me a prescription for a drug called Chantix, a medication I'd heard many nurses say they had used successfully to quit smoking. I wasn't surprised by his recommendations, but I was apprehensive about following them. I didn't know if I could do it. I felt I had only survived as long as I had because of the vodka and the cigarettes and couldn't imagine trying to get through each day without them. If my hamburger meat guts hadn't been so raw and hadn't burned and hurt so badly, there was no way in hell I even would have considered quitting my faithful companions.

Thursday, March 24, 2011

In my attempt to distract myself from the date, I raked leaves and listened to the audiobook, *Water for Elephants*. I didn't add any vodka to my Coke Zero. I hadn't the previous day either because of the endoscopy, but it definitely made the day much more miserable. My stomach burned, and I was nauseous; I could live with those things. Without my mind-altering friend, vodka, I felt the full force of the existing volcano inside me and about living with that, I was much less certain. My senses were sharper so little things I had been missing, I saw—things like Sammy's comb and deodorant which were on the bottom shelf of the mirrored bathroom cabinet, and his allergy medicine bottle with his name on it still next to our other regular med bottles. Every one of those things was like a knife stab to the heart. It hurt to see them, but there was no way I could remove them. They were Sammy's. I couldn't erase things that were a reminder of his existence and then his non-existence as if he had never lived, just to make myself feel better. What a wretched life.

Friday, March 25, 2011

I started taking the medication, Chantix, to help me quit smoking, and a new anti-depressant/anti-anxiety med called Pristiq. I had been taking 75mg of Effexor since my dad's death, but I thought I probably needed to increase my dose, particularly since I was quitting smoking. In doing so, my doctor switched me to a med called Pristiq, which he called the "newer, cleaner" version of Effexor, and I had to wean off Effexor over the following weeks.

The three biggest side effects of nicotine withdrawal are depression, irritability, and inability to focus. In the past, when I had attempted to quit smoking, the biggest challenge had been the blue mood. I was nervous about getting any bluer than I already felt, but I didn't really have a choice. The doctor had stressed that I must quit smoking and drinking vodka at least for a few months so my gut could heal. Even though I absolutely didn't want to, I had to stop using my maladaptive coping mechanisms. They were my friends and had been more faithful to help me feel better over the previous several months than most of my actual friends or family. It totally sucked that in the midst of all of the pain, heartache, and disappointment, I had to give up two of the things I felt had been helping me survive. So what if they had been eating up the lining of my G.I. tract, they had been getting me through each day. Maybe they had been killing me, but they also had been saving me. The vodka, in particular, made my world a little hazier and therefore a little more livable. I wanted hazy. I didn't want my life to be in sharp focus yet. There were too many things I wasn't ready to see clearly.

Sunday, March 27, 2011

In December, Jake worked a job with his brother Jeff in a little town about 15-20 minutes away. I was extremely anxious with him being that far away and told him if he could help it, not to take out of town jobs for a while. I was leaning heavily on my husband and didn't feel ready for him to be out of town. Since then, he hadn't taken any other jobs out of town.

On Sunday, March 27, he told me he and his brother would be starting a job the following day or two at the Lake of the Ozarks. I was surprised and caught off guard. Perhaps because several months had passed since the December job, Jake thought I would be okay with it. I knew he was concerned about money, and the job would pay well. He had been deeply grieving Sammy's death and absence, plus trying to make enough money for our family, be strong for all of us, take the kids to and from school, hold me while I cried every day, and so much more. I didn't want to make his life more difficult by making an issue of the out of town job, but thinking about him being so far away made my stomach churn and turn over.

Monday, March 28, 2011

Late in the afternoon on March 28, I fell down our hardwood stairs. I didn't trip, I didn't slip, and I hadn't had anything to drink (I hadn't had any alcohol since the day before my endoscopy, Tuesday, March 22). While starting down the stairs, I lost my balance and tumbled and banged down each stair until I cracked my head on the tile floor at the bottom. Pain sliced through my head, and my left thigh, hip, shoulder, and elbow, which had all smacked repeatedly against the stairs on my way down. I lay on the tile floor at the foot of the stairs bawling. I didn't even try to get up. The entire left side of my body was throbbing with pain, my thigh felt like it must have split open, and I was seeing stars; I didn't move. I just closed my eyes and cried.

The kids were home for spring break, so Sarah called Jake, and he came home. Jake put ice packs on all of my sore spots, and I took two Vicodin (which a doctor friend called in for me) and 1mg Xanax. Because I hit my head, I should *not* have taken medications that could alter my level of consciousness until I'd had a head scan at the hospital. As a neurology nurse, I was well aware of medication precautions following a head injury, but I wasn't thinking clearly. After several hours, I noticed some pain in my forehead, which continued to worsen, and I started feeling confused. I didn't want to go to the ER, but since I had hit my skull hard on the floor and had a headache and some confusion, I knew I had to go. I needed a head CT to make sure I didn't have a small subdural hematoma (brain bleed). Unfortunately, it was 11:30 pm by the time I had the symptoms warranting a head CT, which meant Jake would be exhausted for work the following day. I felt guilty about that and like an idiot for not having him take me to the ER in the first place, but I thought my fall had only caused bumps and bruises until the headache and confusion started. They X-rayed several bones and gave me a head CT, all of which were negative. I did have a concussion, which explained the confusion, and an enormous hematoma on my left upper thigh (a localized collection of blood in the tissue outside the blood vessels, which looks like a goose egg under the skin and is covered with a large purple bruise. Mine looked less like a goose egg and more like a large, purple, half-cantaloupe sized lump.) It was disgusting to look at and hurt like the dickens. Although the bruising would fade, and the size of the lump would decrease a little, that lump would calcify and never go away. It would become a permanent mark of that horrible week. It was a long night, and we didn't get to sleep until 4:00 am.

Tuesday, March 29, 2011

I awoke nauseated and remained nauseated the entire day. I didn't know if it was a side effect of one of the new meds, Chantix or Pristiq, related to the concussion, or if there was some other cause. I had a little bit of burning in my urethra when I voided, so I worried I might be getting a urinary tract infection (UTI). Having a history of UTIs, I normally kept cranberry pills on hand and at the first sign of an infection, I would start taking them. It nearly always worked to prevent a full-blown UTI. Unfortunately, I was out of cranberry pills. Jake was at work, and I rarely left the house. By evening, I was miserable. My leg, at the site of the hematoma, throbbed and had frequent stabbing pains. I had a headache, my urethra burned, and I was nauseous. I vomited a few times around 8:00 pm.

Wednesday March 30, 2011

I couldn't sleep. I was nauseous, had all kinds of pain, and was all-around uncomfortable. I was surprised when Jake got up at 6:00 am to leave for the lake job. That was much earlier than his usual wake up time, but he had an hour and a half drive to get to the job site. When he returned home at 6:45 pm, I tried to be supportive and encouraging and greet him warmly, but honestly, by evening I was pretty weepy. I had felt terrible all day. I hurt everywhere including my broken heart, and I had no gas left in my tank for living. I don't think Jake had much left in his tank either.

Thursday March 31, 2011

March 31 was a crappy day. My leg, shoulder, hip, and upper left arm all hurt badly from my stupid fall down the stairs. My head was killing me, which I assumed from the concussion. My stomach burned from the GI issues, and I was nauseous. I was very weepy and very blue, but I wasn't sure if that was due to switching antidepressants, nicotine withdrawal, possibly the concussion or some other reason. However, the blueness seemed worse and different from the usual grief sadness. I had some very dark thoughts during the day (meaning, I wondered what would be the easiest way to off myself) which, in spite of everything we had been through, was atypical for me.

Adam was a total grouch. All he wanted was to eat cake and drink soda. At 11:30 am, he asked if he could have a piece of strawberry cake. "Yes, after you eat some lunch," I said. "You can make a turkey or ham sandwich." He argued that he had just woken up at 10:45 am and had cereal, which was really like lunch because of the time. He thought he should just be able to go ahead and eat cake. "Well, you woke up late, so you ate breakfast late. But you still have to have lunch before you can have a dessert," I explained. That was a house rule, the primary purpose of which was to ensure the kids consumed more nutritious food and less dessert.

"Well that is just stupid. The cereal basically *was* my lunch." I didn't have the energy to argue with him, and I knew I couldn't out-logic Adam.

I closed my eyes, took a breath, and said, "Adam, if you want cake, you must eat something for lunch first. I am not going to discuss it further."

"Seriously?" he said and walked off with a huge huff and a big sigh.

Sarah was quiet all day. I felt like I was inconveniencing her when I asked her to fill my ice bag or get me water or a soda. I had hardly been able to walk since the fall, so most of the time I spent lying on the couch with ice bags everywhere. I asked Sarah to heat me up a cheeseburger, which she did, but 30 minutes after I finished it, I felt like puking. I had made a stupid decision. My raw stomach wasn't handling many foods well, and the burger had been entirely too greasy.

After a while, I asked Lydia if we had any chicken noodle soup or macaroni and cheese. Those foods didn't bother my stomach, and I was still hungry. We were out of soup but had one box of mac and cheese, which she made and brought downstairs for me. Then she stated that for some reason, the box hadn't made as much as usual. I asked if we hadn't had enough milk or butter.

She immediately became defensive and yelled, "Why are you accusing me of not knowing how to make it?" I put my hands over my ears as she continued shouting, my concussed head throbbing with her every syllable.

"Lydia, quiet down before my head explodes; I was just trying to figure out why it didn't make as much as usual. Why do you take things like that as a personal insult?"

"Because you are saying I don't know how to make it!" she yelled.

"No, that is not what I was saying, I thought it odd that the same box that is always used would make less than usual and was asking to find out if the reason was perhaps there hadn't been enough of an ingredient?" By then she was wailing and screaming. With my hands still over my ears, I said, "Just go to your room for a while."

She responded by screaming louder, "Well, I'm never making you anything again!" and stomped up to her room.

Throughout the day, I kept thinking about Jake taking the lake job. He was aware of how anxious it made me for him to be out of town for work, and, typically, he was very sensitive to my feelings. I had been shocked the night before, when I asked him how long the job would take and he said six weeks (which meant seven or eight weeks.) That was a long time for him to be working an hour and a half away from home and would make for long 12-hour workdays. I was surprised and didn't understand why he hadn't talked about the job with me prior to taking it. He just told me he was doing it, which wasn't how my husband normally operated. It also upset me that he didn't tell me about it until the night before it was to start. He had to have avoided telling me because he knew I wouldn't want him to take it, but that was out of character for Jake.

When he got home, I told him about my terrible day. Then, I shared with him my frustrations about the lake job—that he took it, that he hadn't told me about it until the night before he was supposed to begin, and that it was going to take six to eight weeks. He didn't seem to hear or understand my feelings or feel sympathetic—again, not normal behavior for Jake—and, eventually, I got angry with him which was rare. He was probably just as worn out with everything as I was. Maybe he hated his life and wanted to be away from home for a large chunk of the day. If that was the case, I didn't blame him. If I could have thought of anywhere I could go where I wouldn't hurt so badly, I would have gone. I hated my life. In fact, I hated everything and everyone.

Friday, April 1, 2011

I almost had another fall! While going down the back deck stairs, I lost my balance and barely caught myself by grabbing the handrail. Although I had managed to grab the rail, the downward motion of my body continued until I was jerked hard. Shortly afterwards, I noticed some pain in my right flank and wondered if I had strained a muscle on the stairs, or if it was kidney pain from a UTI. I was nauseated again and had some other potential UTI symptoms, but my head was a little fuzzy, and I couldn't think clearly enough to figure out anything. With my GI inflammation, nausea was not necessarily a surprise. I wasn't an uncoordinated person though, and I didn't understand why I kept falling. It had happened three times in less than week!

I was miserable and couldn't come up with many things I liked about my life anymore. I had always believed in the power and efficacy of love, so I had invested heavily into my relationships, but I was starting to think that was a complete waste. In spite of feeling I had given my best in my first marriage, it hadn't worked out. Two of my three oldest children were lost to me: one dead, and the other, estranged. I feared Peter was either a sociopath, suffering from Asperger's, or had some kind of empathy disorder. Many of my blood relatives—most importantly my closest sister and mother—had utterly failed to do the right thing and be there for me since Sammy's death. So, what then was love good for? Everything I had poured into many of my relationships felt wasted. All of the hard work and sacrifices seemed pointless. I deeply loved my other three children, but I was no longer certain I would see a return for my labor. I doubted how much effect love could have over genetics.

More and more I was convinced that my children would develop according to the genetic material encoded in their DNA at birth and not because of any great parenting, or training, or because they had been loved so well. So the previous 18 years of my life felt like a complete waste. I was 39 years old, 38 at the time of Sammy's death. I had first married at age 20, so eager to be a loving wife and mother and create a happy, peaceful home. I spent the following eight years, ages 20 to 27, constantly pregnant or nursing. I had home schooled my children starting from age 27 in 1998, for seven years, until I was 33 in 2004. I had remarried at age 35, graduated from nursing school, and settled into a fulfilling job at the hospital. I adored my second husband, our home had been happy, and I had mostly healed from the pain of the divorce and of Peter's choices. My dad's sudden death in April 2009 had been a blow, but it brought sadness, not disillusionment. Sammy's sudden and horrible death, caused (at least it was my suspicion) by Peter, and the subsequent lack of love, care, or nurturing from my family, had completely disillusioned me. Having lost my religious beliefs several years prior to Sammy's death, I had maintained belief in love, family, and the innate goodness of humanity. That was all gone. Being uncertain as to how my remaining three children would develop, I felt the one thing in my life that remained beautiful and for which I lived and hoped was my relationship with Jake. I feared though that after the enormous strain of everything we had gone through, we might have reached a breaking point. I greatly wanted to just spend the evening with my two old, faithful friends Marlboro and Vodka, but fuck me, those were gone too, per the doctor's orders.

Sunday, April 3, 2011

I had a long, uncomfortable, sleepless night. I was nauseated and vomited a few times. I kept having pain on the right side of my back and in my neck. I was hot and restless, and I hurt everywhere. I still wondered if I had strained something when I started to fall down the stairs a few days earlier, but because I felt so miserable and some of my symptoms were similar to a urinary tract infection I had Jake take me to the walk-in clinic.

I did have a urinary tract infection: A whopper of one. When the nurse asked how long I had been running a fever, I had no idea. I hadn't even realized I had a fever. The doctor was concerned the infection had moved into the kidneys and considered hospitalization so I could receive IV antibiotics and IV fluids. I didn't want to be alone in a hospital away from Jake, and I didn't want to be away from the kids and Jake if they needed me at home. The doc agreed to try oral antibiotics first. He told me if I didn't see great improvement over the following 24 hours, or if my condition deteriorated—temperature increased, blood in urine—I was to go to the ER.

I was such an idiot. I had been having the classic symptoms of a UTI and had missed it, which was atypical for me. I had been thrown off my game by discontinuing the Effexor and starting the Pristiq and Chantix. (Upon discontinuing a medication one can have withdrawal symptoms, and when starting a new medication one can have side effects.) Moreover, my thinking had been fuzzy from nicotine withdrawal, the concussion, the UTI itself, and of course, the grief.

Jake and I finally had a good talk. He explained how with our tight budget, he had felt he had no other choice but to take the job. He also shared that.one of the things he liked about the lake job was the long drive there and back. It provided him needed solitude and free-time—not working, with the family, or grocery shopping—so he could think about Sammy. We made a plan about the days he would go to the lake, the hours he would work (which helped me know what to expect), and afterwards we both felt much better and, mercifully, back inside our bubble of love and serenity.

Monday, April 4, 2011

April 4, 2011 marked two long years since my dad's death. I don't know how things would have been different had he still been alive, I just knew they would have been. They would have been better. Dad was always able to make things better. He was also always able to make people better. I missed him. I missed his funny sense of humor. I missed his wisdom. I missed how he looked me straight in the eye. I missed how he cared about me and called me or stopped by to see me at least once a week, and I missed how he believed in me. Most of all, I missed the security, comfort, love, and reassurance of having a parent I was confident loved me and on whom I could depend.

Tuesday, April 5, 2011

I finally felt a little better and was thinking more clearly again, and I took a careful look at the meds I had started over the previous two weeks: Pristiq and Chantix. Normally, I would have checked out new medications prior to taking them, but nothing about me had been "normal" since losing Sammy. When I looked up information about Chantix, one of the side effects was unexplained falling, while another possible side effect was kidney infections. Even more disturbingly, it was a black label drug meaning it could cause suicidal thoughts. I had indeed struggled with some very dark thoughts the previous week. I discontinued the Chantix and started wearing nicotine patches. I also discontinued the Pristiq and went back to the antidepressant I had been on before, Effexor.

Wednesday, April 6, 2011

I had another Sammy dream. I had died, and the place after death looked like a Nintendo game world. If a person wanted to get back to Earth, they had to play and beat the entire game. Some people were attempting to beat each of the different sections in order to beat the whole game and get back to Earth. Others were content to stay in the Nintendo world, lounging at game areas, visiting with each other, and playing games for fun. The air was filled with white puffy clouds, and everyone was wearing long robes and floating (not walking) around.

I immediately set out to play the game. I intended to quickly beat it and get back to Jake and the kids on Earth. I wanted to be with them and I was worried about them. The level of difficulty of each section of the game progressively increased, and I was anxious and sweaty as I moved from station to station. And then I saw him. I saw Sammyboy. He wore a white robe, his hair was a little long as he had worn it for several years, and his face was cheerful and shining. About 20 pretty, young girls surrounded him. They cheered in excitement as he beat a basketball section of the game. "*Sammy!*" I yelled, running/floating toward him. He looked my direction and when his gaze landed on me, he looked happy to see me. As I approached, his eyes flickered back to the girls for a moment, and I realized he was trying to play it cool. I stopped about 15 feet away.

"Hey," he said to me casually. I wanted to rush over, throw my arms around him, and say how much I loved him and had been missing him, but I knew if I did that he would be embarrassed. We stared at each other, and I saw love, peace, and happiness in his gaze. We held eye contact for about five seconds, and then he slowly turned his back to me and started talking to the girls. Somehow, I knew that in the Nintendo world, turning away was a signal that meant the person was happy and content and wanted to stay there. I was crushed. I felt like someone had punched me in the gut and left me winded. I was pissed about all of the pain and heartache we had been suffering since Sammy had died, while he had been completely content and enjoying his new abode. Shocked, I moved on and tried not to think about Sammy. I focused on Jake, Sarah, Adam, and Lydia, who I worried were grieving over my death. I wanted to relieve them of their pain and sorrow. I had to get back home.

The next part of the Nintendo world was very dark. There was a huge lake that I had to cross in a small, paddle boat. Creeping things moved in the water, and I was scared and tired. I started paddling but began to feel there was no way I could beat the rest of the game. I had barely been able to get as far as I had. I was becoming overwhelmed with hopelessness when suddenly I felt the weight of another person in the boat behind me. I quickly turned, and there sat Adam! He was in his Earth clothes, not a robe like everyone else, which meant he wasn't dead like all of us robed people.

"Adam," I shouted in delight, "how did you get here? And you're not dead are you? You're still alive!"

"Hi Mom," he said excitedly, smiling as he hugged me. "Well, I didn't think you would be able to beat the game and get back to Earth to us, so I beat it there, and came here to help you beat it."

"Ohhh Adam, you are wonderful! Thank you. What about Sarah and Lydia? Are they here with you?" I asked.

"They wanted to be. They tried, but they couldn't beat the game," he said with a grin and a satisfied twinkle in his eye. Then, I woke up.

Maybe the dream was my sub-conscious trying to give me a little peace of mind. The comfort of thinking Sammy's spirit existed somewhere, and he was happy and content to be there. I wish I could have believed that. But the rational part of my mind reminded me that no matter how much I wanted it to be true, that kind of thinking was akin to believing in the tooth fairy and had about as much verifiable evidence. Regardless of what my conscious mind thought about heaven or an after-life, the dream did seem to ease my mind ever so slightly. It was the first Sammy dream I had during which I didn't keep trying to see Sammy or get him back. Perhaps, psychologically, I was finally starting to accept that Sammy was gone for good. That seems silly since, obviously, he was gone for good from the day he had died. But, I think we can know something intellectually and still have difficulty believing it, accepting it. I think the dream marked the beginning of my reluctantly surrendered acceptance.

Chapter 26

"Memories are like bullets. Some whiz by and only spook you. Others tear you open and leave you in pieces."

-Richard Kadrey, *Kill The Dead*

April 24, 2011

Six Months After Sammy Died

On the six-month memorial day of Sammy's death, we planted a Red Sunset Maple tree in our back yard. We picked that tree specifically because we thought it was one Sammy would have liked since it would turn bright red in the fall. All of the kids helped dig the hole, plant the tree, and replace the soil around the tree roots. Before we closed the casket on the day we buried Sammy, I cut and saved some of his hair. As we planted the tree on that six-month memorial day, we sprinkled Sammy's hair clippings among the soil so part of him would grow tall and strong with the tree. We bought 14 black balloons (he would have turned 14 in March) and tied them to his tree. We also visited his grave, which we decorated with Easter eggs and bunny rabbit decorations.

May 2011

I didn't want to "celebrate" Mother's Day. Celebrating anything yet felt wrong, and to try and celebrate a day set aside for mothers—when one of the children to whom I had given birth was dead in a grave—felt particularly ridiculous. For the kids' sakes, I thought we should at least go through the motions. They selected inexpensive gifts for me and made cards. I opened my presents, smiled, and gave hugs and kisses, but—just as it had at Christmas—Sammy's absence filled the room. Adam and Lydia seemed to do okay with the day: not great, but not horrible. Sarah had a difficult time with it. A few weeks after Sammy died, when she was very anxious and making somewhat sporadic, unpredictable decisions, Sarah had decided she wanted and needed an enormous bean bag she saw while futon hunting with Jake. We had been doing everything we could to help her feel a sense of control and pretty much had given her anything she thought might help her. We had purchased the $200 beanbag, and many days she would curl up in a ball in it. The first Mother's Day was one of those days. It was pitiful. She missed little brother, one of her closest childhood companions, especially on a day when normally the children would have all been whispering and collaborating to make the day special. I would have done anything to soothe her fractured spirit and crippled heart, but the only thing I could do was be present with her and try to comfort her.

For Sarah's entire life she had been cushioned in age between her brothers, Peter and Sammy, and she had been close to both of them. Before the divorce and because I had home-schooled, the children and I had all been home together nearly 24/7, and Sarah essentially was best friends with her two brothers. I encouraged the bonds between them thinking that as siblings, they could count on each other for life. They spent hundreds of hours together playing all manner of games, make-believe, and toys: matchbox cars, beanie babies, house, trains, dress-up, and Legos. One of the few times Sarah got in trouble and was sitting in time out crying, Peter had asked if he could sit in time-out with her. Of course, I thought what he wanted was beyond sweet, so I said that would be fine. For a while, it became a thing they did for one another. It didn't take them long to realize when they did it, Mom didn't make the child-in-trouble stay in time-out nearly as long. All three of them spent hours outside in the creek behind our house, driving around our huge yard in the motorized jeep and motorcycle and engaged in all sorts of play. Following the divorce, there was some distancing between Sarah and Peter, but he was still in her life as she saw him every Wednesday evening and every other weekend over at Lucas's house. Since Sammy's death, both of her closest two brothers were gone; one, she couldn't get back, the other, she didn't think she wanted back.

There wasn't much I could do for my poor girl. We had figured out that the anxiety we each struggled to control in ourselves, often fed on each other's. Honestly, we made each other feel worse when we tried to talk about things because of the parasitic relationship between our anxious hearts. It was extremely frustrating because Sarah and I had always shared a beautifully harmonious relationship and had been extremely close. However, in addition to the anxiety issue, we also had somewhat different grieving styles. It was strange. Although I was the extrovert and Sarah the introvert, in dealing with the grief we responded just the opposite of our type; I pulled way inside myself and wanted to stay at home and talk to no one, while Sarah wanted to stay busy, do things with friends, and be away from home. Home had always been a joyful harbor for Sarah and associated with love, family tradition, security, and warmth, but it had a different feel to it without Sammy. Her psyche seemed ever aware of the absence of her beloved brother, and while she still loved us and her home, her sub-conscious sensed that something was always slightly amiss. It would take three or four years before that faded, or she learned to manage and live with it. My sub-conscious also sensed something was amiss, but that feeling followed me everywhere, so for me, home remained the most peaceful haven.

In May, I felt the urge to try and mend bridges with at least some of my family members. I missed my family, and I could see that however justified I might have felt, I had been wrong to lose my temper with Vince. I decided to swallow my pride, accept responsibility for my part in the mess, and go visit Vince and Valerie to talk things out and to apologize for losing my temper and saying ugly things.

I thought they would receive my apology warmly and graciously. They didn't. They still maintained anger and resentment toward me and Jake. We tried to explain how difficult Sammy's death had been and continued to be for us, but they didn't want or weren't ready to hear it. They were aloof and resistant. Vince told us he understood loss as his sister had died of diabetes when she was

16-years-old and he was 11-years-old. I attempted to help him see that losing one of your children was very different than losing a sibling, and how Sammy's death, in particular, had been sudden, unexpected, and horrible, which only made it even more challenging. I told him he might have an understanding of our experience if he had found Victoria hanging by her neck when she was 13-years-old, but nothing I said seemed to matter.

Frankly, I was surprised by Vince and Valerie's response. They were cool, closed, and unyielding. They felt they had been wronged, and they weren't ready to forgive. I assumed they would greet us warmly and with kindness, knowing we were trying to carry on after losing our child. Their veiled but palpable hostility that night would only cement in my mind that we were all alone and our separation from my family would continue.

Near the end of May, I returned to my cigarettes and the occasional shots of vodka in my Coke Zero. I had successfully abstained from them both for two months, which fortunately was enough time for my G.I. tract to heal. There were a few end of the year orchestra recitals, plays, and ceremonies I wanted to attend, but my reticence to leave the house, especially if I had to be around other people, was a major problem. The alcohol might not have been ideal, but it did steady my nerves, make me dread leaving the house a little less, and soften the edges of my ever-present screaming heart. I felt I had to attend those events for my living children, but to make myself go I had to push hard and utilize every resource at my disposal.

On Memorial Day, we decorated Sammy's tree we'd planted in our back yard with red, white, and blue balloons and then visited the cemetery. Sammy's headstone was finally finished and had been placed at his grave. It looked beautiful. Well, it looked as beautiful as a headstone for a child *can* look. We all had chosen a symbol that represented a connection between each of us and Sammy, which the stone mason etched onto the stone. The photos of Sammy were bright and definitely made the association stronger between what the stone was marking and who was buried underneath; it honestly became harder for me to visit his grave. I began finding it increasingly difficult to make myself go. On her own initiative, Sarah took over keeping up Sammy's grave and changing the decorations with the seasons.

June 2011

The school year was coming to a close as we entered our eighth month without Sammy. The principal of Sammy and Adam's school contacted me to say there was going to be a small memorial ceremony for the students who were on Sammy's team. Several boys with whom Sammy had taken industrial tech class had built a wooden bench as a memorial tribute to Sammy. An engraved plate with Sammy's name, birth, and death dates would be attached, and the bench would sit in one of the open courtyards of the school. It made me feel a sweet sadness that those boys had been so thoughtful and had done something so kind for Sammy.

When we walked into the front lobby of the school to attend the ceremony, I was caught off guard when I saw Peter. A jolt of pain, sadness, anger, and unease shot through me. I hadn't expected him to come. Standing behind Lucas were his mom and dad, and Bruce's wife and children. Then, I saw my mother, Valerie, Vince, and Victoria standing in a small group next to Lucas. I was shocked. I didn't know they would be there nor how they even knew about it. I hadn't seen any of them in ages. We had last seen Vince and Valerie briefly the previous month on our failed peace-making attempt. Prior to that, we had last seen Vince on October 27, the night of Sammy's funeral, Valerie on November 7 at my house, Mother and Victoria in February at the wedding shower, and Peter on November 3, 2010, when he came to my house and I questioned him. I was astonished they didn't think it would be strange and uncomfortable to have no contact with us, and then, out of the blue, to just show up at a memorial service at Sammy's middle school. Maybe, if they had let me know they planned to attend that might have helped. Had they been behaving like a proper family since Sammy's death, then, of course, I would have wanted them there, but they hadn't, so it was weird. Lucas had to have informed them of the event since I hadn't, which did nothing to make me feel better about it.

The brief service, held outside by the beautiful new bench, was nice. I greatly appreciated the students and teachers and the principal for organizing it. We took pictures by the bench with many of the students who were teary-eyed right along with me. I could barely contain my anger toward my family for showing up unannounced and standing around visiting with Lucas' family, when they had completely neglected us for the past seven months. When I walked past my mother she spoke to me, and said, "I've been praying for you."

I ground my teeth together as I turned to her and said, "You know what? Dad always used to say 'Prayer and action. You need prayer and action.' So, you've prayed. What about the action, Mother? 'Cause I haven't seen much action." Jake, who never misses anything, saw the exchange and immediately made his way toward me. We gathered the children and left.

July 2011

By July, I had reached a strange place in my grief journey where I actively tried *not* to think about Sammy. I spent time raking leaves, mowing the lawn, raking acorns, and watering the lawn by hand with our hose. The lawn watering kept me occupied several hours each day. I have no idea why such a ridiculous thing like watering the entire lawn with our garden hose was a soothing distraction, but it was. The smell of the cool, clean water and fresh, wet soil, the heat of the sun warming my hair and skin, the sparkling, misty water spraying across the grass, all hypnotized me. Every day, I stood outside for hours, holding the hose, squeezing the nozzle, lazily rotating left and right. The water droplets caught the sunlight as they sprayed through the air and settled on blades of grass. It was peaceful and soothing. All summer long, I hand watered our lawn while listening to audiobook after audiobook and sipping Coke Zero and vodka.

I also jogged every day, because that felt like something I ought to do. I hoped to lose weight, or at least to stop gaining. Between December 10, when Sammy's case was made inactive, to the end of June, I had gained 35 pounds and was clueless as to why.

I was eating less not more, and both the Coke Zero and the vodka had zero calories. After a few weeks, the jogging became part of my summer routine; the heat of the July Missouri sun, the vodka buzz, the monotony of the voice of the audiobook reader, and me jogging. My objective was not to give myself a heart attack or a stroke; the jogging was just something I had to do. Somehow, it became part of my therapy. Accepting, and not overly questioning, the why of things was a deliberate coping mechanism I started implementing. I tried putting as little pressure on myself as possible because I really didn't want to crack up, so when I felt moved to do a certain thing—in this case, go jogging—I just went with it and tried not to over-analyze. While the exercise seemed good for me in general, it did nothing for my weight problem; I just continued to gain.

My doctor would later tell me that she thought my body had been stuck, so to speak, in a fight or flight position for that entire first year. The shock of Sammy's death caused my adrenal gland to switch into overdrive, and among many other side effects of the body's stress response, my metabolism came to a screeching halt. By the time the weight gain stopped in September, I was 50 pounds heavier. Whatever. I cared a little, but any potential care I had paled next to how much I cared that Sammy was dead.

From the moment I woke up until I dropped into bed, I listened to audiobooks. It was my way of not thinking about what I didn't want to think about: Sammy feeling scared in the last few moments of his life, Sammy being away from home on the night he died, Sammy being all alone when he died, Sammy hanging from his closet all night, me not being aggressive enough with Lucas about Peter putting his hands on Sammy's neck, me encouraging Sammy to continue going to Lucas's house, my sweet Sarah finding her brother hanging, my innocent girl having to be so responsible because there were no adults in the house, Sammy's skin, his smile, his way of brushing his hair out of his eyes, his muscular body, his sense of humor, his laugh, the ligature mark on his neck, and his pale, lifeless body.

August 2011

Getting the kids ready to go back to school in August can only be described as fucking miserable. I went to the store with the lists, but every shiny notebook and #2 pencil package I put into the cart for Sarah, Adam, and Lydia was a reminder that I wasn't picking them up for Sammy. Previous years, we loved picking up the list at the front of the store designating each school and each grade's necessary items and then running around the store collecting them: bundles of fresh paper, bottles of glue, yellow high lighters, and pink erasers. Without Sammy, it was a list of all of the school supplies I *wouldn't* be getting for him. That thought, on top of being out in public, with the crowds, the noise, and the sensory overload, bested me, and I became anxious and weepy. I abandoned the shopping cart and left the store. I couldn't buy supplies for Sarah, Adam, and Lydia and not buy supplies for Sammy. Jake went back to the store with Sarah to purchase the school supplies.

The first few days of the new school year, Jake took the kids and picked them up again. Then, I took over. I wanted to lighten Jake's burden. Since Sammy's death, he had taken the kids nearly every day and often picked them up (when Sarah had activities and couldn't.) He also had done all of the grocery shopping and cooking for our family. I wanted to try to do something to contribute to Jake's efforts. Taking Adam and Lydia to the middle school Sammy had been attending (with Adam) when he died, was like a direct kick to the gut. I didn't pull up to the front door. I couldn't do it. I pulled up by the side of the school, and Adam and Lydia ran across the grass to the front door. Every day for the first several weeks of school, after I dropped them off I cried all the way home.

I missed my son. I wanted him back. Thinking of him hurt so badly, and everything had become some kind of trigger. Starting around two months after his death, I had stopped turning on the radio. Music had become something I could no longer tolerate. It zipped into my ears and poked straight into my bleeding heart, causing immediate pain and increased heartache. Familiar music elicited memories (all of which were bittersweet because they were all from before my child died. Although music with which I was not familiar didn't draw out memories, it still tapped into my emotion center and made me *feel*, and I didn't want to feel because the first and foremost thing I always felt was pain. Listening to news on the radio was out too, because for some reason it made me feel like throwing up, maybe because the world just kept moving right along without my boy. I moved through time in a sort of hazy blur, and hearing news reports jerked me back into focus. Therefore, our car rides to and from school were without music or news. There would be no music in my life for a long time.

Sarah didn't want to do anything to celebrate her 17th birthday. I understood. It felt wrong to celebrate the day you were born when your dear brother is dead and will never celebrate another birthday. I got her a few small gifts, but I didn't wrap them or make a big deal about giving them to her. I wanted to respect what she wanted, but I didn't want her to feel like I didn't celebrate the day of her birth even though I mourned the death of her brother.

September 2011

By September, I was beginning to think the pain would never go away. His death was just so damn sudden, and my heart would not stop bleeding for him. I couldn't believe it had been 11 months, and I still felt so much pain. How did other bereaved mothers carry on in spite of the misery?

As the new school year started I decided it was time to stop for good. I didn't want to damage my G.I. tract again, I felt like I was as ready as I was going to get, and I was going to be driving to take the kids to school each day and to pick them up. I knew all along it was not an ideal coping mechanism, but considering the circumstances, I had allowed myself the indulgence. Frankly, I don't know how I could have survived the pain without it.

I had absolutely no motivation to plan a 12th birthday party for Lydia. I thought a little about putting together a Justin Bieber themed party (at the time, Lydia was all about JB), but I couldn't scrape up any mojo, and, regardless, we had no extra money.

Fortunately, Jo drove up from St Louis, purchased the party supplies, set up, and, essentially, was the party host.

October 2011

I took a shower, which may not sound like news, but for me since Sammy had died it was. Generally, I got up, threw on whatever I had been wearing for pants the day before (which were on the floor), slid on flip-flops, or once it got chilly again, my Uggs, and that was how I looked all day. I was already wearing a shirt, the one I slept in and had worn the day before. I didn't bother with a bra. I didn't care. I didn't go anywhere except to drive the kids to school and to pick them up, and I really didn't give a crap. I was alive: barely. That was all I could do for time being, and possibly, forever.

In October, I saw something on *The Thinking Atheist* Facebook page that helped me feel a tiny bit less wretched for the first time since Sammy had died 12 months before.

> "Many people say that without 'god' life is just not worth living; it is precisely because there is no heaven that we should maximize every single moment here. The chance of us existing on this rock, in this solar system, in this galaxy, in this universe, in this vast universe is so unbelievable and yet here we are. We got one shot and it is because we reject the idea of an afterlife and heaven and god and superstition that we can and should fully maximize every single second."

For one quick moment I was able to grasp the *magic of being*. Somehow, I came into existence. Somehow, Sammy came into existence. It truly is a miracle that any of us experience life. In spite of the many horrors we all will suffer in life, if we hold onto that truth—the truth that *being*, or existing, is an unfathomable, beautiful mystery, an amazing miracle—it might be just the thing we can always come back to for strength and hope.

Chapter 27

> "You have your wonderful memories people said later. As if memories were solace. Memories are not. Memories are, by definition, of times past, things gone. Memories are what you no longer want to remember."
>
> -Joan Didion, Blue Nights

October 2011- One Year Summary

If I had to say what the worst thing was about the first year of grief, it would have to be the horrible, constant pain, both emotional and physical. The emotional pain of losing Sammy, the heartache, hurt so badly it felt like physical pain. My chest literally ached every day. The pain made everything difficult: talking, moving, showering, every single thing hurt. Being alive while my child was dead was heinous. Many times throughout life I have heard people say, "Parents shouldn't have to bury their children." I have always found that expression simplistic and trite. *Of course*, parents shouldn't have to bury their children. Since losing Sammy, I have a new appreciation for that statement. Perhaps the sentiment could be more fully communicated by saying, "Parents shouldn't have to bury their children because it is *just so wrong, so unnatural*, so not what they expected or how life is *supposed* to work." A child is not supposed to die before his (or her) mom (or dad). It's wrong. That's not the correct order of things. The normal and expected passing of family members is first your mom and dad die, then you die, and later your child dies. When your child dies before you (the parent), it feels hideously wrong. If you looked in the mirror one morning, but instead of seeing yourself (a white female in my case) you saw an Asian male looking back at you, it would be shocking and just *wrong!* If it started raining one day, but blood fell from the sky instead of raindrops—wrong! When your child dies out of order, the immense wrongness of what has happened, the fucked-up-ness of being alive while your child is dead, is suffocating. You have to remind yourself to breathe every minute of every day, for a very long time. The wrongness of their death is infinitely huge and you feel it everywhere, all the time.

The second worst thing about the first year was the unending tears. I cried every day, several times a day. I cried when I woke up, I cried in the middle of the night, I cried at every picture, thought, or conversation about Sammy. I cried and I cried. I would lie on the couch by the fire and cry, lie on my bed and cry (and scream, sob, and wail), or sit outside with a drink and a cigarette, tears running down my face. I learned there were all kinds of different sounds and types of crying. There was the worst, oddest, and most wretched of the crying, when sounds I had never heard before rushed out of my gut, throat, and mouth: uncontrollable wailing, moaning, groaning, and sobbing. Those episodes were probably a mixture of pain and sorrow, rage, bitterness, frustration, and helplessness. It sounded like a mortally wounded animal—it could be said that was precisely what it was. There was the normal boo-hoo crying. There was the crying that came after a big bawling meltdown, when I had no more energy, I thought it was over, the noises had stopped, and yet the tears kept rolling down my dazed, expressionless face. The tears could not, they would not, be quelled. At times I would be engaged in an activity, something would trigger a Sammy thought or memory, and a wail would have already rushed out of my mouth before I even knew it was coming. I have always had a hard time suppressing my tears when I feel like crying, but this crying was like projectile vomiting—there was no stopping it, and it came with force, spewing everywhere.

The despair—the third worst thing during the first year—was horrendous, tainting everything so all looked bleak and miserable. When the regular challenges of living popped up, there was no back-up bag of hope and happiness into which I could dip to help fend away the additional pain and frustration. For example, when the cell phones were turned off occasionally because we couldn't pay the bill. Those moments, and days, were the ones I would find myself thinking, *"What is the fucking point?" I am a fat, saggy, 40-something, with dark hair roots, a dead son, and a son with whom I have no contact because he is either a heartless asshole or a cold-blooded sociopath. I rarely—never— hear from my blood relatives who seem to have little to no concern about me, my children, or husband. We barely have enough money to keep up with our mortgage, utilities, other bills, and groceries. There is no extra for anything else. Even if I wanted to go somewhere or do anything, we have no money with which to do it. My house is a disgusting dump, and I have no energy for living.*

The fourth worst thing about the first year was the violence of every single emotion (the negative emotions, anyway. I didn't feel any positive emotions for the first year.) After the heinous pain, tears, and despair, the power and strength of every negative emotion—anger, sadness, disappointment, bitterness, resentment, hostility, uncertainty, and guilt—was savage. Everything I felt, I felt fiercely. The days when I experienced more shock-like feelings and was numb were a welcome relief in contrast to the passion that filled most of my days. Every once in a while, I would feel some guilt for the numb days, but I continually told myself there was no reason to feel guilty. I had no doubt about my love for my son. My body was trying to absorb the loss, and I needed to go with the flow and not worry about why I was having a numb day or what it might mean.

Some days, the violent emotions with which I was consumed were rage and bitterness. Sammy had been a wonderful, well-behaved, funny boy. He was good, he was just, he was honest, he was loyal, he was loving, and he was innocent. He had never done anything bad to anyone. He didn't deserve to have his life snatched away at his young age. Death had taken the wrong person. My rage at the wrongness and my bitterness at being tricked into thinking life was beautiful, wafted off me like a bad odor. If you came with a certain distance of my proximity, you smelled it, and I could find no special shower to wash the acrid stench off my person. It had to be lived off, and it would be a lonely walk because most people couldn't stomach the odor.

In addition to the anger because this happened to Sammy, was the anger that it happened to me, to my child. I felt I was a decent person. I cared about people, their feelings, their lives, their happiness, and I did what I could to better others' lives. Part of the reason I had loved being a nurse was because it enabled me to be in a position to help people, and that felt good and right.

Aside from my career in a profession of helping others, I felt I was a decent person. Self-evaluation may not provide the most reliable analysis, but I'll offer it, nonetheless. I made concerted efforts to be nice, kind, just, conscientious, open, tolerant, generous, and loving. I wasn't a murderer (some might argue re: the abortion). I didn't steal. I generally played by the rules. When I looked at others around me who lied, cheated, tricked, misrepresented, and snowed their way through life, who took advantage of others for their own gain, and who were disingenuous about who they were in order to get what they wanted, and yet they didn't seem to have had any horrible things happen to them and seemed to be happy, wealthy, and skating through life, traveling the world, eating new foods, and having beautiful children and grandchildren, I was filled with anger.

I had always tried and tried hard. Since adulthood, whether during my first or current marriage, I endeavored to be a good, loving, and patient wife. When I had believed in God, I tried in earnest to honor Him with my life. I had stayed home with my children and invested all of my love and energy into them. I had home educated my children, because I thought it was what was best for them. Yet, in spite of everything, my child had been taken. The rage and bitterness were hard to keep a lid on, and honestly, I often didn't even try. I didn't care if I offended someone. Life was unfair, and I was pissed.

Another thing that was particularly difficult during the first year, was that each person in my immediate family—Jake, Sarah, Adam, and Lydia—was suffering and trying to cope, so none of us were in an emotional place to help and encourage each other. Metaphorically, I was doubled over in pain trying to catch my breath, as were each of them. It made helping each other nearly impossible. If I couldn't even get my own breath, how could I help them? On an airplane, if there is a lack of oxygen in the cabin—by a window breaking, let's say—and the oxygen masks come down, you are instructed to put on your own mask before you help your child. I had to put on my own oxygen mask, because if I ran out of oxygen and passed out, I certainly would be of no help to my children. What if the oxygen mask has no straps to hold it in place? I put my mask on, but I have to hold it with my hands for it to work properly, and I have to do so in the midst of the tumultuous wind caused by the open window so I'm unable to help my children with their masks. What can I do? Hope for, or find and bring in, others who have straps for their masks, who are able to assist.

    Sarah and I realized very early we couldn't be as open with each other as we always had been. We were both in so much pain that if she shared some of her thoughts and struggles with me, I would feel overwhelmed. Hearing my little girl express how heartbroken she was, made my own heart feel like it would rupture. The grief was consuming me, and I didn't have any extra strength to absorb any of her pain. It was the same for Sarah. If I mentioned specific painful thoughts, feelings, or realizations, that knowledge added more pain to what she already felt. We both were fully aware of the other's acute pain and sorrow. Unable to walk straight with our own grief, plus the general awareness of each other's grief, made learning about even more pain too overwhelming. The smallest comment or statement from one of us could send the other to tears, not necessarily because of hurt feelings (although sometimes that was the case) but because of too much pain. We learned to be very gentle with each other and to share most of our specific painful thoughts and feelings with others. We also both tried not to put pressure on each other to be, do, or say, anything. Fortunately, we had grown a strong bond of love and trust between us over our 16 shared years prior to the tragedy, and we were able to give each other the space and the freedom to grieve in our own unique ways. We were also both able to get support we needed, and might previously have gleaned from each other, from different sources.

    I had a gentle, sensitive, dependable, understanding spouse who—in spite of everything—somehow managed to hold his mask and mine at the same time. I also had a strong and brilliant best friend who was very supportive. Sarah had her wonderful, long-time best friend, Susan—who was always mature beyond her years—on whom she could rely as a great source of strength. They had been best friends since fourth grade (they met at the private Christian school and both left in the eighth grade to enter public school). Because Susan spent a good amount of time with our family and in our home before the tragedy, she had known Sammy for years before he died and thus could provide a special kind of comfort to Sarah. Both Susan and her mother Pat were a loyal, loving, strong, and reliable support system, including Sarah in their annual vacations and always opening their hearts and home for her. During Sammy's funeral, Susan sat next to Sarah and held her hand, and I don't think she has ever let go.

In spite of the horrible grief, Jake and I had to continue parenting our still-living children, which was another challenge. Grief is exhausting and often left us with little energy. Although our teenager, Sarah, was generally a respectful, rule-abiding child, parenting was much more taxing from our position of brokenness. Sarah still experienced the typical moods and behaviors of other teenagers, but in our responses, we had to keep in mind she was much more fragile than before and compared to other teenagers. We didn't bring down the hammer often with our grieving daughter, in part because she didn't need it, and in part because we handled her with care. No small battles or differences of opinion or minor scuffles were more important or more pressing than her stability and continued healing. Adam and Lydia required less concerted effort than our teenager during the first year, primarily because they were at that in between period of growing up, after all of the training, character shaping, and physical exhaustion of the first ten years but before the moodiness, independence, occasional belligerence, and mental fatigue of the teen years.

As most of my energy and brainpower was absorbed by grief, I stored the very small bit I had left over for parenting. Little energy was needed for my marital relationship, because for the most part it remained as smooth and relatively easy as it had been from the beginning. Because Jake and I are so similar, meeting each other's needs doesn't take much work. For both of us, our greatest need is to feel loved, and what we each need in order to feel loved, happens to be how the other naturally expresses love. Therefore, that vital, life-sustaining relationship remained strong and a great source of love and comfort without requiring much of my scant energy. I lived on cruise control most of the time, only switching back to manual when necessary. I did everything I could to preserve myself for parenting tasks. I didn't pressure myself to get out of the house but stayed at home. Leaving the house took so much out of me that upon returning, I was completely spent. I would then have nothing left in order to sort through an argument, insist homework be completed, comfort a sad child, or any of the other multitude of parenting responsibilities. So, most of the time I stayed home, and I didn't allow myself to feel bad about it. I was doing what I had to do for myself and for Jake and the kids.

Sarah, Adam, and Lydia all changed in different ways over the year. Immediately following Sammy's death, they all slept in our room for several months, and then slowly in their own time made their way back to their own rooms and beds: Sarah, after two months, Adam, after four months, and Lydia, after six months. Sarah became a bigger risk taker than she ever had been. The first six months, in particular, she was much less careful and cautious than before Sammy's death. Fortunately, due to her naturally over-cautious nature, she could afford to be a little reckless without suffering long-term consequences. She was hurting badly, and her anger sometimes propelled her to be slightly careless. She had a bit of the attitude that when it was her time to go, it was her time to go, and nothing she did would make a difference. Adam seemed to grow up overnight. It was as if he felt he needed to step into the role of the tough brother, which Sammy had always occupied. He became very protective of his sisters and me. He also seemed to lose most of the silliness that had always characterized him. (Adam's silliness would be a long time in returning, but eventually it did, to a lesser degree, during the fourth and fifth years.) Lydia struggled the most with being fearful of things. She wouldn't want me to step outside to smoke after it got dark, during thunderstorms or after she watched a movie or heard a news report that made her feel uneasy, she wouldn't feel comfortable sleeping in her own bed, and she became vigilant about minor safety issues. She checked the doors of our house regularly at night to make sure they were locked. Her mind and state of alertness finally eased a little when we had a security system installed.

An unexpected side effect of the shock and grief was that clear thinking became very difficult and decision making a major ordeal. My mind felt frozen, my critical thinking skills nearly absent, and my ability for recall quite diminished. Perhaps the fuzzy mind was a product of my daily effort to avoid thinking about Sammy hanging, Sammy dead, Sammy alone and scared, Sammy and the rest of his life being snatched away. Whatever the reasons, my mind was a constant state of cloudiness, similar to how one feels following a night of little or no sleep: foggy, out of focus. Maybe that was why I experienced a ridiculous amount of panic when I had to make even the smallest of decisions. In addition, my memory was completely shot to hell: mostly, my short-term memory, but sometimes also my long-term memory. As a person who formerly enjoyed engaging and interacting with others about culture, politics, and medicine, among other topics, my sluggish, muddled thought processes were a big change. My thinking and decision making abilities were so altered I even wondered if at some point during the year I had suffered a stroke.

Personal grooming remained a struggle, not only the first year but even at the time of this writing, well into the sixth year. I didn't bother wearing make-up, putting on a bra, brushing my hair, or changing my clothes most of the time. I rarely showered. It seemed unimportant. Our budget was extremely tight—another challenge because we were living on one very modest income—so I stopped having my hair highlighted. It was an expense we couldn't afford, but I wasn't too bothered by it because I really didn't think much about what I looked like. I didn't necessarily want to look gross, but I had neither the energy to care nor the money to spend, on top of my dread of leaving the house to even go to a potential hair appointment. In September, I bought a box of dark auburn hair color and put it all over my hair. It looked horrendous with my coloring, but it had been quite a while since I had been able to have my hair professionally colored, and my roots looked awful. The all over darker color was a quick and cheap fix. It looked like a quick and cheap fix. Since I first started wearing make-up at age 14, I was fastidious about taking care of my skin every night, removing my make-up, washing my face with cleanser, and moisturizing; that also went by the wayside. I maintained none of the habits I kept throughout my life. I simply lived minute by minute, unable to plan or schedule anything because of the panic, horror, and sadness that surrounded and covered me.

During that first year, the one and only thing that gave me any kind of feeling that at least wasn't negative (I can't go so far as to say it brought happy feelings) was the St Louis Cardinals making it to the play-offs and then winning the 2011 World Series. I had always liked the Cardinals well enough, but I hadn't necessarily been a huge fan of them or of any sport or team. However, my dad had been a Cardinals fan, and I had many memories of Joe Buck's voice on the radio broadcasting Cardinal baseball games into our house or in Dad's car. Jake and I had attended a Cardinal ball-game with Mom and Dad in 2008—the year before Dad's death— and Sammyboy had played baseball (one of his teams was even named the Cardinals.) Whatever the reason, Cardinal baseball took on new meaning for me. I saw the Cardinals as a pleasant thread that ran throughout my life. Watching them play made me feel a little less sad and reminded me of Dad and the happy, carefree innocence of childhood.

To try and describe to others the complexity of the heartache of losing a child requires several metaphors. First, any mother who has had the experience of losing sight of one of her children in a grocery store, and after several minutes of fruitless searching is flooded with panic and terror thinking her child may have been snatched, is familiar with one of the layers of a bereaved mother's heartache. Those feelings of anxiety and terror are one part of the constant pain. Second, any person who has suffered the death of someone with whom they were very close and experienced the pain and sadness of missing them and of knowing they will never see that person again, knows another layer of the grieving mother's heartache. Third—and this one requires a stretch of thinking—if after nine long months of pregnancy and the anticipation of a beautiful baby, instead of a human you gave birth to a pig. (If upon reading "gave birth to a pig" you were totally caught off guard and thought *what the heck*? Good. That's the point. That's how it feels when your child dies.) Imagine the feeling of shock and the horrible over-whelming wrongness, and that is similar to another layer of pain woven into the tapestry of a mother's broken heart. Those three things together—lost child in store/terror, panic, horror; death of someone close/pain and sadness; birth to pig/shock and wrongness—are all part of the heavy heartache with which a bereaved mother lives. Those complex emotions—like smoky, sooty, air— surround, cover, and choke a bereaved mother. The death of one of your children is horrific, it is sorrowful, it is shocking, and it feels very wrong.

One additional thought regarding memories; with deaths other than a child (and possibly a partner, I have not experienced that type of loss) thinking about memories of the deceased is nice, pleasant. Reflecting upon happy occasions shared with a person who is gone, you can feel fondness, warmth, and possibly a bittersweet sentiment. With the death of a child, it is challenging to appreciate the memories of the short time they lived when you assumed you would have an entire lifetime of memories. Every memory reminds you that the beloved child is dead, taken before his time, and brings the pain of knowing it is only a memory and all that is left of the child.

The visceral pain of the first year was hideous, sometimes nearly unbearable. Frankly, I am shocked I survived the year. I am sure every mother has thought about how awful it would be to lose a child. The pain is worse than you could ever possibly imagine.

Chapter 28

"Grief is like the ocean; it comes on waves ebbing and flowing. Sometimes the water is calm, and sometimes it is overwhelming. All we can do is learn to swim."

-Vicki Harrison

October, 2012

The second year following Sammy's death was darker, less vibrant, blazing red, and more charcoal grey, like the surrounding area covered in ash following a volcanic eruption. It was depressing and bleak but then it would have frequent blasts of molten lava. My heart wasn't actively hemorrhaging all the time (as it had been the first year), but the wound was fragile, tender, and easily re-ruptured.

The biggest thing with which I grappled throughout the second year was accepting the reality that Sammy was gone for good. He was never coming back. I would never see him again. The first six months following his death, I constantly looked at pictures of him, sifted through his old school papers and journals, and watched home movies of him multiple times every day. The next six months and throughout the second year, I did just the opposite: avoided all pictures, notes, and home movies. I made every effort to not think about Sammy. It wasn't that I wanted to forget my beautiful boy—as if I could—but everything that reminded me of him caused piercing pain. I struggled with guilt about avoiding Sammy thoughts and had to frequently remind myself that my recovery was imperative, at least for Sarah, Adam, and Lydia. I had to do whatever I needed to recover, and by "recover" I don't mean get back to the person I was before Sammy died. I don't believe that will ever happen. What I mean by "recover" is move through the horrible acute stage of grief and into a more livable chronic state. Looking at pictures of Sammy, notes he had written, old school work, only brought knife gash sensations to my heart. I would see a picture, and—spurt—bright red blood, my heart would be hemorrhaging again. By concerted efforts to distract myself, I could spend more time in the grey, bleak landscape, which—although no place of sunshine and butterflies—at least was not a place spewing hot lava. Even so, the lava still would burst through the surface several times a week. Something, somewhere would trigger a Sammy memory or thought and—like a knife puncture to my heart—blood would spray, the heartache would sharpen, and the tears would run.

Although sleep was a problem the first year, it significantly worsened and became a major issue the second year. Two months before I reached the one-year mark, I stopped adding the vodka shots to my soda. Two months after the one-year mark, I weaned myself off Xanax. Not having the vodka and Xanax made falling asleep very difficult. Upon lying down at any kind of normal bedtime, the image of my boy—hanging—would fill my mind; sobbing would commence. It happened, without fail, every single time I tried to sleep, unless I was so tired I literally couldn't keep myself awake and couldn't keep my eyes open. If not for the Benadryl I started taking, I don't know if I would have slept at all. Two or three hours after taking 50 mg of the Benadryl, I would usually reach the falling-asleep-while-standing place I needed to be before I climbed into bed. Falling asleep listening to my current audio book was also helpful as it lulled me to sleep, as long as I had already reached the heavy-eye-lidded place before reclining. In the morning, I would back up to a part in the audiobook I could remember hearing before dozing off. I didn't pressure myself about the sleep problem just as I tried not to pressure myself about anything. I was trying to survive Sammy's death, and putting pressure or expectations of anything on myself would be counter-productive to healing. I did *not* want to have a complete mental breakdown, so I tried not to do *anything* I didn't think I could do. I stayed up until I start nodding off. I listened to my audio books, and sometimes I watched Netflix shows. The moment I woke up in the morning, the tears started. I would roll over, grab my IPhone, put the earbuds in, and start the current audiobook.

I tried to avoid all thought related to Sammy as I struggled to accept and acclimate to his death. By "accept", I mean recognize that he was gone, and I was never getting him back; I had to acknowledge the futility of attempting to get him back through time travel, parallel universes, magic, or any other means. Even when I didn't reach for fantastical ways to get Sammy back, I struggled to make myself submit to the reality of his death. I also had to "acclimate" to his death, or, to be blunt, I had to get used to it. To do that, I tried to bide my time and keep myself too busy to think. I was hopeful that in the meantime, my heart would keep healing from the worst of the shock, horror, and sorrow. "Busy" for me did not mean physically engaging in an activity. My mind was what I had to keep busy but in a completely stress-free way: In a way that didn't involve decision-making or critical thinking. Listening to audiobooks didn't require much cognitive effort (as long as I picked the right books) and kept my mind distracted from dwelling on other thoughts. Trying to stay busy by doing anything that required leaving the house didn't work because of the anxiety and panic I felt when away from home and the necessity of making decisions while out.

When my difficulty sleeping worsened in January, it was 3:00, 4:00, or 5:00 am before I could finally sleep each night. In addition to staying up late because of my need to feel very tired before I would be able to fall sleep, I think, sub-consciously, I wanted to change my sleeping pattern so I would be awake more at night and asleep more during the day. I probably developed a preference for being awake at night because it was quiet, so there was less sensory overload. Without the vodka and Xanax to dull my senses, everything seemed loud, bright, and crazy; I was easily startled. At night, everyone was asleep and safe at home, and the house/neighborhood/town was dark and quiet. I established a pattern; I would go to bed at the same time as Jake, "tuck him in," and we would have valuable time holding each other, cuddling, crying, and talking. Then, I would get back up. I consistently followed this pattern for most of the first three years.

While I was awake late one evening in February, about 16 months after the tragedy, I noticed a message in my Facebook inbox: an invitation to join an online group for bereaved mothers. I had received an inbox message prior to this, but I thought it was an advertisement or spam and hadn't read it. After looking more closely that night, I joined the group. I wish I had discovered it sooner. One thing that had made me feel so lonely was not being able to talk to anyone who really knew what I was going through because none of my friends had ever lost a child (to my knowledge). To feel heard and understood by others who knew the pain was invaluable. Once discovered, I was on the site every night for several hours, reading other mother's stories, sharing about Sammy's death, and interacting with other moms. Being able to read posts from those who had lost their children three years, five years, and ten years before—and who were surviving—gave me some hope that I could make it through the worst of the horrible pain, and one day possibly even feel some happiness again.

Upon first joining, I never commented but only read other mothers' stories. The relative anonymity of the group was a plus, as well as the fact that I didn't have to leave the house. Sometimes after hearing someone's story I would think, *Oh my God, how is this mother living with this pain*, and *Sammy's death was bad, but that would have been worse*. One mother lost all three of her children at once when they were in an accident while having weekend visitation with their father, the mother's ex-husband. One mother lost two of her four children in a house fire; her husband had been able to reach the two that were saved, but not the other two. Some had lost their children to murder or rape and murder and some to shootings. Some moms endured months of horrible suffering as their children slowly died of cancer, and some had the heartache of turning their heads for a moment, only to turn back to find their child had just drowned. Some of the children had died in car accidents and some had committed suicide. I was no longer so alone with the grief.

I searched for other moms whose children had died by hanging, and I found a small contingent. Some of those had died from suicide, the rest from the activity the police had asked me about: the choking game. I was interested in learning more about the choking game deaths so I could compare them to Sammy's death and look for possible similarities. Sammy was fully suspended, meaning his feet were completely off the floor (in his case by several inches). Within the group, in every choking game death but one, the children were standing on the floor or sitting down, not fully suspended. Those positions provided the opportunity for release of the choking implement—scarf, belt, cord—by the weight of the body falling forward when the victim lost consciousness. The victims died because their strap/belt/rope hadn't loosened as planned when he or she passed out, and since the victims attempted the game alone, there was no one else present to loosen the choking implement. Sammy's complete suspension didn't fit with a choking game death, and the strap wasn't set up in a way to only choke him until he passed out and then to loosen.

When I read posts by mothers who were new to the path, I would comment to let them know they were not alone in their horrid journey—that other mothers were on the road both before them and after them. That awareness alone was reassuring, though it in no way lessened the pain of the loss. Mostly, we shared our child's story, what we were feeling, what struggles we were having, and we posted pictures of our children. Once, the actual topic of conversation was electro convulsive therapy (also known as shock treatment). Some mothers were discussing whether the pros outweighed the cons of being treated with ECT in an attempt to recover and be able to move on with life. If you aren't a grieving mother that might sound extreme, but let it be an indicator of the utter devastation of child bereavement; the deep pain, unending sorrow, and the sense of utter wrongness bereaved mothers must learn how to live with. Most of the moms in the group conversation agreed that regardless of the horrible loss, they wouldn't want to risk losing memories of their deceased child (or children) by having ECT. The group was great therapy, and no matter what time of day or night I logged on, hundreds of other mothers were there interacting. Being a part of that group might have been the single most important thing I discovered to assist in my healing.

At some point during the second year, I realized I had developed a preference for rainy or snowy weather. I think it was because sunny and bright days contrasted too sharply with my constant inner turmoil. Our Midwestern thunderstorms provided the perfect setting for my own inner storms. It was soothing to sit out front on my porch swing, taking in the thick, grey clouds, the loud thunder cracks, the huge sheets of rain coming down, the occasional hail, the wind whipping through the big trees in our neighborhood, the bright flashes of lightening, and the gruff rumbles of thunder. It felt equally right, if not more so, when it snowed, especially at night. Watching the snowflakes silently falling from the sky, landing softly all over our yard, definitely provided the most feng shui environment for my state of mourning: the cold air, the trees covered in the white powder, the bird bath water frozen and shining, the glistening ice crystals hanging off the roof, and the accumulating inches and feet of snow covering everything. Many times during the first two years I even told Jake I thought I would like to move to Siberia.

One thing we did the second year to try and alleviate some of the sadness in our home was grow our pet family. On what would have been the weekend of Sammy's 15th birthday in March 2012, we adopted two more kittens. My intention was to adopt one gold male kitten, but when we arrived at the store to meet him, his beautiful grey and tan sister was curled up close by his side, looking so sweet and attached to her brother that I couldn't leave without them both. Butterscotch and Cinnamon joined the family, and Samantha had pet siblings. The kids were thrilled with the two new additions, and the shadow of Sammy's birthday was not quite as long.

Two days before the two-year memorial of Sammy's death, Sarah's hamster, Evelett, passed away. It was terrible timing. Sarah had received Evelett as a 16th birthday gift from Jo two months *before* Sammy died. Losing her was doubly sad for Sarah; not only did she lose her pet, she lost another connection to Sammy. We decided it must be another occasion to grow our pet family, so for the two-year memorial of Sammy's death, we adopted another kitten! He was a little grey and white male, and because we loved the St Louis Cardinals, especially Yadier Molina, we named him Yadi.

As I previously mentioned, about two months after Sammy's death I became unable to listen to any music. Music had always been something that made me feel alive, so it was strange for me to avoid it; but I didn't want to feel alive because I didn't want to feel anything. When I did, it was only intense pain. Sarah had the opposite experience. Music seemed to be healing for her: therapeutic. She had always loved music, but it took on new passion; it became medicine for her heartache. She was already in choir when Sammy died, but it took on a completely new meaning in her life, particularly her junior and senior years of high school (our second and third years of grieving.)

Singing with her choir became her religion. It soothed her, gave her hope, and lifted up her psyche. It would not be going too far to say music, specifically singing with her choir, was one of the most critical aids in her healing process. Every time she joined in unison with the other choir members, she seemed to let go, become lighter, and fly in the air. In singing with her choir friends, with all of their deep, rich, light and airy voices harmonizing, she temporarily was able to leave most of her grief behind, to see and remember the love, goodness, and beauty in the world.

The music problem continued for me until late during the second year when I finally could tolerate listening to the radio. I did have to quickly flip stations when a Sammy-trigger song started: "Time of Your Life" by Green Day, "Crazy Train" by Ozzie Osborne, "Low Rider" by War, "Eye of the Tiger" by Survivor. Every one of those songs had a strong association with Sammy and every one caused a searing burning rip at my heart when I heard them.

Near the end of our second year of grief in August 2012, Sarah said that for her 18th birthday she wanted a family birthday party like we used to have before the tragedy. Having had almost no contact with my family since Sammy's death, I had zero desire to have a family party. After nearly two years, there was a whole lot of water under that bridge. The hurt we felt by my family's lack of care was deep. However, it was Sarah's senior year, it was her last birthday before she would fly from the nest, and it was what she really wanted.

Sarah lost so much on that horrible day when all of our lives changed. Obviously, the worst loss was Sammy, but she also lost contact with her biological father and with her older brother (albeit by choice, but with the circumstances she didn't feel she had any other option). She lost most contact with her extended family on both her biological father's side—because she wanted to avoid both Lucas and Peter—and on my side—because they all pulled away. I had always prioritized relationships and family in our home, and she also had highly valued them; I knew the loss of contact with so many family members was difficult for her. It was difficult for us all.

After much soul searching and with great effort, I invited my extended family to join us at a restaurant to celebrate Sarah's birthday (our treat). Neither Vince nor Bennet (Victoria's husband) attended—apparently they both had work conflicts—but everyone else showed up, appeared pleasant and seemed to really try to help the evening go well (except Mother who was quiet and cool). It was nice for Sarah to be around extended family, and I did my best not to dwell on negative thoughts or resentments. While I felt a little bit glad to be among them again, I also felt sadness at their utter failure to comfort, encourage, or support me and my family during the previous two years. Mostly, I felt indifferent; by that time I had developed a rough callous concerning my family members. After all, it had been nearly two years, and although I had survived the brunt of the loss it was no thanks to any of them.

One of the reasons I went ahead with a family party was because I wanted to do everything I could to make that school year, August 2012- May 2013 (the end of our second year of grief and most of our third year) a good one for Sarah. In April 2009 at the end of Sarah's eighth grade year, my dad had passed away suddenly and without warning. Two months after we buried dad, Jake was diagnosed with heart failure, and at my insistence for his recovery, he took eight months off from work. Therefore, Sarah's freshman year was marked with sadness over her Papa's death, anxiety over her dad's heart condition, and a tight budget since we only had one income.

Shortly into Sarah's sophomore year in October of 2010, Sammy died; of course, the rest of that year was shrouded in grief and all of death's accompanying horrors. During her junior year, although our home atmosphere had improved a little, it was still primarily a house of mourning. I wanted to do everything I could to make her senior year as happy and perfect as possible. That began with joining together with my family to celebrate Sarah's birthday, in spite of my anger, resentment, frustration, disappointment, sadness, and mistrust.

Following the birthday party, Valerie started sending me a text or two every six months or so asking if I wanted to go to lunch. She had no clue what a recluse I had become since Sammy's death. In addition, she didn't seem to notice, or she ignored, the forgiveness problem; I had yet to forgive her, or the rest of the family, for deserting me, and no one had asked for any forgiveness. My child died, and my sister and the rest of my family got angry with me and didn't (hardly) visit, call, or text for two years. Moving back into any kind of relationship with her would be very hard for me, if it was even possible. The first time she texted, I answered, "I don't do lunch anymore. But thanks!" Then, she texted, "What about breakfast or diner?" I didn't respond. Frankly, I was unwilling to sacrifice any of my time, mental energy, or love for someone who left me alone in the pit of despair, unconcerned if I survived. I didn't even know how to respond to the texts. Perhaps with, "Just the idea of going to lunch makes me feel uncomfortable?" Or, "I don't like people anymore." Or, "I feel like the people who should have been there for me (including you) abandoned me, and now I don't trust anyone anymore?" If I did go to lunch, I didn't even know what we would say to each other. Whatever I might potentially chat about seemed unimportant or irrelevant. It would feel like we were ignoring the elephant in the room. "Hey, isn't it weird that Sammy is dead?" "What in the world happened over there that night that ended with Sammy hanging from a strap?"

And "So, it sure has been tough, you not being around at all for the past two years." That being said, Valerie did at least begin to make some small effort by the occasional text message.

I think the big hole in my heart left by losing Sammy, and everything that went with and followed that event, was slowly being stitched up, but the stitches were placed far apart with more being added all the time to tighten and close the wound. I had to do everything slowly and carefully, or I would bump it, causing a stitch or two to come undone. Sometimes the stitches were ripped out because of the words and actions of others.

I never noticed when the stitches were going in, but every once in a while I felt a slight easing of pain. Jake was responsible for the majority of my stitches. His unending supply of gentleness, kindness, and understanding, and his daily administering dose of holding and spooning me on the couch, his constant physical touch and affection, his complete acceptance of the magnitude of my sorrow and tears with no judgment or pressure to be doing anything other than grieving, in whatever form it took, is the primary reason I survived. His love and care provided the most reconstructive shaping and stitching. He comforted me, he carried me, and it was, primarily, his love that saved me.

In spite of their own pain, Sarah, Adam, and Lydia also placed a fair share of careful stitches. The greatest thing they did, and it wasn't easy, was to extend to me unconditional acceptance of wherever I happened to be on the grief path. They never pressured me to heal more quickly, to do anything I could not, or to be anything I could not. Nor did they resent or harbor anger or bitterness that they were left with a ghost of the mother they used to have (if they did, they mercifully kept it to themselves). Their love, patience, and acceptance—that I was terribly damaged and might never get any better—was, and continues to be, a healing balm.

My best friend of twenty-four years as of this writing in June 2016, Jo, put in a great many stitches, with our regular phone calls (which were the best kind of therapy,) occasional visits, and her coming on special dates and memorial days. She visited and helped out with several birthdays, and she and her partner Carl helped financially on several occasions It cannot be an easy thing to be the best friend of a grieving mother; it must be depressing, grueling, tiring, and not often rewarding, yet she continues. She might have faltered once or twice, but she picked right back up and carried on, and is that not what defines a good relationship? With my condition, she regularly had to be the strong one.

The entire first year my sister Laura provided some stitches by regularly calling and texting me and coming by to visit every few weeks. Throughout the second year, she continued with drop-ins once every three-four weeks and occasional phone check-ins. As the sole member of my extended family to be calling, visiting, or showing concern for me and my family, her faithfulness was priceless.

Our kind Lutheran neighbors, who brought meals occasionally and would continue to do so through the first four years, slipped in several stitches. A few stitches even went in through my Facebook friends, some of whom I had known since grade school or high school, others who I only met online in grief groups. Their caring enough to leave kind messages, or be concerned if I was absent too long from Facebook so they sent private messages, was also helpful.

People say that time heals all wounds, and I suppose to some degree that is true even with the death of a child, but not completely. Child loss isn't just a wound: it is an amputation (and forgive me if this is offensive or presumptuous to those who have suffered amputation; I might be completely incorrect.) With proper care, healing can occur after an amputation, but you still must live the rest of life without that limb. In time, you can get to a place where you are not constantly consumed with the reality that your arm is gone. You can read a book and for that time, you are not actively thinking about your missing limb. However, when you pause from the book, and reach with your other hand for your bookmark, you are smacked in the face with the reality that you no longer have another hand with which to reach.

Chapter 29

> "So it's true, when all is said and done, grief is the price we pay for love."
>
> -E.A. Bucchianeri, *Brushstrokes of a Gadfly*

October 24, 2013, Third Year Reflections

The third year without Sammyboy, I struggled the most with melancholy and inability to move forward. As I have stated, the first year was the most acutely painful and full of despair, rage, horror, and agony, and the second year was depressing, with frequent flares of pain, and consumed with coming to grips that he was gone for good and I would never see him again. The third year, I was weighed down with a lethargy I couldn't shake. To a certain degree, time was helping me learn to live with his absence, and yet, it always covered me like smoke and randomly flared up with red hot flames to lick and burn. The rest of the time, the smoke kept me in a bit of a foggy place. I continued trying to get myself into forward motion, but I found it difficult to carry on with my life knowing my child never would.

Family traditions, many of which had ceased upon Sammy's death, needed to be either resumed or changed. Following my divorce back in 2005, eating at the kitchen table together became tough because of the empty spot where Peter should have been sitting. Following Sammy's death, that discomfort morphed into absolute dread of sitting at the table together. We almost never did it. Instead, we took our plates into the TV room and watched a TV show or a movie while we ate. That wasn't how I ever wanted or envisioned our meal times, but sitting around the kitchen table as a family felt wrong and much too painful.

We did our best to make the year as good as we could for our children, especially our graduating senior. In fact, I had decided if I could accomplish one thing during that year it would be to make Sarah's senior year as good as it was within my power to make it. My efforts to accomplish that began in August 2012, with the family party for her 18th birthday.

After much research and discussion regarding options for college, we—Sarah, Jake, and I—agreed that if she could get in, the best choice for college for Sarah would be Washington University in St. Louis. (Although she had successfully charged along through high school despite of her grief, I suspected attending an ivy league school as far away as the east coast would be too much for her, too far from home). Mid-December, we received the big, white envelope in the mail: an acceptance letter from Wash U. I was so proud of and thrilled for my little girl. She had been through hell the previous two years, yet she had managed to "keep her guts about her" as my dad would have said, and it had paid off. A few weeks later, we received another letter in the mail; combining the scholarships Sarah earned (Bright Flight, Missouri Scholars, to name a few) with the *enormous* scholarship the school offered her, Sarah could attend Wash U on a full-ride.

While I was happy for my sweet girl, I experienced a sensation I had felt several times during the third year. As I hugged and jumped up and down with Sarah upon receiving her letter of acceptance, the happy feelings produced by my brain seemed to hit a ceiling. The happiness started increasing, and then, bump, wouldn't go any higher. I hadn't experienced many happy feelings since losing Sammy, but there had been a few (Adam being selected to receive the Duke Talent Identification Award, Lydia receiving the Presidential Academic Excellence Award, Sarah making National Honor Society and winning Homecoming Queen, and the St Louis Cardinals winning the 2011 World Series.) With each of those, I felt a very little bit of happiness, and then it would stop. I would not and could not feel any happier. It was as if Sammy's death permanently altered my ability to rise above a very limited amount of happy feelings. I was glad I at least occasionally felt some small bits of happiness; it took several years for even that to happen. I hoped, in time, my happy ceiling would rise. (It *would* rise, it would just take several more years.)

Well into the third year, I was still wearing only black clothing; it wasn't even a choice. I had to wear black. I was mourning the death of my child. I had no desire to wear bright or cheerful colors. I didn't feel bright or cheerful. Black perfectly represented how I felt and was a public statement to others that I was mourning Sammyboy; he wasn't quickly forgotten. In April of 2013, two and a half years after Sammy's death, I went shopping. I happened to be right by a clothing store and was feeling strong that day, so I entered the store. I needed a few things to wear to Sarah's graduation and some of the other ceremonies and public events that I needed to attend over the following month or two (most of my clothes no longer fit). Looking at the new spring clothes, I felt I might be ready to start wearing color again, and I knew the kids would be happy to see me back in color. Trying on some outfits I had no guilt or internal struggles, so I purchased a few things and color finally returned to my wardrobe.

In August, I went with Sarah and Lydia to Walmart to get their school supplies (I was able to make myself do it as we approached the third year) when I felt the urge to purchase a planner. It felt good to want to buy a planner. It felt good to feel good to want to buy a planner. I ended up being completely unable to *use* the planner—every time I sat down with it I couldn't write anything, and I would start feeling nauseous—but at least I wanted to buy one again. It was a start.

Near the end of the third year, I had another Sammy dream. In the dream, I got into my bed, and Sammy (around age 6) was lying there sleeping. I slid my arm under his head. Still asleep, he turned his face toward me, scooted in, and slept the rest of the night with his head on my chest in the nook by my shoulder. I kept rubbing my face back and forth over his silky, blonde hair. It was so sweet and lovely, until I woke up and felt the red hot lava spew. It had been over a year since I had dreamed of him, and though it made me feel disloyal to my sweet boy to admit, not dreaming of him had been a relief. When he was in my dreams, the loss pressing in on my heart when I awoke was crushing. The vividness of experiencing him alive—feeling and smelling his hair, talking to him and making eye contact with him—but awakening to the world where he was no more, left me desolate. I loved getting to see him in my dreams, but the missing him once I was no longer connected to him in that dream state was much worse than the usual dull ache to which I was growing accustomed.

A big step in my healing came near the end of the third year, when I finally felt like I was able to start having some perspective again. Seeing things from another person's point of view can be challenging at any time, but Sammy's death caused me to almost completely lose that ability for a while. The best explanation I can give to explain why I couldn't be objective—why perspective-taking was such a problem—would be to say it was like I had a large, gaping, bleeding, oozing chest wound, which absorbed all of my energy, attention, and emotion. My wound hurt too bad, all the time for me to notice or care about anything else. To my mind, other people's daily frustrations, annoyances, or difficulties paled in comparison to the horror of my hanged-to-death 13-year-old son.

In finally being able to look at things from other people's perspectives again, I was able to see things a little differently regarding my family members' responses during the first few years of our great sorrow. It was only 18 months after my father's death, when Sammy died, and we were all (especially my mother) still trying to adjust to life without Dad. My dad was quite the sage, provider, and backbone of our family, to say the least, and his sudden death hit our entire extended family hard. Furthermore, two days after we had buried Dad, Valerie called me crying and upset early in the morning, and I had rushed to her bedside. Circumstances (including our father's death) converged, and she had her own personal struggle over the next year, affecting her immediate family as well as our extended family. It was a sad and challenging year for everyone. Our family endured some hard knocks in a short amount of time (a few others about which I will not elaborate, but in addition to Dad's death and Valerie's crisis).

Sammy's death was yet another punch to the gut of our already weakened family. Unfortunately, it was terrible timing.

It was only near the end of the third year that I was able to start considering these things. I couldn't always keep them in mind, but when I was able to be open to try and comprehend my family's pitiful response, it did help me have more understanding. Reaching that place of understanding took a great deal of effort. It also took forgiveness. It was still awhile before I could reach any forgiveness, but I got there by the end of the fourth year (well, I had moments of forgiveness anyway). Often, when my pain and loss and sorrow surged—a regular pattern with grief—forgiveness would be forgotten. I would only feel the hurt, anger, disappointment, and bitterness again, but at least I was able to achieve forgiveness some of the time. Just as the grief likely will always ebb and flow, so too might my ability to remain in a state of forgiveness.

To mark the three-year memorial of our boy's death, I thought we ought to adopt our first dog. Although Jake and I are cat people, Lydia is a dog person (as was Sammy), and she had wanted a dog since she was very young. As we approached the three-year memorial, I thought it might be just the time. We had discovered that adopting pets to commemorate Sammy's birth and death days helped us better handle the increased pain and sadness around those dates. The weekend marking the third year since Sammy's death, Jo came to visit us. She and I decided a trip to the Humane Society was in order. I saw and fell in love with a Dachshund/Chihuahua mix male puppy and set about campaigning to win Jake's support for the adoption. After plenty of sweet-talking (plus Jo's generous offer to front the adoption fee as well as all the initial puppy supplies) Jake relented, and we brought home our first dog, Louie.

Around the end of year three (August 2013) and beginning of year four, Sarah left home to begin college at Wash U in St Louis. I noticed myself struggling more with increased sadness. In part, it was due to exhaustion after my strenuous efforts to make the previous year—Sarah's senior year—as positive and "normal" as possible. I had pushed myself hard to attend the necessary ceremonies, parties, performances, and social gatherings. I had put on the "fake it until you make it" façade, and it was a relief to return to my life of mostly solitude. The other part of the increased sadness was because the house felt significantly emptier with Sarah gone. I missed her, and I missed the connection she represented for me between her and Sammy and Peter. Because Sarah was a year and a half younger than Peter and two and a half years older than Sammy, she was my fellow memory keeper of all things from Sammy's early life (as well as Peter's). Sarah and I decided more pet therapy was in order to combat the sadness, so my early Christmas gift from Sarah was a nine-week old male, chocolate-point Siamese kitten. When Sammy was still alive, one of the last family tv shows we watched was the BBC series, *Merlin*, so that was what I named my new kitty.

At the beginning of the fourth year in October 2013, I began collating the few short writings I had posted to Facebook or had saved privately regarding my grief. I also gathered all of the notes and lists I made during the investigation into Sammy's death. I then began to write, starting from that horrible morning when Sarah called me in hysterics and said to come to Lucas's house. To clearly communicate everything that happened, I was forced to think through and organize it all. That reflecting enabled me to gain some understanding of certain aspects of our tragedy and its aftermath, and allowed me to see improvements I had made along my grief journey.

Over the years, nearly all of the more experienced women in the bereaved mothers group have consistently reported that the grief will never go away. The grief wont' stay exactly the same, it will fade some, quiet a little, feel less raw—sometimes flair back up and get worse again before simmering back down—but it will never be completely gone. A grieving mother will never be free from the pervading sense of loss, but eventually she will experience moments and periods of happiness again. By the spring of 2016 and into my sixth year of grief, I started having those moments—finally. I wish they happened more frequently, but at least they are happening again, and I understand that my changed sense of awareness, happiness, and contentment are a product of the impact of losing Sammy. I am okay with those changes. They are my psychological stretch marks and will always be a badge of Sammyboy's life and death and of my loving and losing my son.

Chapter 30

"Give sorrow words; the grief that does not speak knits up the o-er wrought heart and bids it break."

-William Shakespeare, *Macbeth*

General Thoughts and Reflections

There are several reasons I felt compelled to write about the hellish experience of losing Sammy and of surviving his death (none of which are because my experience was anything special or different from that of thousands of others). Throughout my life, I have always written in journals and diaries to clear my head, make sense of things, record events, and to understand myself; that was precisely the first reason I wrote about Sammy's death. It was a typical grief therapy exercise with the goal of and hope for continued healing. The second reason I wrote about it was because I thought Sammy deserved for his whole story to be told (even if it was told under pseudonyms). The third reason for writing out what happened was so other grieving moms could read this, and hopefully be helped, soothed, and feel slightly less alone. During those first several hellish years after losing my son, one of the things that helped me to know a little bit about what to expect and to feel slightly less crazy was hearing other bereaved mothers' stories. I finish with a summary of what I have learned through this nightmare, which is probably very similar to what other bereaved parents have lived through, still are living through, or one day will live through.

There is no magic bullet. There has been nothing to make the pain of my child's death go away. I have had to learn to live with it, wade through it, move through it, and grow stronger muscles to carry it. Surviving has been the hardest and most miserable thing I have ever done, but other mothers have done it, are still doing it, and I can too.

In the beginning, the only thing I could do for myself was focus on breathing. Truly. Anything more was too much. Too heavy. Too challenging. Thinking about breathing was something I could do. Getting through the most excruciating period of grief was a little like going through labor at the end of a pregnancy. I had to focus on my breathing and let it come. There was no stopping it. I focused on getting through the next breath. I was engulfed in pain. My whole chest would ache and throb. My heart, my head, my everything felt covered with pain like heavy smoke, so thick it was impossible to see through and made everything challenging. Obviously, the labor metaphor only works so far. After all of the hard work of labor, one ends up with a beautiful, miraculous baby. After the hard work of grief, one ends up with—not a child, but hopefully—the rest of one's life, and the ability to see and enjoy some beauty in life again.

The first year is full of horrified, piercing agony. Every day when I awoke, the burning hot awareness that my child was dead was present in my brain before I even opened my eyes. I also struggled with anger and rage, which was slightly less horrible but still bad the second year. It was a relief when I joined the online group and discovered anger was common among nearly all of the bereaved mothers I encountered. According to Keebler-Ross's five stages of grief, anger is considered a normal part of grief. It seems though that with the loss of a child, the anger might better be classified as rage—with a good portion of bitterness.

I felt as if the world was not the safe place I once thought it to be. I felt cheated. I was disillusioned with life. I questioned everything. No one expects his or her child will die. A child's death is not "normal". In time, I learned to accept the truth that *sometimes* children *do* die.

There really weren't many good things anyone could say to me. Nothing was going to bring back my child. Nothing was going to fill the huge hole in my psyche left by my child's death. The best anyone could do was be there, give hugs, listen, call, cry with me, and be present with me and for me. The few simple things a person could say to me were, "I'm so sorry," "I am thinking of you," and "My heart goes out to you." Also, it was fine to ask me, "Could I please do something for you and your family?" However, it was pointless to ask what I needed because I couldn't answer. I didn't know. It was best if someone simply *did* something, anything.

In our immediate family, we all needed therapy. We all were grieving and were stricken and weak. We each needed to be able to share our thoughts, feelings, frustrations, and struggles with someone who was not emotionally involved and who could listen and provide insight, support, and encouragement. The role of the therapist wasn't to "cure" us or to solve our grief. Her role was to guide us down the dark and unfamiliar path, alert us to potholes in the road and other obstacles, and advise us how to jump over those potholes. Her role also was to be a safe person with whom we could share every thought and emotion without worry of how it would affect her.

I was in survival mode for quite a while. I had to be gentle to myself. I had to allow myself to do and be, or not do or be, in order to make it through each day. It was not the time to worry about what I ate, what I drank, how I dressed or anything else. It was survival time. I didn't pressure myself. Over time and very slowly I have been able to do more, but I have never tried to push myself or rush it. (I did *not*, and still do not, want to have a complete mental breakdown—in other words, a break with reality involving hallucinations or delusions). I accepted that I was grieving and that grief was hard work. Putting no pressure on myself to be at any particular emotional milestone, or to be doing any particular thing, allowed me the time and freedom to move through the grief at my own pace *without* losing my mind or succumbing to suicide. There were many times when I would feel a little disgusted with myself and my lack of improvement. When I would voice this to Jake, he would say, "Oh no, Sweetheart. You are in a much better place now than you were six months or a year ago." Those kinds of comments encouraged me that I was truly experiencing slow healing and allowed me to feel okay continuing at my snail's pace. I sometimes found myself doing things that made no sense to others, but if they weren't harmful to anyone and if they made me feel better, I did them.

    I didn't want to continue certain family rituals or routines in which we had engaged when Sammy was alive. It didn't feel right to do some of those things without him. Eventually, I developed new routines and rituals, and, in time, I was able to pick up some of the old ones again. We used to go to a Christmas tree farm each year to cut down our Christmas tree. I wasn't able to do that for the first two years, but by the third year (for the kids and with great effort) we were able to start doing it again. (I suppose I *did* push myself a little about certain things, but *only* if I thought it would be substantially beneficial for the kids or Jake and wouldn't be too much for me). If I hadn't been able to get back to doing the Christmas tree farm, that would have been okay too. Eating dinner all together at the table continues to be impossible. We don't do it. We take our food to the living room and eat off TV trays and often still watch TV while we eat. Eventually, Jake remodeled our kitchen and built a long bar where we began to sit on stools and eat. Eating together at the bar didn't have the same wrong feeling to it as eating at our kitchen table.

    The second year, I would characterize as mostly grey, bleak, and sorrowful, with frequent stabbings of pain often brought on by triggers. There were also intermittent days of numbness. On the numb days, the pain wouldn't be as debilitating, not as sharp. Sometimes, just when I thought I was doing better coping with the loss, I would feel the acute pain again. I learned that the grief was unpredictable. It started coming more in waves. I would have a day or two of feeling mostly numb. I would feel relieved for the numbness. Then, another wave would slam into me, and I would feel the full-force of the pain and loss all over again. I had to tell myself not to feel guilty for the numb days. It didn't mean I no longer cared about Sammy. It didn't mean that I was "getting over" his death. It was just part of the grief path and of gaining my strength to carry the grief. As time passed, the waves of pain would get a little further apart and sometimes decrease in intensity.

The third year, the chronic heartache became ever so slowly, less raw. It was still there, but felt less acute, less piercing, I would still have days when it would flare up again, but not as frequently and not as painfully. I didn't return to work. I don't know if I will ever return to work, or if I do, if it will be in nursing. I am a very different person than I was before Sammy died. I don't know if I could even hold a job anymore. I struggle with depression and anxiety, and I rarely leave my house. (The more I stay at home, the less anxious I am.) I feel like a vase that was dropped, shattering into a million pieces and then glued back together. The vase looks more or less like a vase again, but it is very fragile and when it occasionally gets bumped, pieces and sections fall off and have to be glued on again. The repaired vase can no longer hold water, because it seeps out through the cracks. Essentially, the vase is not really good for any practical use anymore, but those who really loved the vase in all of its pre-shattered glory, still love the vase, in spite of all the cracks, glue, and lack of function.

Early on, when others wanted to donate to help with all of the expenses, I felt uncomfortable accepting money and directed them to donate in Sammy's name to the Humane Society. It would have been better if I had set up a special account or fund and accepted the donations. People wanted to help; for some, it was the only thing they felt they *could* do. Funerals are expensive: the service: the casket, the burial plot, the headstone, the flowers. The therapy, which was so important, was also expensive, and we were compelled to discontinue only two months after Sammy's death because we no longer had the funds to pay for it. At least for several days and weeks following a child's death, employment of both parents is interrupted, and bills begin to accumulate. Sometimes, the family must move forward living with only one income if one parent is unable to return to work. It is a terrible thing to be in despair over your dead child and not have enough money to pay the bills or take your living children to the dentist.

The grief journey is scary, especially the first three years. One of the best things I did to help myself was to become active in online grief groups, particularly the one for bereaved mothers. Reading the stories of others, seeing where they were on the journey, and being able to talk with those who had experienced and knew the pain I was in was helpful. In part, it helped because I could see others who had lived through child loss. They were further down the road and yet were still going; that encouraged me. It also was helpful because it made me feel less alone carrying all of the pain, knowing others were also walking with it. I might have been helped had I been able to attend live, local groups, but because of the anxiety and of not wanting to leave the house, I couldn't. Many others in the bereaved mothers group had that same problem (anxiety and difficulty leaving home.)

One thing which made the enormity of the loss worse was the disappointing response of my extended family. When I learned that nearly every other mom in my grief group felt let down by their family's responses, I looked at why those supposed to be closest to us failed during the worst time of our lives. Thinking it unrealistic that all 20,000 of us (in the group) had thoughtless, uncaring, mean-spirited families, I considered what else might account for the problem. Since everyone said the same thing, I had to admit the problem didn't *merely* lie with the families. The problem is that we grieving mothers lose our ability for perspective taking. Because we are suffering such tremendous pain, shock, and horror, we are overwhelmed, and there is no energy or brain power to see anything from anyone else's viewpoint.

For example, I couldn't understand why family member, X, never called, or why family member, Y, didn't come visit. When my ability to take another person's perspective returned, I had more understanding for X and Y. I could see they might have thought I wanted space or solitude. I could recognize that although I lost a child and my world came to a screeching halt, they still had to go to work, pay bills, and carry on other activities of daily living. They still had fights with their spouse about the budget and had to discipline their teenager for missing curfew. I was finally able to see they might not have been intentionally ignoring or neglecting us, they might have just caught up in their own lives. They didn't have bleeding hearts.

Another consideration was that family and friends might have been doomed to fail. I don't think anyone who isn't a trained therapist who regularly works with grieving parents, can anticipate, recognize, or tolerate the enormous emotional impact, strain, and response of a grieving parent. The pain the parents experience is heinous, and if our intense sorrow doesn't scare people off, our raging, explosive anger likely will. Following any death within a family, it is not uncommon for there to be fights, misunderstandings, and hurt feelings and many family members will act irrationally. Everyone is in shock and hurting. When the death involves a child, these things are hugely magnified. Just as it devastates, crushes, and buries the bereaved mother, it confounds, overwhelms, and scares the extended family members (whether they realize that or not). No one is at fault. Everyone is at fault. The broken mother doesn't know how to get through the worst of it, but neither does the rest of her extended family. The devastated mother has no choice; she is buried under the grief and can't run from it. The extended family does have a choice; they can choose to remain busy, not have time, or even become angry with the bereaved mother, thus distancing themselves from the horror. Those who are able to remain by the side of the angry, sad, devastated mother sometimes will become weary and sometimes will be lashed out at by the bereaved mother. They might feel like anything they do isn't helping or isn't appreciated. It *is* helping, though results might not be visible and appreciation might not be evident for many years. It will eventually be recognized and greatly appreciated. One day the grieving mother will be able to manage the pain and sorrow and will look with gratitude at those who got under the grief with her, provided oxygen, brought sustenance, and did their best to assist.

The depth, width, and weight of the grief has diminished incrementally throughout the last five years. It has very slowly become more manageable. I suspect it will always remain as I will always miss and always love my child. I don't feel I am yet able to carry it in my pocket, but I am able to hoist it onto my back, carrying it as a large backpack. It continues to weigh me down, make living more tiresome and prevent me from running, but I just keep walking, putting one foot in front of the other, doing the next thing.

    I am certainly a very different person than I was. I doubt I will ever return to the me I was before losing Sammy. Short of having a stroke and forgetting large portions of the last five years, I will always remain a bereaved mother. I am different. That I have changed is no secret to me; I am aware. I can look back at Me Before and see the differences compared to Me After. I no longer have much of a burning desire to conquer the world, to be a perfect wife, mother, daughter, sister, friend, or perfect anything. I just want to live in peace. I simply want to spend time with my husband and children. I like sitting outside on the porch swing listening to an audiobook. I enjoy lying on the couch by our crackling fireplace. I still like to spend most of my time at home with my pets and with my loved ones. The changes that have occurred in me through losing my son and trying to survive his death are not superficial, they are bone deep. I couldn't go back to Me Before even if I wanted to and tried.

    I will never "get over" my child's death. Although I have described "healing" or "improving" or "recovering" throughout this account, I don't mean to imply that I think I will reach a place where the grief has finished or has been settled and put away. I live with the under-current of grief constantly swirling beneath the surface. That under-current is a combination of my love, my sadness, and my missing my son. It is slowly becoming more manageable as I continue to learn to live and move with the grief. Like a person who lives with chronic illness and/or chronic pain and discomfort, I accept that I will live with chronic heartache (heart-scream is more accurate) for the rest of my life.

Conclusion

I seek a life of truth, not a life built on illusions that I have created or blindly swallowed to make living more palatable. Lying to self—believing things to be true because they are what I want to be true—makes life feel superficial and brings dissatisfaction. Life is complex, and understanding self is difficult even when you strive for intellectual honesty. When you lie to yourself, it is impossible to have both happiness and peace because your psyche feels the rifts between the lies and the truth, causing feelings of discontent.

I always wanted the truth about Sammy's death. If the evidence had pointed to suicide, I would have accepted that reality and adapted to that truth, or if information had been uncovered to support it was a prank, I would have done the same. To me—and I am, admittedly, no detective, police officer, private investigator, or lawyer—the details of Sammy's death scene looked like a set up, so others would assume his death was a suicide. At the end of the day, I don't know how or why Sammy ended up being hanged. I only know what my gut tells me and what makes the most sense to me, which is that another person was involved. Who that was or how that played out remains a mystery. Maybe Peter was responsible. Maybe he wasn't. Although I have no contact with my oldest son, I do love him, and because of him, I had serious reservations about sharing this story. After considering everything, I still felt compelled to put the story out there. I thought it was the right thing for Sammy and he was the one who lost his life.

To my first-born son, forgive me, if I hurt or offend you in telling my version of this tragedy. Certainly, I could be wrong. I could be blind to some of the facts. I could be seeing the events from a narrow perspective and not even realize it. However, what I can say definitively is this was what I experienced, and these are the facts as I saw them. I have told it as I perceived it. I know that I love you, have always loved you, and will always love you. I hope you are not responsible in any way for Sammy's death, or if you were, you come clean about it one day for everyone's peace of mind. I don't know if we will ever be able to share in a meaningful relationship, but I do wish you love and happiness. I wish things had turned out differently.

To my extended family members, I apologize if I hurt or offended you in the way I reacted within the first few weeks, or anytime following Sammy's death, or in sharing my perspective of this tragedy. I continue to struggle with anger, disappointment, and bitterness over how things unfolded, particularly the first two years, but I have come a long way in my efforts to forgive, and to reach a place of understanding. Please extend the same mercy to me.

To my ex-husband, I apologize if my telling this story pains you. My objective was not to vilify you or misrepresent the facts. My intent was to present the confounding mystery of Sammy's death, and to share my experience with child bereavement for other grieving mothers.

To anyone who has interest, if you want to help a mother who has lost a child, it might be helpful to think of her and treat her as if she were a sick, hospital patient (at least for the first few years). She is indeed sick—with grief. Her sickness has no cure. She will continue to struggle—possibly for her entire life—with the weight of the grief she must learn to live with and carry.

If you were a nurse, and she was your sick, hospital patient, you would do what you could to comfort and support her—so do that. Check in on her regularly so she feels as if someone cares, stop by her house, call and text her. When you are with her, remember there isn't any specific thing you should be saying or doing. Just be with her. By simply being there you can help her to feel less alone as she deals with it. You can comfort her with your presence. You can take her flowers, candles, firewood, potpourri, bubble bath, bath oils, pillows, blankets, muffins, pastries, bread, tea, chocolate, candy, magazines, books, heating pads—anything that you might take to a patient in the hospital also would provide comfort to a bereaved mother. Take her a meal, order pizza for her family, give her gift cards, pay to have her house cleaned or clean her house for her. Anything is better than nothing.

It takes a great deal of emotional and physical energy to care for a bereaved mother. She will not ask for help because she doesn't even know how to help herself and can't begin to think what to tell others. She might not seem to appreciate or even care about your efforts—in time, she will. Try to remember that one of her children is dead. She has no extra emotional energy to be gracious or appreciative. She will almost certainly be angry and bitter, so it is best to put on your thick skin before you begin to care for her as you will likely be snapped at as her grief rages. In those moments, keep in mind it really has nothing to do with you; it is all about the heinous sorrow and anger over her dead child.

It would be helpful to remember that your good work in caring for the bereaved mother will not cure her ailment, but it will be a salve to her ruptured heart. She will never return to the person you knew before she lost her child because a part of her died with her child. She will always live with a portion of her heart missing, and you will observe changes in her because of that missing piece. She will be very fragile for a long time as she learns to carry on living with the constant grief.

I know how arduous it is to continue living after one of your children has died. I have seen despair looking back at me from my mirror, and I have closed my eyes or looked away so as not to be consumed by it. I have seen the vast, pitch-black expanse of grief over and all-around me, and I have looked up from the bottom of the pit, searching for just one speck of blue sky and finding none. Yet, I survive. I hope one day not to be merely surviving, but to be actively living. I am not yet there, but I have found myself occasionally feeling awe that Sammy—and I, and Jake, and my other children—ever came into existence at all. I have glimpsed an occasional, ephemeral ray of sunshine, so I *do* have a little bit of hope that someday I will once again enjoy sunny days.

Made in the USA
Middletown, DE
10 July 2016